OUT IN CENTRAL PENNSYLVANIA

OUT IN
CENTRAL PENNSYLVANIA

THE HISTORY OF AN LGBTQ COMMUNITY

WILLIAM BURTON with **BARRY LOVELAND**

THE PENNSYLVANIA STATE UNIVERSITY PRESS, *University Park, Pennsylvania*

KEYSTONE BOOKS

Keystone Books are intended to serve the citizens of Pennsylvania. They are accessible, well-researched explorations into the history, culture, society, and environment of the Keystone State as part of the Middle Atlantic region.

Map of Pennsylvania by Erin Greb.

Library of Congress Cataloging-in-Publication Data

Names: Burton, William, 1950– author. | Loveland, Barry, author.
Title: Out in central Pennsylvania : the history of an LGBTQ community / William Burton with Barry Loveland.
Description: University Park, Pennsylvania : The Pennsylvania State University Press, [2020] | "Keystone books." | Includes bibliographical references and index.
Summary: "Examines the rise and development of an LGBTQ community in the heart of Central Pennsylvania, and how gay identity and social and advocacy networks form outside of a large urban environment"—Provided by publisher.
Identifiers: LCCN 2020007713 | ISBN 9780271084794 (paperback)
Subjects: LCSH: Sexual minorities—Pennsylvania—History. | Gay liberation movement—Pennsylvania—History.
Classification: LCC HQ73.3.U62 P43 2020 | DDC 306.76—dc23
LC record available at https://lccn.loc.gov/2020007713

The Pennsylvania State University Press is a member of the Association of University Presses.

It is the policy of The Pennsylvania State University Press to use acid-free paper. Publications on uncoated stock satisfy the minimum requirements of American National Standard for Information Sciences—Permanence of Paper for Printed Library Material, ANSI Z39.48-1992.

contents

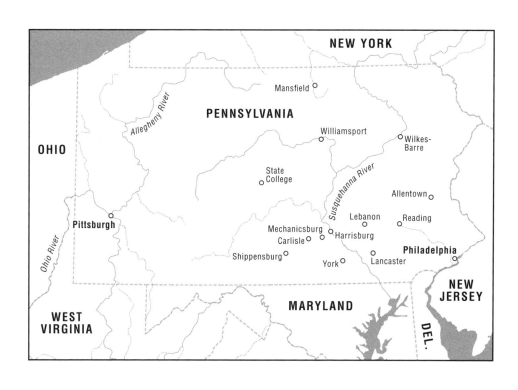

foreword

LGBTQ in Central PA
A Missing Chapter in Pennsylvania History

BRENT D. GLASS

In 2002 Penn State University Press published a landmark study of state history, *Pennsylvania: A History of the Commonwealth*, a handsome volume of more than seven hundred pages filled with an abundance of maps, illustrations, and photographs. An impressive group of scholars contributed chapters that covered every major historical period, and a separate section called "Ways to Pennsylvania's Past" explored art, architecture, geography, folklore, and other disciplines, offering a variety of perspectives. I was pleased that the Pennsylvania Historical and Museum Commission (PHMC) copublished the book and that, as the commission's executive director, I had the opportunity to contribute the foreword that surveyed state history through the lens of historical places.

Despite the critical praise we received for this major work of historical scholarship, the book barely mentioned LGBTQ history and gay political activism and the creative achievements that have animated research and writing about this subject. Fifteen years later the publication of *Out in Central Pennsylvania: The History of an LGBTQ Community* by Penn State University Press is a significant achievement that adds depth and nuance to our changing understanding of state history. This book provides a missing chapter in civil rights history in Pennsylvania and is deeply relevant to understanding state and national politics today.

During my tenure at PHMC, one incident took place in the summer of 1993 that brought the struggle for gay rights directly to my office. A white supremacist organization called the United States of America Nationalist

Party (ANP) requested a permit to march and pass out leaflets at Washington Crossing Historic Park. Their purpose was to protest LGBTQ activism with a special focus on New Hope, Pennsylvania, located two miles north of the park. By that time New Hope had become a political and cultural center for the LGBTQ community. Washington Crossing, owned and managed by the PHMC, is a symbol of patriotism and liberty. This is, after all, the place where George Washington embarked with 2,400 troops across the Delaware River on December 25, 1776, to launch successful attacks on British and Hessian forces in Trenton and Princeton. By choosing the park for their protest, the ANP hoped to link their cause to Washington's legacy.

At PHMC we were faced with a challenge. Our written policy gave us little discretion to deny the permit request. But I did not want to be the state official who approved a march by a group who promoted homophobia, racism, and anti-Semitism. I decided to follow the MAD principle: maximum administrative delay. But the Philadelphia branch of the American Civil Liberties Union soon informed me that they were representing the ANP and that we were violating their First Amendment right to assemble. Within a few weeks I found myself in a federal courtroom trying—unsuccessfully—to defend our inaction. Our delaying tactic, however, paid off. While the court ordered us to issue the permit, we were able to delay the march until the fall season, when the park had fewer visitors. On November 6 we closed the park to the public except for a group from New Hope supporting gay rights. Although the opposing groups threw insults—and rocks!—at each other across the Delaware Canal, we avoided any major conflict, thanks to hundreds of state police who outnumbered the protesters. Happily, we never heard from the ANP again, and New Hope today proudly promotes itself as "the gay-friendly centerpiece of Bucks County's breathtaking countryside."[1]

During my years at the Smithsonian, two events—one positive, one negative—stand out. In 2006 I had the honor of meeting Frank Kameny, a pioneer in LGBTQ civil rights. Kameny was an astronomer with a PhD from Harvard University. He lost his job at the Army Map Service in 1957 for being gay. He petitioned the Supreme Court, arguing that the federal government's treatment of him was an "affront to human dignity." He was the first person to make that civil rights argument to the nation's highest court. His petition was denied, but it launched the modern LGBTQ rights movement. In April 1965, four years before the Stonewall riots, Kameny and a few colleagues picketed the White House and the Pentagon to demand equality. On July 4 that same year, he joined around forty protesters who marched outside Independence

Hall in Philadelphia with signs that read, "Homosexuals ask for the right to pursue happiness." In 2006 Kameny donated his personal archive to the Library of Congress and his collection of protest signs to the Smithsonian. One sign reads, "First Class Citizenship for Homosexuals"; another, "Discrimination against homosexuals is as immoral as discrimination against Negroes and Jews." When the National Museum of American History displayed these signs in our *Treasures of American History* exhibit, the *Washington Post* commented, "the Smithsonian display of gay rights memorabilia is . . . a major milestone."[2]

Unfortunately, the celebration of including the LGBTQ story in America's historical narrative turned out to be premature. In 2010 a pathbreaking exhibition at the National Portrait Gallery called *Hide/Seek: Difference and Desire in American Portraiture* was the first major museum exhibition to focus on LGBTQ artists and subjects in modern US portraiture. Within weeks after opening, this critically acclaimed show faced condemnation from the Catholic League, an organization based in New York City. The league called attention to one of the works in the exhibition, a 1987 video by David Wojnarowicz called *A Fire in My Belly*, which includes a brief scene of ants crawling on a crucifix. Under pressure from congressional leaders, the Smithsonian secretary ordered the removal of the video from the exhibition. This decision sparked a new round of protests, this time from artists, LGBTQ rights advocates, and proponents of free speech who saw—correctly—that the Smithsonian, a major cultural institution, had retreated from its fundamental core values of engagement and openness.

Today we see the growth and acceptance of intolerance and exclusion in our national political life. That is why we need this new volume on LGBTQ history in central Pennsylvania. It is a timely and necessary contribution that will expand our appreciation and understanding of a shared heritage.

acknowledgments

Many people were involved with helping, investigating, and creating this book, and their efforts and work need to be acknowledged. First, Barry Loveland had the vision to create the History Project of Central Pennsylvania and recognize that the history of LGBTQ people of central Pennsylvania needed to be documented and recorded. Without this permanent record this history would have been lost, and this book would have never been written. An important part of the historical record of rural communities would have been missing from the study of LGBTQ history. His work and contributions throughout the writing of the book have also been invaluable. Barry has been not only the visionary for the book but also the guide, main researcher, and editor.

Malinda Triller Doran, librarian at the Dickinson College Archives and Special Collections, provided exceptional access, assistance, reading of the manuscript, and advice that made this book possible. She also supervised and made available the following interns working in the Archives and Special Collections, who assisted in research for the book: Amanda Donoghue, Liam Fuller, V. J. Kopacki, Andrew Strahosky, and Kailey Zengo. Many thanks go to all these interns for their enthusiasm and assistance with the research.

I am grateful to the staff and board of the LGBT Center of Central PA for its continued support of the History Project and of this book. Many volunteers shared their stories; conducted, recorded, and transcribed interviews; and donated, collected, and processed documents, photographs, and artifacts for the History Project collection. Michael J. O'Malley Jr., retired editor of publications for the Pennsylvania Historical and Museum Commission, edited the manuscript for this book. Also many thanks go to Elliot Rebhun for his keen and incisive editing to finish off the final manuscript.

I thank Dr. Brent D. Glass, director emeritus of the Smithsonian National Museum of American History, for his insightful foreword to this book; Dr. Lonna Malmsheimer, professor emerita of Dickinson College, for her support, critique, and encouragement to write this book; Sue Blosser, who volunteered her talents as photographer for many of the archival collections that appear here; and all those pioneering activists in central Pennsylvania and throughout the nation, in places large and small, who took risks, fought hard for equality, and made a difference in the lives of so many LGBTQ citizens. Finally, thanks go to Bradford Voigt, who was the first one who read the initial drafts of each of the chapters. His input and advice was always spot-on, and his support and counsel were always readily available.

Introduction

Most people automatically associate lesbian, gay, bisexual, transgender, and queer/questioning (LGBTQ) communities with large urban areas. Cities such as New York, San Francisco, Los Angeles, and Boston all feature iconic gay enclaves: Greenwich Village, the Castro, West Hollywood, and the South End. The majority of LGBTQ people migrate to major urban centers because they are considered safe havens and have a large number of bars, clubs, and organizations that cater to the way they live. Such cities provide anonymity (for those who want it) and social support that LGBTQ people often cannot find in smaller and more conservative places. Many cities have distinct gay neighborhoods, and a number have passed antidiscrimination laws that protect LGBTQ citizens' jobs, homes, and access to public services. In addition, big cities are usually more progressive in their social and political views, making it easier for LGBTQ people to live openly and to create a thriving community.

I was one of those young gay men who left his home (in my case, Arizona) and moved to Houston in 1974—at the time the nation's fifth-largest city. Although Houston was located in a "red state," there I found a gay neighborhood, the Montrose District, with more than a dozen gay bars and clubs and a thriving gay and lesbian community. In the early 1980s I relocated to Boston, where I found a utopian existence: a progressive city and state, a gay neighborhood, and a well-established gay and lesbian community, with plenty of bars, clubs, restaurants, bookstores, activist organizations, and medical facilities all catering to LGBTQ people. In 1989 Massachusetts became the second state in the nation to pass an antidiscrimination law protecting gays and lesbians in employment, housing, and all public accommodations.

After living in Houston and Boston, I moved to Philadelphia in 2015. This was my third city with a well-established gay district, the Gayborhood. There

I became aware of the LGBT Center of Central PA History Project, headquartered in Harrisburg. In coordination with the Dickinson College Archives and Special Collections in Carlisle, Pennsylvania, the all-volunteer organization was in the midst of collecting and archiving oral histories, photographs, artifacts, and ephemera of the LGBTQ community in central Pennsylvania. I met Barry A. Loveland, the founder and chair of the project, who gave me fifty transcripts of oral histories. They both shocked and mesmerized me. There were stories of rejection, prejudice, discrimination, threats and acts of violence, and the daily minutiae of simply coping with the challenges of being LGBTQ in central Pennsylvania. These stories captured how the LGBTQ community evolved and how its social networks developed, but predominantly—and this is what startled me—in a nonurban environment. The challenges faced in these contexts had not yet been well documented or researched. It was a story that needed to be told.

At the same time I realized that I had been living in a bubble for the past thirty years. I had endured none of these hardships because I had been living in environments that were safe havens. LGBTQ people who live in smaller or rural communities face very different circumstances that require different survival skills and support systems. In rural and even urban central Pennsylvania, there were no laws to protect LGBTQ people. Much of the region is culturally conservative and has stereotypically been seen as backward.[1] This dismissive caricature, however, fails to do justice to the actual experience of inhabiting central Pennsylvania. Pittsburgh and Philadelphia have long had thriving LGBTQ communities and neighborhoods protected by antidiscrimination laws. But throughout the rest of the state and even in Harrisburg, the state capital, few such laws existed. The vast majority of central Pennsylvania's LGBTQ citizens remain unprotected to this day.

I told Barry that no book had ever been written about the varied geographic cross-sections of LGBTQ communities outside of a large city. To be sure, books have been written about growing up or living as an adult gay or lesbian in rural America. Those books focus mainly on the southern and midwestern rural gay and lesbian experience and center on the development of queer identity, gender nonconformity, and the particular characteristics of each region. They detail how race, class, religion, and gender affect gay identity. Some share coming-out stories, while others explore how gays and lesbians meet and socialize. None of these books, however, has explored the development of a gay and lesbian community in a rural and conservative area in the eastern United States. *Out in Central Pennsylvania: The History of an LGBTQ Community* is the story of the people and the LGBTQ community that formed over decades in central Pennsylvania in the late twentieth and early twenty-first centuries.

Gay life has always existed outside of large urban areas, but generally in secret and hidden from public view. As Nan Alamilla Boyd and Horacio N. Roque Ramírez state in their book *Bodies of Evidence: The Practice of Queer Oral History*, "Recognizing that queer histories often go unmentioned in mainstream historical texts, activists and scholars have used a variety of methods to gather data and, thus, evidence of the existence of queer lives."[2] This book uses oral histories to understand and document the history of the development of the LGBTQ community in central Pennsylvania. More specifically, it takes up a suggestion from *Bodies of Evidence* that "oral history transcripts might allow historians to comprehend better how a person or group of people make sense today of successful or disappointing experiences that took place years ago."[3] Like *Making History: The Struggle for Gay and Lesbian Equal Rights, 1945–1990*, by Eric Marcus, *Out in Central Pennsylvania* uses oral histories and an assortment of recollections to represent "a cross section of people, from high-profile leaders to little-known and largely forgotten contributors," who built this community.[4]

The communities that settled in the fertile lands of central Pennsylvania still remain embedded in their agricultural and industrial past and retain their religious inheritances. Like much of the rural United States, many families in the region hold morally conservative values. Growing up gay or lesbian in a small-town environment in central Pennsylvania meant that many people never had the opportunity to have homosexuality explained or even acknowledged. Many, too, endured discrimination and harassment. Without the benefit of urban attitudes, protections, amenities, or defined neighborhoods, sexual minorities in central Pennsylvania had no choice but to find other ways to unite and build their community. LGBTQ residents of small cities and towns such as Lancaster, Harrisburg, Lebanon, Williamsport, State College, and York formed grassroots support organizations that reached gay people beyond the bar scene.

The primary focus of this book is the region generally known as south-central Pennsylvania, or the Lower Susquehanna Valley. The geographic range of this book occasionally ventures beyond this territory to provide a broader context, but the primary area of study comprises the three small cities that are the heart of this region: Lancaster, York, and Harrisburg, with their populations of 59,000, 43,000, and 49,000, respectively, as of 2018.[5] These cities are in turn surrounded by associated suburbs and other small boroughs and towns. The Susquehanna River is a defining geographic feature, as are the mountains of the Alleghenies, which provide a picturesque forested break in the landscape from towns and farms.

Harrisburg, York, and Lancaster have been sanctuaries, in some ways, offering more liberal politics and inclusive communities. But beyond these areas, hostility often remains acute. Out of this inhospitable environment, both urban and rural, have emerged brave pioneer gay and lesbian activists who managed to find one another, create networks, and build a community that enhanced the quality of life in the region.

The stories chronicled in this book are of coming out, contending with family reactions, navigating bars and social life from the 1960s to the 1980s, facing AIDS, and dealing with a culturally conservative society. They tell how the LGBTQ residents of central Pennsylvania organized for their civil rights protections and how they secured their quality of life. Amid inequities, harassment, and discrimination, courageous but unheralded leaders stepped forward to create social networks and political organizations that would ensure their treatment as citizens with equal dignity under the law.

Chapter 1 focuses on early gay life in central Pennsylvania, starting in the mid-twentieth century with the emergence of gay bars in Harrisburg and Lancaster. These initial sites of community building were accompanied by a brutal police crackdown on gay men in Harrisburg in the mid-1960s. More broadly, this chapter recounts personal stories of growing up in central Pennsylvania, coming out, and facing family reactions, reflecting what life was like for those growing up in the mid-twentieth century.

Chapter 2 details the emergence of social networks for lesbians and gays. As the gay community moved into the 1970s, a growing awareness of the need for more social outlets (aside from the scant number of bars) provided the impetus for the formation of new organizations and outlets, such as Dignity/Central PA, the Gay and Lesbian Switchboard of Harrisburg, and the Metropolitan Community Church of the Spirit, along with the *Lavender Letter* newsletter and the *Gay Era* newspaper in Lancaster. In this chapter we introduce a "profile" section, which also features in most of the subsequent chapters. These profiles share personal stories that reflect the impact of powerful events on the people telling the stories. In chapter 2, Joe Burns talks about his participation in the first Gay Pride parade in New York, the year after the Stonewall riots.

Chapter 3 delves into the wave of activism that spread across college and university campuses after Stonewall. This era saw the formation of Homophiles of Penn State (HOPS) at University Park in north-central Pennsylvania in 1971. From its inception, the fledgling organization faced fierce opposition: the university first granted, then immediately revoked, the group's charter, setting up a fight for reinstatement. The struggle took a toll on one of the members of HOPS, Joe Acanfora, who fought to teach in the classroom as an openly gay man. We also learn about The Lesbian Connection, known as the TLC, and other early organizing efforts by the women's community in north-central Pennsylvania. The chapter includes a profile of Dan Maneval, who was harassed and had his home vandalized. He was eventually forced to move out after his neighbors learned that he had protested an appearance by antihomosexual crusader Anita Bryant in Bloomsburg.

Chapter 4 opens with the precedent-setting establishment of the Pennsylvania Council for Sexual Minorities in 1975, launched by one of Gov. Milton J. Shapp's executive orders, the first of their type in the nation. It was the result of a unique and unlikely partnership between many brave gay and lesbian activists and a governor who was ahead of his time on gay issues in the mid-1970s. This in turn led to the formation of the Pennsylvania Rural Gay Caucus, a seminal network of organizations from small cities and rural communities throughout central Pennsylvania that became the catalyst for rural gay activism. Chapter 4 also profiles Tony Silvestre, who chaired the council, as well as Mary Nancarrow, who was chair of the caucus and president of the Pennsylvania chapter of the National Organization for Women.

Chapter 5 chronicles the horror of the AIDS crisis. When the epidemic struck rural Pennsylvania in 1983, its victims and those who helped them were treated as pariahs. The gay and lesbian communities came together to take care of themselves. The stories of these grassroots organizations—and those of their leaders—are powerful and emotional. We meet Joy Ufema, a nationally known pioneer of hospice care who founded the AIDS hospice in York, and Rick Schulze, whose compassionate work with AIDS patients is truly inspirational.

Chapter 6 moves us from the 1980s into the 1990s and the fight for the passage of antidiscrimination laws in Harrisburg, Lancaster, and York. This was a time of activism but also of rancorous arguments and staunch opposition to gay rights. We hear the uplifting story of folk singer Bobbi Carmitchell, who was at the center of a burgeoning women's music scene in central Pennsylvania, and her efforts to create the Women's Music Festival. The chapter tells the disturbing story of the firebombing of Nancy Helm's gay and lesbian bookstore in Lancaster, and we also meet Dan Miller, who recounts that he was fired, with no legal recourse, for being gay.

Chapter 7 explores the history of central Pennsylvania's celebration of Gay Pride. Large urban areas began celebrating Gay Pride in 1970, one year after the Stonewall riots. Social expressions of gay culture, however, developed differently in rural areas than in metropolitan ones. A Pride festival in central Pennsylvania was not held until 1985, some sixteen years after Stonewall. Called the Open Air Festival, it did not even use the words gay, lesbian, or pride in the name of the event because of the region's cultural homophobia. This chapter traces central Pennsylvania's celebrations of Pride through their various incarnations from the 1980s until the present.

Chapter 8 leads us into the twenty-first century and the maturation of the LGBTQ community in central Pennsylvania. We hear the case of Jennifer Harris and her lawsuit against Maureen "Rene" Portland, head coach of the Penn State University women's basketball team, for race and sex discrimination. This era also saw the transgender community come together to form TransCentralPA and launch its groundbreaking Keystone Conference. The organization left a lasting impact on the region and the nation by advocating for trans visibility and hosting educational programs. Finally, we hear a story of unity, as the community came together with the founding of the LGBT Center of Central PA in Harrisburg. The development of this center and its programs reflect how cooperative this LGBTQ community has become. We meet MJ Dougherty, whose compelling story of survival after the horrific September 11, 2001, terrorist attacks on the World Trade Center is an emotional tale of overcoming bigotry and discrimination and, ultimately, one of strength and courage. We also get to know Mara Keisling, founder and executive director of the National Center for Transgender Equality, as we follow her journey as a transgender woman and activist.

The broader message from this chorus of voices is that LGBTQ life exists and can even flourish outside of large urban areas. In central Pennsylvania, LGBTQ citizens have shown tremendous resilience in the face of hardship and have built an amazing community. I am inspired by their strength and courage, and I hope you will be too. This is their story.

A Note on Terminology

This book focuses on periods from the late 1950s to the present. During these years, different terms were used to refer to the LGBTQ community. In the 1950s, people with same-sex desires were known as homosexuals. Today historians commonly refer to the homophile movement of the 1950s, referring to the early activist days of the Mattachine Society and Daughters of Bilitis. By the mid-twentieth century, gay came into wide use and theoretically could apply to everyone. Lesbian feminists promoted the use of the term lesbian, which became the preferred designation among activists and nonactivists by the 1970s. By the next decade, the movement commonly referred to itself as gay and lesbian.[6] In the late 1990s and early 2000s, it became increasingly common to speak of the LGBT movement, with the increased visibility of the transgender movement and the acknowledgment of bisexual members of the community. And LGBTQ has recently gained traction as an inclusive term. Since this book chronologically covers LGBTQ history in central Pennsylvania, I have generally used the terms appropriate to the periods being discussed.

CHAPTER 1

Discovery

There was a time
I carved a heart on a tree in Pennsylvania
Using the knife from our picnic basket.
You, watching me in distress, whispered,
"Don't put our names in the heart!"
So fearful they would come upon us,
Finding our crop of love
Too foreign to accept,
And, like some Taliban sect,
Would raise up stones to put out our eyes.
Your eyes, blue and frightened
Implored me to leave the heart
Empty.
Having no armor for your fears,
I relented.
And returning the knife to its place in the basket,
We both leaned against the marred tree,
Shoulders touching—
The best we could do in a hostile world,
And silently we ate our tuna on rye.

—FROM LORRAINE KUJAWA, "THERE WAS A TIME"

In 1973 Jerry Brennan wanted to connect with other gay people in the small city of Harrisburg, Pennsylvania. He was frustrated with going to the few gay bars in the state capital, and he wanted other options for meeting and socializing. By 1975, Brennan had organized a church for the gay community that provided not only spiritual inspiration but also social activities and, depending on the event, drew in dozens of people each week.

More than eighteen years later, in May 1991, when Nancy Helm opened a gay bookstore in Lancaster, Pennsylvania, she received hate mail and death threats. By August her store had twice been firebombed. In January, fearing for the safety of her customers and herself, Helm closed her beloved bookstore.

During the 1970s, gay churches and gay bookstores were commonplace in large urban areas. Gay people living in large cities had plenty of social outlets where they could meet others, without resorting to gay bars. Metropolitan gays and lesbians in the 1990s certainly would not have expected a gay bookstore to be bombed. In central Pennsylvania, however, forming alternative social outlets and opening a gay bookstore were groundbreaking events, even though gays and lesbians had long been living there. The struggle to form a gay community in central Pennsylvania would face many hurdles that had long since been cleared for gay citizens in large urban centers. The history of the formation of a gay community in the heartland of Pennsylvania is told here. But gay culture dates back further and would eventually impact the formation of gay communities in the heartland of Pennsylvania.

Though same-sex attraction was by no means new in the early twentieth century, it was then that a gay subculture began to develop in earnest in the United States. Urban population growth in a rapidly industrializing country meant that for the first time, many men and women who found themselves attracted to others of the same gender could begin to connect, identify their attractions, socialize, and build networks.[1] By the 1930s, the community was taking shape in large cities across the country; after World War II, these urban enclaves also offered a social space for gay veterans. Though homosexuality was still illegal, gays and lesbians could live relatively openly within these cities, which became destinations for many young gays in rural areas seeking refuge and acceptance.[2] The Cold War era of the 1950s ushered in a wave of conformity and rendered homosexuality suspect, which further increased the hostile attitude toward gays and lesbians.[3]

In central Pennsylvania, smaller cities such as Harrisburg—the state capital and a railroad throughway—also underwent industrial development. The surrounding area was home to a small steel industry and a host of other manufacturing activities. In the postwar era, Harrisburg, York, Lancaster, and other small central Pennsylvania cities saw population growth, which spurred the opening of a few new gay bars. Despite the advances, there were no gay neighborhoods or formal social networks, and the formation of gay identity and gay culture in the region would prove not only difficult but also, for many people, traumatic.

Many decided to stay in central Pennsylvania, in both urban and rural areas. In most cases they led double lives, unable to come out to their straight friends, neighbors, and colleagues for fear of being fired, arrested, institutionalized, or turned away from their church. Nonetheless, these central Pennsylvania cities—along with State College, Williamsport, Carlisle, and other large towns and small cities in the region—were starting to become hubs in a wider rural area where same-sex attracted people on farms or in small towns lived in secret with very little or no connection to others like them. These connections would strengthen as time went on, but in the 1950s and 1960s the groundwork was still being laid in the region and a "gay consciousness" had not yet been widely developed.[4]

In this environment, the journey to self-discovery and the acceptance of gay identity were a struggle for many, and the opportunity to find others like themselves was virtually nonexistent. Reactions of their families when confronted with their sexual orientation were at times harsh and cruel. The stories of realizing their sexual identity, coming out, and seeking out others like themselves are riveting. Many felt as though they were alone, but they found others and soon began to build the beginnings of a community in central Pennsylvania. According to historians Nan Alamilla Boyd and Horacio N. Roque Ramírez, "Queer oral history as a genre works in many ways to generate a series of intelligible (or predictable) sexual signposts that mark the queer body's passage through time. . . . [It generates] explicit speech about sex, sexuality, and pleasure, and the no less valuable but more highly coded articulations about how sex and desire have shaped individuals and communities in history."[5] The following personal accounts look back at life in central Pennsylvania at midcentury, granting the reader a window onto the individual journeys of men and women whose lives were shaped by this environment.

Nobody Talked About It

Many individuals in central Pennsylvania, like those elsewhere, had experienced same-sex involvement prior to their high school years. Larry Wilson, the owner of two gay clubs in Harrisburg in the 1980s, remembers exploring his sexuality with neighborhood friends: "Nobody thought anything of it; nobody put a label on it. To us back then, especially in a small town, there wasn't anything known as gay or homosexual. It was a nonexistent thing. Nobody mentioned it; nobody talked about it. Now, as you got older and talk of homosexuality would come out in conversation and rumors about people in town [surfaced], then you learned what it was."[6]

For Larry, there was a distinct disconnect between a same-sex experience and the definition of sexuality. During his high school years in Huntingdon County, Larry was not aware of any gay people. But he remembers one man who was quite effeminate. "People talked about him," Larry recalls. "He was very isolated. He had no friends. He worked at the newspaper as some type of copyeditor. To me, that's what gay was. It [was] my only observation of somebody that was gay, and it was my only reference to what gayness was. And I knew I wasn't that. . . . So that's the reason it took me until I was twenty-six years old to actually realize and accept the fact that I was gay and to do something about it." It was only after meeting another gay man who did not embody the outward gay stereotype—and was someone to whom Larry could relate—that he accepted his own sexuality.

When Larry finally came out to his parents several years later, on the surface they were accepting but, as time went on, he was not as easily accepted by his mother as he was by his father. "She had a real problem with it on many different levels," Larry explains. "Primarily, it was her concern for me that I would not have a normal life. . . . Their concern was that you're not going to get married, have children." Like so many parents of that generation, they were placing their own values and life choices on their son. "You're going to have a lonely existence. That's what they felt, which hasn't been the case, but this was a concern on her part," Larry adds. "My dad, on the other hand . . . if you would ask him [now], he's glad I'm gay. He likes that I'm independent, different, my own person, that I'm not like the others, that I take charge of my life, and he has on many different occasions told me how proud he is of me for the life choices that I have made."

Talked in Whispers

Born at the end of World War II and raised in a fundamentalist religious family in York, Pennsylvania, Donald Fitz was baptized in a river by the Church of the Brethren at an early age. "I can't ever recall, growing up, hearing anything negative about homosexuals. I never [heard] anything—even the word *homosexual*," he says.[7] "There were people that were talked in whispers about, but not me, not to kids. I had a cousin by marriage that people said was a little weird, but nobody ever talked to me about what that meant, but I kind of knew that that was something that shouldn't be, and it was acted [on] with other men." Never having had any sexual feelings for girls growing up, Donald became the girls' best friend. The first awareness he had of his sexuality was late in elementary school, around the age of twelve, when he went to see a baseball game featuring one of the teams that his father sponsored. "There was a gentleman on one of the teams," he remembers. "His name was Junior. . . . I didn't tie it to anything sexual, but there was something about him that gave me chills, and I wanted to go back to that game again to see him play. So that's my first experience that there was something between me and . . . other men." Donald adds, "I can't say I didn't think it was natural. I just didn't know what it was." Donald kept his sexual feelings repressed for years, doing what was expected of him, dating girls, even having serious girlfriends, but there was "nothing sexual" about those relationships.

An identical set of twins, Donald and his brother, Ronald, were popular with the opposite sex. Ronald was athletic and excelled in sports, while Donald was studious and enjoyed music and the arts. The brothers were so close that they could finish each other's sentences. While his brother gained notoriety on the athletic fields, Donald hated gym class and anything sports related. "I felt bad about that," he recalls, "but I didn't tie it to anything sexual." When he entered college, Donald continued having relationships with women, but they were not sexual: "I never thought about that." One night in college, after a double date with a friend, the other male initiated sex with Donald. "I was in the car with one of my best friends . . . and we had gay sex. We both had girls, we were both involved with women, but the interesting thing about that is that we were never friends after that." The next sexual experience Donald had was in the Peace Corps, serving in Mumbai, India. "I was walking down the street, and a guy picked me up and took me back to his apartment, stripped me down, and he tried to have anal sex with me. It didn't happen, but I did ejaculate. . . . As soon as it happened, as soon as I came, he did not—I jumped back, got dressed, [and] got out of there. It was just not me. It was not me. I was not queer. So I came home, got married."

For the next several years of his marriage, Donald suffered a tormented existence. After their marriage, Donald and his wife moved to Harrisburg, where he began his teaching career and raising a family. Throughout his marriage, there were isolated stops at various men's rooms in the city, where he watched men masturbate but had no contact with them. He made frequent visits to a store in downtown Harrisburg that sold magazines for gays, where on one occasion he was picked up by a young student at the Harrisburg Area Community College. Suddenly things changed. "We must have driven for an hour, just talking. . . . Overnight, that was my coming out. Overnight, I was queer. Overnight, every part of my body was, 'Oh my god!' I cannot tell you the release. It was like being born again." Donald says, "I really knew, from that moment on, I was a queer man, and I was okay with that. . . . I didn't know what I was going to do about it, though, 'cause I had a very loving wife, a wonderful family."

Donald went back to his wife and immediately told her. She was in disbelief, constantly asking, "What's wrong with you? What's wrong?" They lived together for one more month and then eventually separated and divorced. Not much later, Donald came out to his twin brother. They were driving in his brother's car when Donald told him. Ronald immediately stopped and kicked him out. When Donald told his parents, his father fell to the floor, crying, rolling back and forth in anguish. His mother pleaded with him to move back home, where they would buy him a house and send him back to college, so he could change his career and his "wicked ways."

Donald eventually moved to Florida, where he continued his career in education, becoming the principal of an elementary school until his retirement in 2012. Donald has since moved back to the Harrisburg area to be near his two children and five grandchildren.

Act Like a Lady

Lorraine Kujawa was born in Brooklyn, New York, one of two children raised by a longshoreman father and a stay-at-home mother. Her life took a dramatic turn when she was fifteen: her father suddenly left, forcing her mother to take the children and move to Wilkes-Barre, Luzerne County, in northeastern Pennsylvania's hardscrabble anthracite coal region, where her grandparents lived. Lorraine was suddenly thrust into a conservative, Catholic factory and mining community, a vast contrast to the urban setting of her early years. Always a tomboy, continually roller skating and playing baseball, she drew harsh criticism from her mother, who was strict and constantly admonished her, "Behave yourself, act like a lady." Lorraine remembers that she was a tomboy. "I liked to play baseball, and I had a really good right arm. So I played with the boys."[8]

In looking back on those early years in the 1950s, Lorraine says she was not in touch with her lesbian identity. "I wasn't aware of anything in those days and [people] never even said the word gay. And I'd never even heard the word lesbian until I was out of college." She adds that she didn't realize "that there was another way of living" until after she had graduated and was working as a counselor at a Girl Scouts camp. Lorraine dated occasionally in college, but, as she recounts, "I wasn't really that interested and I hung out with my girlfriends. And I really just wasn't involved. . . . I wasn't into dressing up and . . . didn't feel quite a part of what was going on until I got out of school."

It was at the summer camp that she met someone "more knowledgeable than I was, and then I got involved with that person. And that was my coming out, and that led to getting to know other people." Lorraine says that "one of the hardest things for gay people to face is that silence of not speaking about their actual lives, and that followed me through to [my teaching career], too, because, of course, I could never tell anyone I was working with that I was a gay person."

For the next thirty-two years, Lorraine remained silent about her lesbian identity in the workplace. Although she has been partnered for more than three decades, her coworkers had assumed she lived alone. The reason for her silence is Pennsylvania's lack of laws banning discrimination in the workplace. Lorraine could have been fired for being gay. She has never told her parents or her brother. "It was a different age," says Lorraine. "I didn't really feel that I [needed] to burden [my mother] and try to explain it, so I never said anything to her."

I Just Felt Different for Years

John Folby was raised in a strict Catholic household in the early 1950s. Very early in his life, he knew that he was different. He was not attracted to girls. He did not know what it was called; he just knew he was different. "There was an expectation that I would date, I would go to functions with girls and take them out, and go to proms, and all of the typical stuff that you do when you're in school. So I did it, really just to please my parents."[9] As John recounts, "I just felt different for years." Someone at college recommended that he read *The Sexual Outlaw* by John Rechy. "It was about all of [Rechy's] sexual [exploits] in San Francicisco. . . . And by reading that book I started to learn more about [the] gay lifestyle." The man who recommended Rechy's book started introducing John to other friends, "and bit by bit I met people and started dating and going out, and feeling a lot more comfortable about my preference."

John did come out to several friends in college, but not to any of his siblings. He came out to his parents quite by accident. When his mother visited Harrisburg years later, when John was living there, she found a handful of gay magazines and confronted John. They talked about John being gay for hours; finally, she reluctantly resigned herself to John's sexuality. John and his father never broached the subject or discussed John's sexuality, even up until the day his father died. "Someone said to me, 'You have to remember your dad was ninety-four years old. [For] his generation, . . . for a son to be gay or a daughter to be gay, you just didn't talk about it. You didn't address it. And you're lucky—maybe if you had told him he [might] have kicked you out of the house." John went on to become the AZT coordinator for the Commonwealth of Pennsylvania during the AIDS epidemic, and his brothers, even knowing what John did for a living and the importance of his position in the common-wealth, never acknowledged the fact that John was gay or commented on the impact and contribution of his work.

It Was a Pretense

Sam Deetz, the son of a fundamentalist minister who was a pastor of God's Missionary Church, was one of eight children. During the course of Sam's early life, his father went from church to church, accepting "the call" as a minister, moving as far away as Colorado. Sam's mother's health brought the family back to central Pennsylvania, where Sam completed his schooling in a Christian high school. It was at this juncture in his life, at the age of sixteen, Sam remembers, "I became aware that I really had some differences that were going to affect my life. . . . I realized that I was attracted to men and had absolutely no attraction to girls."[10] By the late 1960s, Sam was severely conflicted. His father would claim Sam was "born again" at the age of three and often mentioned this in his sermons to illustrate that accepting Christ as your personal Savior could happen at a young age. According to Sam, when his father would recount that story, "[I'd] feel kind of guilty because I knew that it was a pretense. . . . But at that point I started praying silently and screaming in my own mind, 'God help me. God, somehow solve this problem. Take this away.'" In the twelfth grade, Sam reached out to one of his instructors. He told him there was a situation in his family that was very important, and he had to determine how to handle it—and it would have to be soon. As Sam remembers, "I didn't come out and name it. But I made it very clear. I'm sure that my instructor at that time probably [wondered], 'Well, what could this be?' but we never could talk about it."

The internal conflict continued for several years. For a while, Sam lived at home. He started working in the field of accounting and began to lead a double life. "I was living a life that was very secret because even though I was living with my family and even for a while was attending church regularly, I started dropping off going to church for any little excuse." Sam explains, "I was going to different places, seeking some sort of community. Some sort of feeling of belonging. Some acceptance. And so I was going to bathhouses and things like this." But Sam's conflict did not disappear: "I couldn't handle living alone in the city, even though I enjoyed the night life, and the cruising and all that. [It] really was getting on my nerves living alone and not having somebody that I really knew well to depend on." At the same time, Sam was hoping that his same-sex desire would evap-

Fig. 1 Sam Deetz. Courtesy of the LGBT Center of Central PA History Project, Archives and Special Collections, Dickinson College, Carlisle, Pennsylvania.

orate, "that I would get over it and find a way to love the opposite sex and get married and raise a family like the rest of my siblings."

As the years went by, Sam went through many stages of self-realization and growth. He discovered he liked the people he met at the bars in Harrisburg—the Neptune Lounge and the Silhouette. He became aware of the riots at the Stonewall Inn in New York and the changes in the stance of the American Psychiatric Association's position on homosexuality, and he slowly began to feel comfortable with himself. Sam discovered that the answer to prayers for the past eight years was no answer at all. "My answer, if it came from God or whatever, [was] 'you are what you are . . . and make the best of it.'" Sam came out soon after and went on to become a gay activist.

Sam's activism led to his coming out to his family at the age of twenty-four, with "a lot of crying [and] a lot of stunned silence on the part of my family."

My eldest brother was the assistant president at the Penn View Bible Institute [which] I graduated from. I had nieces and nephews and cousins attending there. I knew the bulk of their churches were in the central Pennsylvania area. . . . There were churches of the denomination all over, so everybody knew who I was. I had one nephew that said he was embarrassed because somebody at work said, "Are you related to that guy who was on the front page of the Sunbury Daily Item?" I don't know what my nephew said, but, apparently, he wasn't happy about it because later he moved to Florida and told me how embarrassed he was, and what a hard time it gave him on the job. I had a couple calls from relatives with hang-ups [i.e., hung up calls].

Over time there has been some acceptance from his immediate family but, as Sam explains, there is still a "gulf." His extended family has never truly accepted it.

Here All This Time, but I Couldn't See It

Born in 1960, Nancy Helm grew up in Lancaster. At the age of six, she was aware that she was gay. "I knew I was different from everybody else around me. But I didn't understand it, but I knew I had a crush on the gym teacher. I couldn't make heads nor tails of it at the time, 'cause of course you didn't hear about it. Ever. You know, you thought you were the only one."[11]

Like many gay men and lesbians, Nancy reaffirms what others have said: "I'll be honest, you didn't hear anything about *gay* back then, at all. You never did. I mean, this is why I always assumed I was the only one, because I never heard of it, never saw it, never knew anything about it. We were very sheltered here. You know, it's 'Farmville.'" In looking back at her early life, Nancy reflects that she didn't really date, but instead "just hung out with friends. I didn't know where to go with all that, or what to do, or where to meet [gay] people, or anything like that. So I just hung out with my friends, and I didn't even come out to them until much later. And when I did, I lost the majority of them."

Knowing she was a lesbian and different so early on in life, Nancy had a difficult time envisioning how she was going to live her life or what she was going to do. "I think I put it away, because it didn't seem like something that would come to fruition. It seemed like a boat out on the ocean with no motor and just no contact. Because there weren't other people like me that I knew of."

But things started to change for Nancy when she started socializing with one of her cousins who happened to be gay. One day, one of her cousin's friends approached her and said, "You're gay," an accusation Nancy immediately denied. With her defense mechanisms up, Nancy backed off the confrontation, unable to accept being called out so bluntly. According to Nancy, "It really freaked me out." She went home and started wondering, "Why did I do that? Why didn't I just say, 'Yeah?'" The following weekend, Nancy says, "I went back down and I was like, 'Yeah, and?' And they were like, 'Okay, let us introduce you to the world.'" After that, her life changed. She suddenly started meeting other lesbians and gay men in the Lancaster area. "I was blown away by the size of the community in Lancaster. I really was. 'Cause here all this time it was all around me, but I couldn't see it."

I Started to Become Fair Game

Growing up in the small town of Gap in eastern Lancaster County, David Walker, one of three children, was raised in a strict Evangelical United Brethren home by a stay-at-home mother and a father who was a former World War II veteran and army reservist. Well known in Gap, the Walker family had been around for generations and ran the local feed mill, delivering and picking up grain from local farmers.

Growing up in the 1950s and 1960s, David always knew he was different.[12] "[By] seventh grade, I became [known as] 'Gayzie,' right along with the old song 'Daisy, Daisy' ["Daisy Bell (Bicycle Built for Two)" from 1892], so that kind of hurt. . . . But by senior high, because I was a different person—I was totally different from the other hundred people in my class—I started to become fair game." David recalls being an outsider, someone interested in art, music, and the theater. "I got two varsity letters," David says. "One was because I was manager of the basketball team, and the other was because I was a cheerleader." According to David, these two varsity letters humiliated his father: cheerleading and managing only confirmed to his father that his son was not normal. His parents were always very strict with his siblings, but, David explains, "They had just given up with me, as the third one. And again it was because I was different. They sensed something about me from day one." So, David, says, he was "given free rein on a lot of stuff." And as for his artistic interests, "they never encouraged me, but they very seldom discouraged me."[13]

After graduating from high school, he spent the summer before going off to college working in a summer theater, where he fell in love with the leading man. This was essentially David's coming out. "I had experimented before that [in school], . . . but that was the first affair of any length." The relationship continued into freshman year. The two stayed in contact through letters, David says, since "he lived in New York, and I was in Annville [in Lebanon County, Pennsylvania]."[14]

David's coming out to his parents was the result of his military classification. This was the time of the Vietnam War, and David had received his draft notice. When he appeared at the induction center for his physical, David "checked the box," stating he was homosexual. He was given 4-F classification, unfit for duty, and rejected for military service. His father, with his awareness of the military, knew what a 4-F rating meant; it was another source of humiliation for his father and a continuation of the friction between them. As for his mother, she was accepting and understanding. The family friction, however, continued throughout David's life. He is not invited to family functions such as Thanksgiving, Christmas, or summer picnics. But as David reflects, "That's okay, I don't mind." He adds, "One of the finest things [my sister] ever said to me was . . . that whenever she heard [Cass Elliot's 'Make Your Own Kind of Music'], she thought of me—that you have to make your own kind of music, sing your own special song."[15] And that's what David has done.

I Was Different

Kathy Fillman was born in Coatesville, Chester County, and grew up in the small town of Loag's Corner at Elverson. Even though Kathy describes her life growing up on her grandparents' farm as idyllic, it was also troublesome. Her mother was not around much. Kathy remembers that after her mother divorced her father, "my mother, my aunt, and my two uncles, they were pretty much drunks. So I spent a lot of time in bars when I was a kid. Probably more time as a kid than I did as an adult. They were always out drinking somewhere."[16] For the first twelve years of Kathy's life, she lived with her grandparents and attended a Catholic school. After her mother had remarried again, Kathy had an urgent desire to live with her. She left her grandparents and moved in with her mother and her new husband. It was a disastrous decision. As Kathy recounts, "That was hell, 'cause they were both drunks. He was a raging alcoholic and very abusive. . . . [It] was pretty traumatic being around that all the time." Kathy felt that she couldn't go back to her grandparents, who had retired. "They had sold the place and they were, you know, living in a trailer." She left as soon as she turned eighteen.

While growing up, Kathy had an awareness of her sexuality at an early age. "I knew it, about age five, that I was different. But I didn't know what that meant. And I remember, in Catholic school, somebody called somebody queer, and I didn't know what that meant. And I asked my grandmother, and she said that's when men and women do bad things. So I still had no clue what *queer* was, but I wasn't allowed to use that word." Kathy recalls that growing up and watching television in the 1950s was all Fred Astaire and Ginger Rogers. "I wanted to be suave and debonair; I didn't want to be the women. I always had crushes on them."

Things became clearer to Kathy in high school. She began to develop crushes, all on women. She developed a friendship with one woman, and they began to write notes back and forth to each other, but Kathy had no idea that the woman was gay. The woman later had an affair with another girl, which became public knowledge. The couple was ostracized. Because of Kathy's prior friendship with the woman, people then started accusing Kathy of being gay, even though nothing had ever transpired between the two. Kathy had not yet had a same-sex relationship, but she now knew her own identity because of what had happened and the nature of her feelings toward the woman. Kathy finally came out to her mother at the age of twenty-one. As Kathy remembers, "The first thing out of my mother's mouth was, 'What did I do wrong?' And I was like, 'Well, I can think of several things. But nothing having to do with me being gay.'"

You Don't Know How to Put That Together

Born in 1949, Marlene Kanuck was raised by a father who was a Lutheran minister and a mother active as both a stay-at-home mom and a pastor's wife. Marlene grew up in a strict, religious household, eventually attending three different schools during her high school years. Wanting to become a doctor, Marlene applied for admission to Muhlenberg College, Allentown, her father's alma mater. The college had been coed for only a few years at the time, and she was denied admission. Marlene applied to Penn State and was accepted, but her father insisted she attend Thiel College in Greenville, Mercer County, in western Pennsylvania.[17]

Once there, Marlene rebelled and began dating an older man from her church. She married him by April of her freshman year. After two children and eleven years of marriage, Marlene left her husband. "The marriage was just not working out—it was pretty emotionally abusive." She remembers, "I had tried leaving many times before that, and for various reasons, I would come back. It's hard to leave a marriage."

After her divorce, she started dating, then living with, another man named Bill. Marlene and Bill soon became close friends with another couple who were dating at the time, a woman named Anne and her partner, also named Bill. Anne and Marlene quickly became close friends. They both were divorced mothers of two children who were nearly the same ages. Marlene and Anne were constantly together, doing lots of things. One night Bill asked Marlene if she ever thought she was gay. "I said 'No.' I was just even shocked that he brought it up. . . . I said, 'Well, why?' And he says, ''Cause I think you're in love with Anne.'" Upon reflection, Marlene believes, "I probably was, but I wasn't ready to admit it." Bill pursued his questioning, asking her if she had ever considered same-sex relationships. This launched Marlene on the road to self-discovery.

She initially decided she might be bisexual. She was living with a man, but she had feelings and deep affection for a woman. But upon reflection, she identified earlier crushes: "I definitely had a lot of fantasies about my best [female] friend in high school." Like many others of that era, "I think what I realized is I didn't have the words. . . . I had never heard the word gay in respect to a woman." Marlene recounts the only time that she heard the word gay was in association with a man who was a student pastor at her church when she was growing up. Suddenly, one day he was gone. "It was all hush-hush, because [he] had left. And then it was [said that he] had left because he was gay. . . . So it was all negative." And, she adds, "I certainly had never heard of women being together. Even though you have feelings, you have fantasies, you don't know how to put that together."

Twenty years later Marlene faced her sexuality and decided she should do something about it. Bill was understanding and helped Marlene on her journey, sometimes accompanying her to gay bars. She eventually moved out and began building a new life to accept her lesbian identity.

Immoral and Indecent Conduct

Born in 1927 in Berrysburg, a small Dauphin County borough thirty miles north of Harrisburg, Richard Schlegel lived in various small towns in Pennsylvania while he was growing up. He entered Penn State University, graduated in 1949, and then moved to Washington, DC, acquiring a master's degree and taking a job with the federal government. Richard received many promotions

Fig. 2 Richard Schlegel (*second from right*) with other officials from the Pennsylvania Department of Highways, giving a presentation on the agency budget. Reprinted with permission of the family by Robert Deibler.

and transfers that earned him some of the highest civilian job classifications and security clearances in the US government. His career ended in 1961, when he was fired for "immoral and indecent conduct" after investigators secretly trailed him as he went about his personal life. He appealed his case, *Schlegel v. the United States*, which went all the way to the US Supreme Court, where he eventually lost.[18]

Richard returned to central Pennsylvania in late 1962. On a whim he sent his résumé to the Governor's Office of Administration, Bureau of Personnel, in Harrisburg. Newly elected governor William Warren Scranton was just beginning to fill his top appointed positions, and Richard was in the right place at the right time. In early 1963, he was interviewed and hired as director of finance for the Department of Highways (reorganized in 1970 as the Pennsylvania Department of Transportation, or PennDOT) and began enjoying success in his new position.

In Richard's private life, he knew several leaders of the Janus Society, which was a gay organization founded in 1962 in Philadelphia. He had attended some of the group's meetings. The president of the Janus Society contacted Richard and encouraged him to establish a central Pennsylvania chapter. Richard recruited a small membership and opened a post office box in Harrisburg to receive society correspondence. This is believed to be the first gay organization created in central Pennsylvania. It would not last long.

Richard immediately sensed something was wrong when he was unexpectedly summoned to his supervisor's office one day in the late summer of 1965. To his surprise, there was a postal inspector in the room. He had experienced similar feelings several years before, having undergone a federal investigation of his private life and losing his job. Now he was being confronted by another federal official, this time for receiving material in a post office box from the Janus Society, which postal inspectors deemed obscene. An investigation of his private life in Harrisburg ensued, and he was fired from his high-profile state position. Richard moved to Philadelphia and the central Pennsylvania chapter of the Janus Society folded.

Seeking Out Others

As these individuals and other young gays and lesbians in central Pennsylvania during the 1950s and 1960s began to accept their homosexuality, they had a need and desire to seek out others like themselves. The only place they could turn to meet others were the few bars that catered to a gay clientele in Harrisburg. Looking back on that era, John Folby recalls, "When I was growing up the gay bar was your haven. The place where you could go to be with people who were like you, to feel safe, hang out, meet people, socialize, [and] have a really good time."[19] Paul Foltz, a founding member of the Harrisburg Gay Men's Chorus and the founder of Lily White and Company, a troupe of men who performed in drag and raised money for gay causes, remembers the feeling of isolation. "You will commonly hear from people of my generation that when they were [young], they felt like they were the only gay person in the world because there was no way to know that there were other gay people in the world. Because the only [places] you could encounter other gay people were either in bars or in much more steamy places."[20]

By the 1960s, urban centers had gay neighborhoods and numerous gay and lesbian bars. New York had Chelsea, Greenwich Village, and Harlem, and San Francisco had the Castro and the Tenderloin District, where gays and lesbians could live, socialize, and move about freely. Philadelphia had a dozen or so gay bars between Spruce and Locust Streets, west of Broad Street, forming what has become known as the City of Brotherly Love's iconic Gaybor-hood.[21] In central Pennsylvania communities there were few gay bars and no gay neighborhoods where gays might relocate. In Harrisburg, a city whose major employer was the state government, being out was dangerous.

In 1938, Harrisburg's first gay bar, the Clock Bar, opened. Located at 400 North Second Street, the bar had an art deco neon sign that hung out over the street. Inserted inside the letter *O* of the word *Clock* was a depiction of a time-piece. The theme continued inside the bar, where many different clocks displayed various times zones throughout the world. A long narrow rect-angular bar filled about 70 percent of the space, accommodating approximately twenty people. In the back were tables and chairs and one lone booth for the balance of the thirty or so patrons in the bar. Also in the rear was an area for danc-ing, with a mirror-covered wall. The bar was not well lit, but once one's eyes adjusted to the atmo-sphere, the music and camaraderie soon made for a welcoming environment. For the occasion of going out, people dressed nicely. Harrisburg resident Bob Kregis remembers, "Saturday night was coat and tie." Larry Wilson adds, "You dressed up and put on your best."[22]

Fig. 3 Location of the first gay bar in Harrisburg, the Clock Bar, at 400 North Second Street. The bar opened in 1938 and closed in 1965, then became a series of gay bars, including the 400 Club, the Apple and the Frenchman, the Dandelion Tree (as pictured here, ca. 1978), and finally La Rose Rouge (closed in 1990). It later turned into a series of restaurants and bars. Photo: John Koch. Reprinted with permission of Dr. Eric Selvey, editor, *Crossroads Magazine*.

The laws enforced by the Pennsylvania Liquor Control Board (PLCB) required that a bar have a seat for every person in the establishment. The Clock Bar could accommodate only fifty people at a time. As each patron freely moved about the bar, the bartender kept track of the seating. Wilson recalls, "To the LCB [it was] a head count and a chair count." If you wanted to meet someone, you'd ask the bartender to send him a drink. If the response was positive, you could go over to meet him, and the bartender would "protect" your seat.

Dancing was a big draw on the weekends, especially on Saturday nights. During the 1950s and 1960s, it was the main reason patrons flocked to the bar on weekends. During that era the bar was continually aware of the possibility of raids and harassment by the police.

You always had someone monitoring the door back in the '50s and '60s, so that when the cops were coming, they would turn the lights up. The first thing they would do was turn the lights up, turn the music down—I mean, there was a checklist, and it worked like clockwork. It was beautifully orchestrated. And once the lights went up, and it wasn't last call, you knew that if you were two guys you couldn't dance any more. You'd better go find a seat, because they are going to leave you alone if you are sitting somewhere.

The system did not work flawlessly at all times. In 1965, the PLCB cracked down on the Clock Bar, revoking its liquor license.[23] The bar reopened the following year under new ownership as the 400 Club and continued to function as a series of gay bars under different owners and names until 1990.

Along with the Clock Bar were also Johnny Kobler's, a restaurant and bar, and the Hotel Warner. Both were places where gays could gather and socialize. The major difference was that these two establishments were primarily heterosexual. Johnny Kobler's, located at the corner of Strawberry Alley and Court Street in downtown Harrisburg, opened in 1937. It was a welcoming place for gays and became a hangout during the 1940s and 1950s. In 1953, the owner, Johnny Kobler, died, and the lawyers for his estate ran the restaurant and bar. By 1957, the establishment had "turned gay" and was functioning as Harrisburg's second gay bar. Gays would frequent both the Clock Bar and Johnny Kobler's for their social interactions. By the end of 1961, the estate was finally settled, and Johnny Kobler's closed.[24]

The Hotel Warner was located just off Market Square in downtown Harrisburg on Second Street. The hotel had an extremely large circular bar on the first floor that soon became a draw for many gays and lesbians. "It was frequented by gays, but it was a very mixed crowd—it was never a gay bar," Larry Wilson remembers. "It was just frequented by gays because they had a gay bartender behind the bar, and you had an accepting place that didn't throw the gays out."[25] The Warner Hotel bar continued as a popular local spot for gays well into the early 1970s. The building was demolished in 1987 to make way for a parking deck for the new Hilton Hotel.

The bars were a white male–dominated world. During the 1960s, a few lesbians would frequent the three bars, but the preponderance of the clientele was white gay men. "We were a gay bar community downtown of white males, period," says Wilson. "There were eight to ten lesbian women that were allowed in. They were accepted as part of the crowd. There were eight to ten black men that were allowed in and that were very much a part of the crowd.

Fig. 4 Matchbook from Johnny Kobler's restaurant and bar. Johnny Kobler's was one of Harrisburg's gay-friendly mixed bars in the 1940s and 1950s. Photo: Sue Blosser. Courtesy of the LGBT Center of Central PA History Project, Archives and Special Collections, Dickinson College, Carlisle, Pennsylvania.

Fig. 5 The Hotel Warner, one of Harrisburg's gay-friendly mixed bars in the 1950s and 1960s. Image: *01A8 Market Square, Harrisburg, PA*, 1960, MG-214.1, Warren J. Harder Collection, Pennsylvania State Archives, Harrisburg.

A Harrisburg Centennial Celebration Souvenir Photograph 1960

There were no drag queens. You were only allowed to dress up on selected gay holidays. You know, Halloween, New Year's Eve, if you're having some kind of presentation. . . . These were rules that were strictly enforced by the management, by the owners and by the bar managers." This was a predetermined business decision by the bar owners. They wanted to control who patronized their bars, feeling that if they let certain groups come in, they would eventually take over the bar.[26] In 1975 the region's first lesbian bar, the Silhouette, opened on North Front Street in Harrisburg to counter these restrictive policies and practices toward women. A year later, it would change ownership and become the D-Gem.

While these bars dominated the bar scene from the 1940s through the 1960s in Harrisburg, in the nearby city of Lancaster, the Tally Ho Tavern opened at 201 West Orange Street in 1968. Prior to its opening, the only bar in Lancaster open to gays and lesbians was located in the basement of the Village Night Club. The main level of the club was reserved for its straight clientele. In the early 1960s, George Centini went to work as a bartender for Ebey's bar on West Orange Street. In 1966, when the owner died, Centini decided to buy the liquor license from the owner's widow and purchase the building. It was then that he renamed the bar the Tally Ho and continued to run the operation as it had been, catering to a straight clientele. When the Village Night Club closed in 1968, Centini decided that he would begin catering to the gay crowd. To do so, he remodeled the bar and changed his marketing approach. He changed the interior walls from knotty pine to shingle and wagon wheels, a custom Western theme, and added a huge rectangular bar. As he remembers, "We had a forty-seat bar, and it was the biggest bar in the city."[27] He changed the dress code, did away with draft beer, and just served mixed drinks and bottled beer. These changes, along with instituting a two-dollar cover charge at the door, were aimed at keeping the "rough guys" out and maintaining control of who entered. Those who paid the two-dollar cover were given a ticket for a drink at the bar.

By 1971, Centini and his partner, Gary Hufford, decided to take over the rooming house upstairs and open a restaurant. They worked for more than a year remodeling the space, they hired a chef and, by 1972, The Loft opened. Centini and Hufford now had two booming businesses. The restaurant attracted a mixed crowd and received rave reviews. Downstairs they introduced dancing and soon were attracting large crowds—well more than two hundred customers on weekends. They began to throw seasonal parties on Halloween, Christmas, and New Year's and to organize bus trips to Atlantic City for their patrons.

The Tally Ho Tavern and The Loft restaurant were then the dominant gay and lesbian hot spots in Lancaster.

In State College, located in Centre County, the earliest known gay bar was the My-Oh-My, likely opened in the early 1960s. What made this bar unusual is that one half of the bar catered to heterosexuals and the other half to homosexuals. As one former student from Penn State, Tony Silvestre, recalls,

> We had a gay bar in State College, actually it was half a bar, called the My-Oh-My. The entrance from College Avenue, the main drag, led down some steps into the bar. And then as you walked further into the bar and made a left, you walked into the straight end of the bar, where they usually had scantily-clothed women dancing [*laughs*]. And so it wouldn't be unusual for the Steel Worker's Convention to have a bunch of their delegates watching the women and of course on the gay side have a bunch of gay men and women. But things were touchy back then, so we weren't allowed to dance in the bar because that's how rigid society was.[28]

A letter of complaint was printed in a 1972 edition of the Alternative, the newsletter of Homophiles of Penn State (HOPS), which lamented that the gay section of the bar had been allowed to deteriorate while money had been continually spent on the straight side of the bar. This indicates how long the bar had been open. The article further describes the gay side as "dark, smoky, run-down, with a poor collection of music, poor drinks, and poor bar service."[29] The My-Oh-My's liquor license was revoked in 1977 on a charge of offering lewd entertainment. The owner lost on a court appeal and the bar closed.

In the small rural town of Spring Grove, near York, Altland's Ranch opened in 1967 at 8505 Orchard Road. The region's second lesbian bar, the Sundown Lounge, opened in 1976, in Lancaster. These bars were a major expansion of gay life outside the Harrisburg area, surviving in the small cities of central Pennsylvania.

Fig. 6 Advertisement for Altland's Ranch in Spring Grove, York County, from the *Gay Era* newspaper, June 1976, 14. Courtesy of the LGBT Center of Central PA History Project, Archives and Special Collections, Dickinson College, Carlisle, Pennsylvania.

It was not unusual during the 1960s and 1970s for gays and lesbians in central Pennsylvania to drive hours or hundreds of miles to go to a gay bar

Fig. 7 Flyer advertising Halloween celebration at Altland's Ranch in Spring Grove, York County. Courtesy of the LGBT Center of Central PA History Project, Archives and Special Collections, Dickinson College, Carlisle, Pennsylvania.

to meet someone. Dan Maneval, from Williamsport, tells the story of how he learned of a gay bar—Castaway's Inn in Cresson, in the western part of the commonwealth—through a gay newspaper. He decided to drive the two hours to the bar. Upon entering, he went up to the bartender and asked, "Do you know anybody at all here from Williamsport?" He was surprised when the bartender pointed out a gentleman at end of the bar. Maneval went over and introduced himself and asked the man where he lived. When the man responded that he lived on Beaver Street, Maneval was taken aback—so did he. Pursuing it further, Maneval found out that he lived just a few houses away from him. The two had never met, but each had traveled more than two hours just to find a neighbor.[30]

In the 1960s and 1970s, there were two places where gay men could go to cruise for sex. One was the bar at the New Plaza Hotel in Harrisburg, which was known for its gay-friendly bar but even more for its infamous men's room downstairs. Sexual encounters occurred regularly in the hotel's bathrooms.[31]

Even more notorious and frequented was the cruising area along State Street, near Front Street, in downtown Harrisburg. The street had a center island that one could drive around continuously. Along the street, men—not infrequently male hustlers—would stand, waiting to be picked up. The area was occasionally raided by the police. After the bars closed, the traffic would increase, along with the danger of police arrest. As Harrisburg resident Richard Hause recounts, "If you were stopped by the police, your name and address would be in the paper the next morning."[32]

The aftermath of being caught and arrested could be devastating. The *Daily Patriot* and the *Evening News* would report these stops and arrests as "Homosexual Nests" or "Homosexual Rings," sensationalizing each incident.[33] Pennsylvania would not repeal its sodomy laws until 1980, and the men cruising along State Street were taking a calculated risk of arrest and possible prosecution. In an era when homosexuality was considered a threat to society and a moral perversion, the county and state would take legal action against those arrested. In July 1965, the newly sworn-in county district attorney, LeRoy S. Zimmerman, decided to crack down on the homosexual activity occurring in the State Street area and the Clock Bar by conducting a monthlong investigation that led to a series of raids and arrests. Twenty-six men and a male juvenile, ranging in age from fifteen to sixty-two, were arrested and taken into custody. All were charged with soliciting to commit sodomy, while others also faced charges of corrupting the morals of a minor. Their names, ages, and addresses were published in the local newspapers, adding to their disgrace. More than thirty state and city police, together with PLCB agents, took part in the arrests.[34]

When Richard Schlegel lived in Harrisburg, he had a front-row seat to these events from his apartment on State Street. As Schlegel remembers, LeRoy Zimmerman pursued charges, and "these people were arraigned and they were charged with this and that and the other thing. Some of them eventually came to trial. . . . I don't remember what the sentences were anymore. These were older men sometimes; sometimes [they were men] still in their twenties. . . . Some were tried, some skipped, some pleaded guilty,

Fig. 8 The New Plaza Hotel, another of Harrisburg's gay-friendly mixed bars, with a notorious men's room in the basement. It closed in 1976 after a major fire destroyed most of the building. Photo: Sue Blosser. Courtesy of the LGBT Center of Central PA History Project, Archives and Special Collections, Dickinson College, Carlisle, Pennsylvania.

and some killed themselves." Schlegel remembers the suicide of one young man:

> That one suicide I will never forget. . . . He was in the full bloom of life and had no real reason to be doing this, other than having this inflicted on him. The funeral was held [at] St. Patrick's Cathedral. I looked out of my living room window when I saw that casket being hauled out. I will never forget that. At that point I swore eternal hatred to this man Zimmerman, because I thought that this was so totally unnecessary. It was only for his political aggrandizement. And I will never say anything other than that. He used [these arrests] to advance his own political career.[35]

Zimmerman commented in a statement he issued about the arrests, "This is no one-shot deal. This is a continuing investigation. Some definite course of action must be taken to rid our community of this infectious disease."[36]

The men who were arrested were from many of the small cities in central Pennsylvania, including Harrisburg, Lebanon, York, Mechanicsburg, Steelton, Halifax, and Lancaster. The arrests continued over the ensuing month, and when the men went to trial, the sentences and fines varied. Some were sentenced to jail, while others were fined and placed on probation (as long as thirty-three months in jail and up to $300 in fines).[37]

The harassment of gays and lesbians continued when, on October 27, the PLCB announced it had revoked the license of the Clock Bar. The charges were that the bar was "maintaining a disorderly house and permitting the solicitations of patrons for immoral purposes."[38] By the end of 1965, the city of Harrisburg had clamped down on its homosexual population, severely limiting its gay social meeting places.

Even with all the risks, gay men continued to cruise the State Street area well into the late 1980s. When Mayor Stephen R. Reed began encouraging the development of new restaurants in the area in the early 1990s, the idea soon ballooned into a large-scale development project. The entire Capitol Hill area of Harrisburg was reshaped and later, with the redesign of the paving and streetscaping of State Street, the days of cruising abruptly ended.

Indicating that the larger community lauded the antigay policing, friends of Judge William W. Lipsett, who presided over the cases, and District Attorney Zimmerman held a testimonial dinner for the pair on October 19, 1965. More than seven hundred people attended the dinner, held at the former Penn-Harris Hotel in Harrisburg. There was no distinct award being bestowed on

Fig. 9 The interior of the building at 400 North Second Street in Harrisburg, when it was La Rose Rouge. Note the clock, which is a holdover from the original Clock Bar. Courtesy of the LGBT Center of Central PA History Project, Archives and Special Collections, Dickinson College, Carlisle, Pennsylvania.

either of the two men, just their friends getting together to honor them. The dinner came in the midst of the heated crackdown that both men were involved with in the city of Harrisburg. Both men received portraits of themselves. The *Harrisburg Patriot-News* pointed out that Judge Lipsett was a bachelor, while Zimmerman was married and the father of two children.[39]

Zimmerman achieved a high political office. He went on to become the first elected Pennsylvania attorney general, serving from 1981 until 1989.[40] In 2011, however, he resigned as chair of the Hershey Trust after the trust was placed under investigation by Attorney General Kathleen Granahan Kane for diverting funds from the Milton Hershey School to a money-losing golf course.[41]

By 1970, the Stonewall uprising rocked New York City but had little impact on gay life and activism in central Pennsylvania. The early gay bars had all closed. The closeted life that gays and lesbians led continued as usual. In Harrisburg, the Neptune Lounge, formerly a bar catering to heterosexuals, was purchased by Jim Bortzfield in 1972, who immediately spread the word to its existing clientele that it was now a gay bar. It was an immediate success. Bortzfield established happy hours and organized theme parties throughout the year.[42] During the 1970s, five other gay bars opened in Harrisburg:

Fig. 10 Advertisement for the Tavern in the Town, York, from the *Gay Era* newspaper, June 1976, 13. Courtesy of the LGBT Center of Central PA History Project, Archives and Special Collections, Dickinson College, Carlisle, Pennsylvania.

The Ark, Strawberry Inn, Class One, Orpheus, and Shadows. Bars had also opened in other cities, like the Tavern in the Town in York, the Fiddler in Lancaster, the Palmer House in Northumberland, the Scorpion Lounge in State College, and several others. The world for gays and lesbians had finally started to change.

Not all gays and lesbians frequented bars. Many avoided the bar scene entirely, choosing instead to socialize privately on their own. People would sometimes host cocktail and dinner parties for groups of friends. Some hosted dinner parties regularly, twice a month. These gatherings ran the gamut from informal to formal, and guests always came wearing their best.[43]

Sometimes the private parties turned into major events, as in the case of Will Kratz and Vince Grimm. Kratz began performing in drag in 1959 at the Zanzibar, a gay bar in the Berks County seat of Reading. Two years later, he met Grimm, who had just returned to Reading after a two-year deployment with the US Army in Korea, at another gay bar in Reading, the Big Apple. The two would forge a relationship lasting more than fifty years, while helping to create a unique series of social events for the gay community in central Pennsylvania. In 1961, Kratz wanted to stage a much larger and more elaborate choreographed drag show, so he made arrangements with the owner of the Big Apple bar, whose relatives owned a nearby picnic area with a building and a pavilion, to rent the facility. Kratz, Grimm, and their friends staged four shows a year to an ever-increasing audience, eventually reaching more than 600 attendees.[44]

The shows needed money to survive, so Kratz and Grimm decided to put on three picnics a year and charge admission to fund the performances. The drag shows and summer picnics were held from 1961 through 1979. The picnics became legendary, with people coming from as far away as northern New Jersey, Baltimore, and Washington, DC. Attendance would top 1,500 people. Some people arrived in themed buses; one group arrived in costume as Vatican officials, including the pope. A lesbian arrived one year riding on the back of an elephant, accompanied by two tigers she borrowed from a local circus.[45]

As gay activist Joe Burns recalls,

> The Reading picnics were well known. They featured a chicken and corn roast, and the beer was free for the price of admission. The gate of the picnic was protected by off-duty police, but the real appeal of the picnics was the unfettered freedom of what I call "the hundred-acre woods" beyond the picnic shelters. The picnics provided funding for amateur, almost professional quality, drag shows. I remember having to cross a very small foot bridge over a stream to get to the barn where the drag shows were staged. The regular performers were well known from appearing year after year, including comedians, [and] lip sync and real voiced performances.[46]

Kratz and Grimm did not realize at the time that what they were doing was unprecedented. Eight years before the Stonewall riots, they were helping to build a gay community in central Pennsylvania and putting it on the map.

As the gay and lesbian community started to grow in central Pennsylvania during the 1960s and 1970s, a larger demand for expanded social networks developed. Going to a bar in Harrisburg or a dinner party at someone's home was simply not fulfilling the social needs of the community. There were no distinct gay and lesbian neighborhoods to move into. More social outlets and activities were needed where gays and lesbians could meet like-minded individuals. By filling this void, the foundation for establishing the gay and lesbian community in central Pennsylvania would be laid.

CHAPTER 2

Sparks!

Ignited by the Stonewall Inn uprising and subsequent demonstrations and riots in late June 1969, a firestorm erupted that forever changed the gay movement. Word quickly spread throughout the country that something huge was happening in the gay community, and the sparks from those flames soon spread.

Prior to Stonewall, gay men and lesbians had begun the fight for their civil liberties with the first activist action in what was known as the homophile movement. The publication of Alfred Kinsey's scientific study *Sexual Behavior in the Human Male* in 1948 received widespread media coverage and provoked an intense national discussion about homosexuality; Americans became increasingly alarmed and concerned about its prevalence. The results from the Kinsey study—which showed much more homosexual contact among men than anyone had expected—shocked the public.[1] For gays, the study confirmed that they were not alone: there were thousands of homosexuals in the United States. Homophile activist organizations such as the Mattachine Society (founded in 1950) and the Daughters of Bilitis (founded in 1955) gained attention, and members, with social events, lectures, newsletters, and political discussions.[2]

By the mid-1960s, US society was experiencing dramatic change. Young people were promoting shifts in sexual attitudes, with music and the arts reflecting ideas of sexual freedom and blurred gender roles. The antiwar, feminist, and civil rights movements were in full swing. Strikes, protests, and political assassinations contributed to the sense of social upheaval. Some in the homophile movement identified with other oppressed minority groups and felt the same sense of frustration with the slow pace of progress.[3]

By 1969, the stage had been set for the public expression of gay and lesbian discontent—for combined action and political resistance. On June 28 at the Stonewall Inn, a gay bar in Manhattan, gays, lesbians, and transgender people, including people of color, resisted arrest, and thousands went to the streets in violent protests and riots lasting more than three days. Those who had participated knew that something powerful had been unleashed, but there was little newspaper coverage in the mainstream press; the story was generally relegated to the back pages. In the aftermath of the uprising, the question became how to keep the momentum going. A former member of the New York Mattachine Society, Jack Nichols, along with his partner, Lige Clarke, wrote to a gay newspaper with an urgent question: "Will the spark die?"[4]

The spark did not die. Across the country, gay men and lesbians—once reluctant to become involved—now began to join or create new activist organizations that would supersede the early efforts of the Mattachine Society and the Daughters of Bilitis. By the 1970s, gay and lesbian activist, religious, and campus groups were spreading across the country, even reaching into the heart of central Pennsylvania. The new activists began to lobby, protest, and demand their civil rights. Change was now under way, but a long road lay ahead.[5]

Sparks Land in Central Pennsylvania

In the Keystone State, Jerry Brennan proved to be one of those activists who was spurred into action in the aftermath of the Stonewall uprising. Born in 1943 in the small community of Shamokin in northeastern Pennsylvania, Brennan grew up in a devout Irish Catholic home. His domineering father operated an automobile repair shop, and his demure mother was a homemaker. His deep religious roots and his emerging homosexuality confused him at an early age, but it also instilled in him a lasting empathy with the disenfranchised, the oppressed, and others like him who were ostracized and relegated to the fringes of society. By the time Brennan had finished his senior year in high school in 1961, he had decided to pursue the priesthood. He first attended the seminary at St. Jerome's University in Kitchener, Ontario, Canada, and later matriculated at the seminary of St. Bernard's Abbey in Cullman, Alabama. It was in Alabama that the social and civil rights upheavals of the 1960s would affect Brennan and irreversibly alter his life's path.

It was in Cullman, Brennan recounted later to friends, that he saw a large billboard that addressed African American people with a racial slur, followed by "don't let the sun set on your black ass in Cullman, Alabama."[6] Brennan's sense of injustice was enraged. The civil rights movement was just beginning, and he immediately related to the plight of those who had been marginalized, though it was not because of his race but for his sexuality. The denial of equal rights to the black population struck a chord deep in Brennan. In March 1965, he decided to become involved and joined the historic five-day, fifty-four-mile march from Selma to Montgomery, Alabama, led by Dr. Martin Luther King Jr. The experience was transformative, and Brennan decided to focus his life on making a difference for others. He was also coming to terms with his own sexuality and decided the priesthood was no longer an option.

In autumn 1966, he entered Penn State University at University Park in Centre County, working toward a degree and a career in social work. In June 1969, after finishing his junior year, Brennan received a telephone call from a gay friend living in New York. The friend encouraged Brennan to come to New York to experience what was happening, including an uprising after police raided the Stonewall Inn. Brennan's activist instincts immediately engaged, and he committed himself to spending part of the summer in New York.

In the heat of the newly energized gay rights movement following Stonewall, some women and men in New York City formed the Gay Liberation Front (GLF). This was a militant activist organization, modeled in the radical political style of the New Left.[7] Soon after its creation, a few members of GLF split off and founded the Gay Activists Alliance (GAA). The GAA's mission was entirely different and focused solely on obtaining civil rights for gay and lesbians.[8]

Brennan attended the meetings of both GLF and GAA that summer, witnessing the unprecedented burst of anger and action fanning the sparks of the gay movement. Brennan learned from these groups that the first step toward freedom was to come out of the closet. This act fused the personal and the political. How could you fight for your own equality if you did not make yourself known? His awareness continued to grow, and from these groups he hypothesized two basic approaches to achieve social change: advocate for the reform of laws, public policies, and practices so that lesbians and gay men could experience equal treatment, and create and nurture institutions to allow for a strong, cohesive, and visible gay community. He finished his senior year at Penn State, but he returned with a new attitude toward gay life and activism.

Brennan graduated from college in 1970 and immediately entered the army. Following his discharge from the military in late 1972, he moved to Harrisburg, where he soon took a position with the Commonwealth of Pennsylvania as a social worker at the Harrisburg State Hospital, founded in 1851 and known for many years as the Pennsylvania State Lunatic Hospital. Gradually making several gay friends and connections in the state capital through gay bars, Brennan enjoyed the gay life but was frustrated and wanted something more than just socializing at bars. He knew he wanted to put to work the principles he learned from GLF and GAA, as well as pursue his activist instincts. Outside of the gay bars there were few social networks for lesbians and gay men to socialize or be politically active in their area. The Lehigh Valley Homophile Organization formed in 1969 and the Homophiles of Penn State (HOPS) in 1971, but they were small groups and many miles away.

No one knew how to connect with one another outside of gay bars. How could a cohesive and visible community be built and sustained with no organizations or networks to connect it? How could you advocate for equality when all you had were gay bars? Many of Brennan's friends felt the same way. He was active in the antiwar movement going on at the time. When brothers Daniel J. Berrigan and Philip F. Berrigan, members of the Josephite order of priests who were both involved in the antiwar movement in the 1970s, came to Harrisburg for a peace demonstration, they stayed with Brennan, who now wanted to put his energies to work for the gay community in the capital city.

In 1973, he formed an organization called Gay Community Services (GCS). No records of this group remain, but it started as a small discussion and social group of about fifteen members, meeting with the goal of trying to determine what services the community needed and wanted.[9] In late 1974 it became clear that at least two areas were in need—one spiritual and social, and one informational. After a young man committed suicide, GCS members decided it was imperative that something be in place for an individual in crisis and established a hotline. The members also decided that an alternative to traditional churches, which had rejected the presence of gays and lesbians, needed to be established—a spiritual and social venue that would not only offer a safe haven where lesbians and gays could worship but also provide an alternative social outlet outside of the gay bar venue. An informational organization was also needed to provide the community with peer and crisis counseling, as well as referrals to gay-friendly businesses, gay and lesbian social and political activities, and health and legal services.

Not long after the Stonewall uprising, a vibrant gay life began to flourish in large cities across the country. Gay men and lesbians in sizeable cities could easily find and connect with one another just by living in the gay neighborhoods that had been established. The cities had a preponderance of gay bars, discos, clubs, bathhouses, coffee shops, bookstores, and various types of social and political organizations. Gay political and activist organizations were already lobbying city councils and state legislatures for civil rights protection.

By the mid-1970s, nearly half of all the states had repealed their sodomy laws. None of this was happening in central Pennsylvania, however. Gays and lesbians were isolated, with the gay bar as the only social outlet. No neighborhoods had been settled, and few political or activist organizations had been established to fight for their rights. It was a community waiting to find supporters and activists to develop alternative social networks and build some sort of solidarity.

Under Brennan's leadership, two new organizations were formed. Dignity/Central PA began meeting in early 1975 and would file for and obtain its charter from Dignity/USA in July 1975. As a Catholic, Brennan knew about this national organization for gay Catholics that had been founded in 1969 in response to the Catholic Church's position on homosexuality. In April 1975, GCS initiated the Gay Switchboard of Harrisburg, later renamed the Gay and Lesbian Switchboard of Harrisburg. With the founding of these two groups, Brennan began to realize the activist ambition that had taken hold of him in the aftermath of Stonewall.

At the time of Dignity/Central PA's creation, Dignity chapters already existed in Philadelphia, Pittsburgh, Baltimore, and Washington, DC. The national organization of Dignity offered a category of membership called "at-large" for individuals living in the hinterlands, away from large urban areas. Dignity/USA required a minimum of ten interested people in an area before granting a chapter-in-formation status. Brennan convened a total of eighteen individuals, and he traveled to the national conference in the nation's capital to apply for an official charter. On June 23, 1975, the national president, Paul Diederich, encouraged Brennan to form a chapter in central Pennsylvania.[10]

The first meeting was held on July 12, 1975, in Reading, at the home of the Reverend Jim Miller. A liturgy and discussion, followed by a supper and social hour, made up the first evening. The events were reported back to the national organization, and on August 23, 1975, Dignity/Central PA was officially established, with Jerry Brennan appointed as coordinator. The chapter used a combination of religious observance, dialogue, and social interaction, a model that allowed it to gain a foothold with the lesbian and gay community.

Dignity/Central PA's first major task was to find a permanent meeting place. In the beginning, Brennan wrote to nearly every religious denomination in the area—except Catholic, which he knew would be a lost cause—to find one that would rent space to the organization. All the churches that he'd approached rejected the request; not one wanted or would authorize a gay group to meet in their facilities. There was a single exception. The Religious

Society of Friends, popularly known as Quakers, agreed to rent space to the organization and allow use of its fellowship hall. In late 1975 Dignity/Central PA finally found a home at the Friends Meeting House at North Sixth and Herr Streets in midtown Harrisburg. Members continued to meet there for three decades.

The next challenge was to find priests to conduct masses on the first Sunday of every month. Brennan happened to know a local Catholic priest, the Reverend Wallace E. Sawdy, stationed at the Sacred Heart Church in Harrisburg, whom he had met when Father Sawdy was an assistant priest at Brennan's parish church in Shamokin. Brennan and several members of Dignity went to Sawdy to explain their mission. Father Sawdy fully supported their cause and immediately called on Harrisburg diocese bishop Joseph T. Daley to let him know that there was a need for a ministry to the gay community, along with his desire to be involved. The bishop gave Sawdy his tacit approval, and Sawdy served as chaplain for Dignity/Central PA for twenty years, leading masses and arranging for other priests to participate in religious services.

More importantly, he became the spiritual counselor and guide to many in Dignity/Central PA. As part of his ministry, he conducted separate Bible study and prayer groups in his home, with those in attendance often seeking his spiritual guidance. Father Sawdy "was a part of that gay consciousness-raising," remembers John Barns. "[He] did workshops, trying to [help you reconcile] your sexuality as a gay man [or a] gay woman with your Christianity." He adds that Sawdy "really fought for gay rights" and became a "father confessor" for the community.[11] Many members echoed similar sentiments. Thurman Grossnickle recounts of those times, "I don't know what I would have done without that man. He was a tremendous influence in my life. Dignity—Father Sawdy, especially—I think helped relieve a lot of people's anxieties."[12]

While the organization's initial appeal was its religious aspect, discussion sessions and social events soon began drawing large numbers. Attendance at mass would range between fifteen to twenty people, but discussions and potluck dinners drew larger crowds of forty or more, with the special events welcoming upward of one hundred or more individuals. To increase awareness of the organization and its schedule of services and activities, Dignity began publishing a newsletter, the Keystone, which members handed out in gay bars in small cities and towns throughout central Pennsylvania. The Gay and Lesbian Switchboard referred interested callers wanting to know where they could meet gay men and women to Dignity and its events.

Fig. 11 The Reverend Wallace E. Sawdy, preparing to offer mass for members of Dignity/Central PA at the Society of Friends Meeting House in Harrisburg. Courtesy of the LGBT Center of Central PA History Project, Archives and Special Collections, Dickinson College, Carlisle, Pennsylvania.

Discussion topics offered by Dignity/Central PA varied from workshops on Gestalt psychology and relationships to discussions on rape, public health, and coming out. Dignity/Central PA formed both women's and men's "rap" groups, which met separately to discuss gender-specific issues. The discussion sessions also had a host of provocative programs, films, psychologists, and speakers, such as the Reverend John J. McNeill, author of *The Church and the Homosexual,* and the flamboyant Quentin Crisp, a famous gay British writer and storyteller, who spoke and entertained at Dignity's tenth anniversary dinner.[13]

Social events were quite successful. After each mass, there was a dinner and social hour, and from that other special events soon evolved: lawn parties in Bellevue Park, an attractive suburban-style neighborhood in Harrisburg; evenings at dinner theaters; gatherings at restaurants; camping trips; bowling outings; potluck suppers; and card nights. The two most successful and popular events were summer picnics at Pine Grove Furnace State Park at Gardners in southern Cumberland County and weekly volleyball games at the Police Athletic League's gymnasium on North Third Street in midtown Harrisburg. These events continued from the late 1970s through the early 1990s.

What Jerry Brennan achieved with Dignity/Central PA went to the heart of his mission. He built a viable spiritual, political, and (most importantly)

SPARKS!

Fig. 12 Members of Dignity/Central PA gathering in 1985, at the organization's tenth anniversary celebration, with invited speaker and entertainer Quentin Crisp. *Left to right*: Jerry Brennan, founder; Richard Hause; Crisp; and William Clifford. Courtesy of the LGBT Center of Central PA History Project, Archives and Special Collections, Dickinson College, Carlisle, Pennsylvania.

welcoming dynamic social network for the gay and lesbian community in central Pennsylvania. "Dignity/Central PA was the only act in town," recounts Richard Hause. "There were no other gay organizations. And our membership, at its height, had swelled to, like, 120 people. We had religious services that I could take or leave, but we had a lot of social activities. Most of the members were Protestant or Jewish—there were very few, [only a] handful of Catholics. . . . We had picnics at Pine Grove Furnace State Park. We would have dinner nights out throughout the year, all kinds of events, seminars, and it was really a dynamic organization."[14] It was this accompanying social aspect that Dignity provided that drew people.

According to John Folby, "It would be four, six, eight of us at mass, and then we would go downstairs for [the] potluck supper, and there would be forty, fifty, or sixty people." The fellowship of the meal was what they needed. Folby also remembers the Pine Grove picnics at the beginning and end of the summer; those would draw up to three hundred people. "This was the only other [social] outlet, other than the bars at the time," he recounts. That was their ministry in the community.[15]

Fig. 13 One of the first Dignity/Central PA picnics, August 22, 1976. Courtesy of the LGBT Center of Central PA History Project, Archives and Special Collections, Dickinson College, Carlisle, Pennsylvania.

The weekly volleyball games, played every Tuesday and Friday evening at the Police Athletic League in Harrisburg, attracted both gays and lesbians, who formed team rotations. "It didn't matter if you knew how to play . . . it was fun, it was fellowship," John Folby recalls. "At one point we formed a team that participated in the city league."[16] John Barns remembers an enthusiastic Jerry Brennan exhorting people to "come play volleyball, you know, get to know other gay people outside bar life." He would say, "Life does not exist around the bars!"[17]

In keeping with his philosophy of coming out, Brennan organized bus trips for Dignity members to attend Gay Pride celebrations in Philadelphia and New York. (Central Pennsylvania would not have its own Gay Pride events until 1984.) Brennan took it upon himself to arrange these outings and give people the opportunity to march in the parades. In 1979, he organized a bus trip to the first National March on Washington for Lesbian and Gay Rights. He wanted to make sure that gays and lesbians living in central Pennsylvania could attend and participate in defining and historic moments in gay and lesbian activist history.

To get the Harrisburg Gay Switchboard up and running, Brennan invited the director of the Philadelphia Gay and Lesbian Switchboard to consult with GCS members for this initiative. GCS volunteers also consulted CONTACT, a social service organization, which provided necessary crisis training for volunteers. Brennan immediately turned the Switchboard's operation over to others in GCS to run, as he was more interested in working with Dignity/Central PA. The Switchboard started in April 1975, initially located in the garage of a house belonging to a gay couple at Verbeke and Penn Streets. Conditions were bleak. The garage was cold and its roof leaked. Nevertheless, volunteers persisted and staffed the helpline out of dedication to their mission.

A new location for the Switchboard was found in a room above the Strawberry Inn, a gay bar, on North Second Street in downtown Harrisburg. Tragedy struck in January 1984, when a five-alarm fire broke out and ripped through three buildings, killing one person.[18] All of the Switchboard's equipment, records, and files were lost in the blaze. Over the course of the next few years, the Switchboard would move several times before settling into its final location in a building at North Third and Verbeke Streets in Harrisburg's midtown neighborhood, opposite the Broad Street Market (one of the oldest continuously operated farmers' market houses in the country, opened in 1860).

Fig. 14 Brochure advertising Dignity/Central PA, circa 1985. Courtesy of the LGBT Center of Central PA History Project, Archives and Special Collections, Dickinson College, Carlisle, Pennsylvania.

Over the decades, the Switchboard proved vital to the gay and lesbian community. Remembering his experience, Folby says, "It was a hotline, that if people in the LGBT community needed help or felt they were in crisis, we would refer them to the crisis hotline, or counseling hotline. We, ourselves, were not counselors. We were not social workers, but we would direct them: 'Here is the appropriate agency you can call.' Sometimes people would be visiting from out of town and just call and say, 'Where are the bars?' So to me, given that it was such a conservative community, that in itself was a form of activism."[19]

There [was] a handful of gay bars, but no one knew how to find other lesbians and gay men. You know, there were some potlucks, and there were some small gatherings of friends and so forth. . . . [But] there was no central place [such as the Switchboard] for somebody to call to find out what was going on, and there was also nowhere to call—for that young person out there in Sunbury or wherever—to just talk to another gay person to just know that they weren't criminals or mentally ill or perverts, so that if you were having these feelings for someone of the same sex, that you weren't weird. . . . So we provided that peer connection to people.[20]

The Gay and Lesbian Switchboard proved to be a significant asset in serving the LGBT community. Dan Miller remembers that when he returned home to Harrisburg and searched in the blue pages of the telephone book, he came upon the listing for the Switchboard. "Of course, I called it, but somebody was only there certain hours. So I called back, and that is the way I came out. So I'm very thankful to the Switchboard. And they said there was gay volleyball on Friday nights . . . and, of course, part of me was petrified, part of me was very anxious to go. It was a big, big night in my life."[21] Miller later became a leading activist for the LGBT community and served as co-director of the Switchboard.

Fig. 15 Business card advertising the Gay and Lesbian Switchboard of Harrisburg, circa 1993. Photo: Sue Blosser. Courtesy of the LGBT Center of Central PA History Project, Archives and Special Collections, Dickinson College, Carlisle, Pennsylvania.

The Gay and Lesbian Switchboard wove the community together. There was someone to talk to. There was a way to find gay or lesbian activities. There was a place to call for help. There was a way to find legal help. The Switchboard shut down operations shortly after the turn of the century, a victim of changing times and the new technology used to obtain and exchange information.

Jerry Brennan's spark of activism ignited the fires that burned brightly with Dignity/Central PA and the Switchboard but also encouraged others into activism. Gary Norton, originally from Williamsport, Lycoming County,

SPARKS!

had been active in starting the Homophiles of Williamsport (HOW), a small group of gay men that formed in the early 1970s. Its purpose was to galvanize support for the gay community in Williamsport. In 1979, Norton moved to Harrisburg and began searching for ways to become involved with the gay community in the state capital. He joined Dignity, but, not being Catholic, he wanted to start another church, an affiliate of the Metropolitan Community Church (MCC). MCC was originally founded in Los Angeles on October 6, 1968, by the Reverend Troy Deroy Perry Jr., as a nondenominational church to serve the gay and lesbian community.[22] Norton had founded an MCC church in Williamsport, but it did not last long after he moved. He reached out to the MCC in Philadelphia and asked its leaders to help him organize a church in Harrisburg.

In 1980, MCC of Harrisburg was founded as a ministry extension of MCC of Philadelphia, with the Reverend Bruce Hughes and Gary Norton as leaders in planning and developing the church. The first three years were difficult. They went through two different pastors.[23] The church suffered a tremendous blow when Norton died of AIDS in 1983. He is thought to have been the first known AIDS case in central Pennsylvania and the first individual to die in central Pennsylvania from complications due to AIDS.

From its inception, MCC tried to follow Dignity's model, holding monthly events. Generally, they were potluck dinners, worship services, Bible study classes, and workshops. In general, however, MCC's focus was on its ministry to gays and lesbians: to provide a place to worship and to profess the love that God had for members of the LGBT community.

In 1983, the church called the Reverend Pat Lichty as its first pastor and changed its name to MCC of the Spirit, and by 1986 it had named the Reverend Karon Van Gelder as minister. MCC, like Dignity, would meet in the Friends Meeting House, and it continued to do so for eight years. In MCC's early years it had a strong relationship with Dignity, which would have its mass in the Friends Meeting Hall, followed by a potluck dinner and program downstairs in the Fellowship Hall. MCC would schedule its service in the Meeting Hall following the Dignity potluck so that its members could attend the dinner. The simple act of the two groups sharing a meal reinforced a feeling of one community. In 1991, the Reverend Eva O'Diam was installed as pastor, and she spearheaded the drive for the congregation—with more than 120 members—to purchase its own facility on Jefferson Street in Harrisburg. MCC of the Spirit has continued as a leading voice in central Pennsylvania for LGBT rights and spirituality to the present day. It performed countless same-sex unions prior to the Supreme Court ruling in June 2015. MCC also raised funds for Equity for Gays and Lesbians, AIDS education, and Help Ministries. MCC of the Spirit continues to create an open, safe, respectful, multigenerational, and healing church, where all are welcomed and unconditionally loved. They are radically committed to unity, freedom, and social justice in world.[24]

In Lancaster, Arthur Runyan, a student at the Lancaster Theological Seminary, and his partner, Al Johnson, decided to found an MCC church in 1981. It was hosted at the local Unitarian church. But the first six years of the church were turbulent. Shortly thereafter, Johnson succumbed to AIDS. Runyan served as pastor until 1984, followed by the Reverend Bucky Williams-Hooker, but membership dwindled as a result of the AIDS crisis. In 1987, the Reverend Mary Merriman (who had just moved from Florida) was hired as pastor.[25]

Merriman had her work cut out for her. She had to rebuild the church, whose membership had plummeted. She immediately instituted an outreach program, not only to the gay and lesbian community but also to people with AIDS, their families, and their children. The church moved to new facilities on Plum Street and began to hold services there. Merriman's outreach program was successful, and the congregation burgeoned. The church changed its name to Vision of Hope Metropolitan Community Church and, besides its core ministry, became active not only in the Lancaster AIDS Project but with other LGBT rights issues as well.

In 1993, Vision of Hope MCC became the second LGBT church in the area to purchase its own building. The Trinity Reformed United Church of Christ of Mountville was selling its building, and Merriman led efforts to raise the funds to buy it. With an anonymous gift of $20,000, the congregation was able to raise funds to pay for a bond issue for the balance. With most MCC churches in the country either using or leasing space in buildings or other churches, it's quite remarkable that in central Pennsylvania, in the cities of Harrisburg and Lancaster, two MCC churches own their own buildings. The resilient commitment of the gay and lesbian congregations propelled these two churches to surpass their founders' own aspirations.

Dignity/Central PA is the oldest continuously operating LGBT organization in the region. Both MCC churches are vibrant and actively involved in their communities. Growing from Jerry Brennan's initial vision, these organizations created a strong, cohesive, and visible community. They instituted the social networks that began to unite the gay and lesbian community in central Pennsylvania.

In 1977, an all-male social club called the Pennsmen was organized as gay leather/fetish lifestyle social club. The group primarily sponsored "runs," excursions to a designated location for a gathering at leather/denim bars or other venues, sometimes in conjunction with other similar groups from nearby cities. They also had a secondary purpose: to raise money or to provide other support to gay community causes. Originally all male in its membership, it was not until the early twenty-first century that the group allowed female members, and today it now more fully includes the entire LGBT community.[26]

Fig. 16 Pin commemorating the seventh anniversary, in 1984, of the Pennsmen, a leather-fetish social organization based in Harrisburg. Photo: Sue Blosser. Courtesy of the LGBT Center of Central PA History Project, Archives and Special Collections, Dickinson College, Carlisle, Pennsylvania.

Richard Twaddle, a member of the Pennsmen from 1980 through the early 1990s, has many fond memories of the events, some of which are captured in a photo album of their runs and parties during that time. When Twaddle joined, the group was rebuilding its membership after its founding president had withdrawn. The exit had precipitated a dramatic drop in membership. Twaddle recalls that Gary Norton, who was active in MCC, then joined the Pennsmen and took an active role in recruiting new members and rebuilding the club.[27]

The Pennsmen was also affiliated with the American Motorcycle Coordinating Council (AMCC). "People would call it a motorcycle club, and maybe half of the guys owned bikes, but I never rode or owned a bike in my entire life," Twaddle said. "On occasion we would fund-raise for charities and other things—hosting fund-raiser[s], but the club never took in that much money. It was mainly a social club. You had your dues and whatever, and [we would] have our bar nights and raise a bit of money for the club, and then we would donate money to organizations and so forth. It was mainly entertainment—fun."[28]

Similar groups started in central Pennsylvania after the Pennsmen, including the Reading Railmen in 1978, the Pocono Warriors in the early 1980s, and the Northeast Pennsylvania Leathermen in Scranton.[29] All these groups continued to provide alternative outlets to bars and expanded social networks for the growing gay community.

Fig. 17 Program advertising annual "run" event of the Pennsmen, 1999. Courtesy of the LGBT Center of Central PA History Project, Archives and Special Collections, Dickinson College, Carlisle, Pennsylvania.

Fig. 18 Leather spats worn by a member of the Pennsmen at various events. Photo: LGBT Center of Central PA. Courtesy of the LGBT Center of Central PA History Project, Archives and Special Collections, Dickinson College, Carlisle, Pennsylvania.

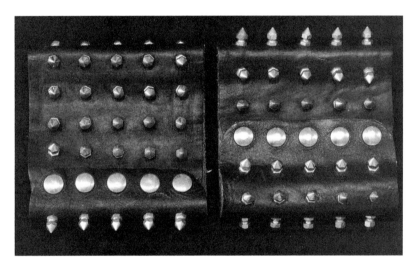

Sparks Land in the Women's Community

In the 1970s, gay bar life in central Pennsylvania was male dominated. Of the dozen or so bars in central Pennsylvania, only two bars catered to women. In Harrisburg, the Silhouette opened in 1975 at 4425 North Front Street and was renamed the D-Gem the following year. Not long after, Lancaster's Sundown Lounge opened in 1976 at 429 North Mulberry Street. The options for lesbians to meet and socialize in this period were scant, and, given the antigay animus that permeated central Pennsylvania, many women remained closeted. Such was the case for Lorraine Kujawa, a young teacher who had just moved from Marysville, a small borough in Perry County, to take a teaching job across the Susquehanna River at the Central Dauphin School District in Harrisburg.

Because of social pressure, Kujawa had tried dating men and even joined a dating service. "You were supposed to get married," she says. "I went about looking for someone and, you know, nothing clicked." She tried dating various men—a "hippie type," a "professional," and others. "It took me until I was twenty-nine, and I said, 'What am I doing?' I much prefer to be with my women friends than to be married."[30] After this realization, Kujawa made the decision to meet more women and accepted her sexuality.

Kujawa attended the convention for the National Organization for Women (NOW) at the local community college. She attended a workshop titled "The Woman Alone" and afterward struck up a conversation with the two leaders who were giving the workshop. They invited Kujawa over to their house the following Sunday to read the *New York Times*. "There was a whole gaggle of women there," she recalls, "and then we stayed for dinner. And, before you know it, I was in my own little group." This was the beginning of Kujawa's coming-out process. Eventually, she made her way to the D-Gem, the lesbian bar in Harrisburg.

At first, Kujawa remembered, bar life was exciting. One would take a nap in the afternoon, since nothing would start happening until late at night. "On a Friday or Saturday night you would go out at 11:00 and stay until 2:00; [then you would] go up the river. There was a Howard Johnson up there, and then maybe we would go for breakfast." Kujawa would usually go out on a Saturday night. There was music and dancing; it was the late 1970s, and disco was the rage. As she recalls, "The music was nice, but I am not a big drinker. And [the bar] was just one aspect of life." Kujawa eventually made a connection with a woman, but it soon ended.

The D-Gem tended to attract the same group of people. According to Kujawa, the lesbian community in Harrisburg was very cliquish and scattered, with little groups of friends that tended to socialize only with one another. After she broke it off with a woman she was seeing, Kujawa went out socially with another friend who had also just broken up with someone. She and her friend were discussing the fact that, when they were seeing someone, they were socializing only with a certain group of people. Kujawa and her friend had an epiphany. "We said, you know, once you [break up], you cut off that group of friends and there is nobody. You don't know anybody."

Kujawa discovered she was totally isolated. With one bar in Harrisburg and one in Lancaster welcoming lesbians, and given the scattered nature of the

Fig. 19 Lorraine Kujawa (*right*), presenting an award to Cindy Lou Mitzel at the first Community Recognition banquet, at Miss Garbo's Tea Room in Carlisle, circa 1992. Courtesy of the LGBT Center of Central PA History Project, Archives and Special Collections, Dickinson College, Carlisle, Pennsylvania.

lesbian community, there were no other social venues in which women could meet or connect. "I said, well, there must be other places to go or things to do for gay women in this area, but we just don't know about them." Kujawa contacted five of her friends—Mary Nancarrow, Cindy Lou Mitzel, and three others. They were from diverse circles, including "somebody from the sports group, somebody from the bar group, somebody in a political action group."

The five women met at Kujawa's house and agreed to publish a monthly newsletter of events for women that were occurring in central Pennsylvania. They named the newsletter the *Lavender Letter*. The events, whether sports related, political, or social, were listed and designed so interested women could knowingly go and, once there, have the possibility of meeting other women. Kujawa remembers, "If there wasn't a local event that was going on, we would make one up. We would say, 'Potluck at such and such a house. Call this number.' And then, we would make sure that we were there so that it would at least be three of us. Or picnic at Knoebels Park and we would have balloons hanging up, lavender balloons just hanging out around the area that we would meet that day. And so, it started out as three or four people and it ended up maybe fifteen to twenty."

For the first newsletter, Kujawa and her crew printed one hundred copies with seed money of twenty dollars. They went to the D-Gem and to each event listed in the first newsletter and handed them out. Kujawa or another one of the group members made sure one of them would go to all the events. It immediately took off. "People started sending us money. And then they also started sending us information about events that were going on." Women were saying, "I always wanted to have this kind of group." Kujawa would encourage them to put things in the *Lavender Letter*, and after a while, "we didn't have to make anything up anymore because people would start having their own activities."

The initial distribution of the *Lavender Letter* was through the bar and events, but a mailing list soon developed. Because many of the women were still in the closet and concerned about their privacy, the *Lavender Letter* was mailed in a plain envelope with no return address. Within the first few months, the mailing list had accrued more than one hundred names, and within several years the list had topped five hundred names. The event listings also reflected the fears and concerns about privacy, with only a phone number and the first name of the person to contact. For example, one entry reads, "Saturday, March 17th, 7:30 p.m., Lancaster Women's Potluck. Bring a dish or a carafe of your favorite beverage to share. Call for info," followed by a phone number.[31] Interested women would have to call to find out the location and any other information, and callers would go through an informal screening process to ensure that they were sincere in their intentions.

During the early 1980s, the events were mainly social gatherings. Besides holding potluck dinners throughout the area, some women formed restaurant groups, meeting at different eateries once a month, and sewing or sports groups. At her house, Kujawa hosted a cultural evening once a year: "We would have a turkey and people would bring food. Then you would have to read a poem or play the violin, whatever it is, dance, or whatever, to contribute

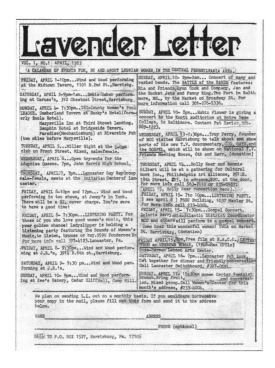

Fig. 20 First issue of the *Lavender Letter*, April 1983. Courtesy of the LGBT Center of Central PA History Project, Archives and Special Collections, Dickinson College, Carlisle, Pennsylvania.

to the cultural evening." "One of our people [Roe Robusto]," she continues, ". . . wrote some wonderful plays. We would practice them and put them on at our house in front of the fireplace to an audience of about twenty. And then, there was a place called Altland's Ranch, which was another gay bar [located in Spring Grove, near York] off of the woods somewhere. We had a week where we put the plays on all week there, and that was a much larger crowd."[32]

The *Lavender Letter* also began to sponsor dances, but, like Dignity/Central PA, it had difficulty finding organizations that would rent space to them. According to Kujawa, "They would say, 'Oh sure, you can have the space at such and such a date,' and then we would have to tell them that it was going to be an all-women thing and there were gay people, and they would say, 'Oh no, we don't rent to gay people.'"[33] Fortunately, Lakeside Lutheran Church was willing to rent space to them, so the *Lavender Letter* started holding their dances there. They were a resounding success, with more than 150 women attending. By comparison, on a Saturday night at the D-Gem, the crowd would number only between 75 and 100 women.

In Lancaster, a group formed and started holding a monthly potluck. They had twelve women with large houses who volunteered them for a different month during the year. New attendees were prescreened by group members to ensure that the person was not a risk to the group. The screener would vet them and then give them the address of the potluck. Even given the high degree of scrutiny, they had 50 to 60 people each month at these dinners.

By the mid-1980s and well into the 1990s, the *Lavender Letter* had expanded beyond social gatherings. It carried a regular listing of events sponsored by organizations such as Dignity/Central PA and the MCC churches in Harrisburg and Lancaster and various gay and lesbian support groups throughout central Pennsylvania, such as Parents of Gays, Reading Gay Alcoholics Anonymous, Gays and Lesbians Older and Wiser (GLOW), and *Harrisburg Area Women's News* (HAWN).

The *Lavender Letter* also began to list various workshops available to women throughout central Pennsylvania. Topics ranged from a multiracial conference on aging to lesbian history, women in the creative arts, problem solving, and parenting. Eventually, political activism became a key feature, with listings not only of Gay Pride events throughout Pennsylvania and New York but also of issues dealing with the AIDS crisis and the fight for gay and lesbian equality. Women in central Pennsylvania, wherever their interests lay, now had a resource to connect them.

In addition to its annual subscription fee, the *Lavender Letter* began running advertisements from local businesses to help raise money to fund the publication. Restaurants, bars, and hotels, all catering to gay and lesbian clientele, were soon advertising. The reach of the newsletter went beyond Harrisburg and Lancaster into small cities and towns such as York, Chambersburg, State College, Reading, Elizabethtown, Shippensburg, and Mechanicsburg. Whether it was through a workshop, a social gathering, a support group, or a political event, women in these small towns could now connect.

Lorraine Kujawa's initiative connected the lesbian community. Her vision to create the *Lavender Letter* helped women find one another and meet in the small cities and towns throughout conservative central Pennsylvania. A single gay bar or two could not have done this. A viable and focused lesbian community began to evolve; the women just needed to find one another. Kujawa lit the way.

Sparks Land in Lancaster

Born in 1955, in the small town of Columbia, Lancaster County, twenty-eight miles southeast of Harrisburg, David Leas was the oldest of five children. Both of Leas's parents worked to support their large family, his father in a foundry and his mother in a textile factory, providing a loving but strict Catholic home in which they raised their family. Growing up, Leas attended grade school in Columbia, eventually graduating from Lancaster Catholic High School.[34]

A turning point occurred for Leas when he became sixteen and landed a job as a busboy at the Accomac Inn, a tiny French-inspired restaurant across the Susquehanna River from Columbia in Wrightsville, York County. The waiters wore tuxedos, and the busboys wore white jackets with bowties. "I saw a world that I did not even know existed. . . . It was just this whole world that I wanted to know more about," Leas recalls. "That steered me in the restaurant business, because that's basically what I [have] done, up until seven years ago, when I left." At this time, Leas was also dealing with his sexuality. "[I was] struggling with the issue of being a gay teenager and meeting other gay people." He adds that he "wasn't necessarily sure that I [knew] that word [*gay*] or what to do about it. I mean, there was no support group, other than people that I worked with who might also be that way."

After high school graduation Leas felt compelled to leave town, so he took the dramatic step of moving to Saint Thomas in the US Virgin Islands. After a year of working and sowing his wild oats, he returned to Lancaster, confident in his gay sexuality and ready to carve out his life. Upon his return, he reacquainted himself with an old friend, who took him to the Tally Ho Tavern in Lancaster. This was the first time Leas had ever been in a gay bar. "There was a certain level of nervousness—which definitely dissipated within fifteen to twenty minutes—to be in an environment with other people who were like me." It was here that he soon became friends with Bari Weaver and Sam Wilson, who told Leas about the group they were forming, Gays United Lancaster (GUL). The focus of Lancaster's first gay organization was not just political but also social and did not revolve around the bars and alcohol. Leas was intrigued.

At the first meeting in Bari Weaver's home, Leas found that he was in the midst of about twenty-five fellow potential members interested in forming the group. Many were still not out publicly and expressed fear of exposure. According to Leas, they would say, "Oh, we can't do this, it's too public . . . it's too radical." But there were more reasons to do it than not, so GUL was formed. In the early years, Leas felt that he had found a home, not just for political activism but as an alternative social outlet. GUL held various social functions, such as dances and spaghetti dinners, at venues like the Moose Hall in Lancaster or the Union Hall on Manor Street. These events soon grew popular and began to draw large crowds.

David Leas's work with the GUL led him to his most significant contribution for the lesbian and gay community in central Pennsylvania: the creation of the region's first gay newspaper. GUL had been publishing a monthly newsletter for its membership detailing the activities of GUL and other groups. It soon became evident that the information they were reporting on, the fight for gay and lesbian rights, should be distributed to the larger gay and lesbian community in central Pennsylvania. The only other gay newspaper in the state at the time was the *Philadelphia Gay News*, not readily available in the region. Leas, along with fellow GUL member Harry Long, decided to take the newsletter and expand it into a newspaper, and the *Gay Era* was born.

The newspaper covered gay and lesbian–related stories around central Pennsylvania from places like Northumberland, West Chester, Reading, State College, and Williamsport. It detailed the struggles for gay rights and women's rights, along with reporting the activities of local organizations. More importantly, the newspaper reported stories from around the nation, taken and credited from reports from shared sources, including the *Philadelphia Gay News* and Boston's *Gay Community News*. Suddenly, gays and lesbians in central Pennsylvania were reading stories from New York, Baltimore, Los Angeles,

San Francisco, and other large urban areas. The *Gay Era* brought all the news of the nationwide struggle for gay and lesbian rights to the region.

With headlines such as "Gay Press Barred from All Federal Prisons" and "Consensual Sodomy Legal in More Than One-Third of Nation" to "ERA Set Backs" and "Lesbian Mothers Rally in NYC," readers of the *Gay Era* were now in touch with their gay brothers and sisters throughout the country.[35] The publication extensively covered Gay Pride parades and festivals in New York, Los Angeles, Philadelphia, and San Francisco at a time when no Pride celebrations were occurring in central Pennsylvania.

The newspaper covered the fight in California when conservative Republican state legislator John V. Briggs of Orange County introduced Proposition 6, legislation that would require school boards to fire or refuse to hire teachers who advocated or committed homosexual acts. The proposal was resoundingly defeated. The *Gay Era* closely followed Anita Bryant's "Save Our Children" antigay campaign and her nationwide advocacy for discrimination against gays.[36] The newspaper helped rally gays and lesbians to stand up and fight against those denying their civil rights, and it brought the world to the doorsteps of gays and lesbians living in central Pennsylvania.

Fig. 21 Cover of the one-year-anniversary issue of the *Gay Era*, March 1976. Courtesy of the LGBT Center of Central PA History Project, Archives and Special Collections, Dickinson College, Carlisle, Pennsylvania.

But the path to publishing a newspaper was challenging. "I played a major part in the paper and keeping it going," David Leas remembers.[37] "I basically financed it, 'cause it did not make money and there was always a printing bill." Finding a printer was itself an arduous task. "We were always looking for a printer. We had multiple printers [who printed for us] . . . and then told us to go away." The reason for their refusal was that the printers felt that the newspaper was pornographic, and they did not want their employees exposed to the paper. The newspaper did contain some sketches of men kissing, women in a loving embrace, or an erotic sketch of a man or a woman. A few issues had photographs of nearly nude men, but with no genitals exposed.

The paper did meet with success, starting out with a few hundred copies and eventually reaching a distribution of more than one thousand copies. "We were selling it for fifty cents," Leas notes. The paper was distributed in the bars and various bookstores. The major difficulty was the printing and distribution effort. The monies collected were returned on an honor system, so it was very hard to make money, and advertising revenue did not cover the costs.

After nearly four years of publication, in 1978, Leas was frustrated with the struggle. "It was just a real financial drain. I didn't really want to do it anymore. I was done with financing it, you know, after a couple hundred dollars every month in printing bills." The *Gay Era* ceased publication, but it left a tremendous historical record of the time from 1974 through 1978 in central Pennsylvania. Not only did the paper record the events of the gay and lesbian community in central Pennsylvania, but it also brought to the community an awareness of the world that they were living in and made them part of the national community of gays and lesbians.

Sparks would continue to land in the small cities, towns, and college campuses throughout central Pennsylvania. Activists would continue to form political, social, and educational organizations in their communities throughout the region. Their ability to effect political and policy changes was limited only by the number of their members interested in gay rights activism and the resources of the groups. But change was in the wind.

Profile

JOE BURNS

Joe Burns grew up during the 1940s and 1950s in the small town of Butler, Butler County, thirty-five miles north of Pittsburgh. It was here, at the age of thirteen, that he had his first same-sex experience. In this industrial town of twenty-three thousand, there was no one to talk to about his feelings or his experience. Because of his environment, Joe remained silent and kept his budding sexuality hidden. When he graduated from high school, Joe decided to enroll at Moravian College in Bethlehem, and he left home for the first time in his life.[38]

Joe stayed in college for a short time but soon returned home. By 1967, he returned to Bethlehem, ostensibly to return to college. As Joe remembers, "I told everybody I was going to go back to school and went out there in January, in time for school. . . . I was away from home, which is what I wanted to be." Joe was twenty-seven and, he says, "[I] wanted very much to be away and be my own person. [I] didn't have a way to do that, and so I kind of used this excuse to get out."

Prior to Joe's return to Bethlehem, he had had another same-sex experience and knew he was gay. Now, away from home and on his own, he wanted to understand and learn more about the new world he inhabited. Joe would go to the Moravian Book Shop in Bethlehem and buy any book he could find on the subject of homosexuality. He also visited libraries in the Lehigh Valley to research the subject. "I went to the five libraries in Bethlehem's area; this would have been Moravian College, Lehigh University, Muhlenberg College, Lafayette College, and St. Francis De Sales, a little Catholic college off in Allentown. There were no books that I could find in the card catalogue that started with the word *homosexual*. There were no books. There were no books on *gay*, which was a new term to me." In Joe's search for answers, labels were important.

> I didn't know [the word] *gay* when I started, actually. I'm not sure when I was even comfortable with the term *gay*. It was foreign to me for a long time. It took me a while to get used to that whole term. And I didn't know it until I moved away and began to . . . value the difference between *homosexual* and *gay*. *Homosexual* is the old word; it was the word that was laden very heavily with all the [negative] freight [that] people could put onto it. . . . So *gay* was what I knew, and *gay* is what I called myself all this time.

Joe finally struck gold when, with the help of a librarian at the Moravian Library, he found the address of the Mattachine Society in New York. He remembered a feature report on the television program *CBS Reports* that Mike Wallace had done on the society in 1967. The Mattachine Society was founded in 1951 in Los Angeles to fight the discrimination and oppression that homosexuals faced. The purpose of the group was to unify isolated homosexuals, educate them to see themselves as an oppressed minority, and lead them toward their own emancipation.[39] "I had seen a program with Mike Wallace," Joe recalls. "He was interviewing with homosexuals and he, in fact, showed the [front] door of the Mattachine Society in New York. I wanted to be there. . . . That was my key."

For Joe, the world in 1967 was a sad, lonely place. Living in a small town in rural Pennsylvania, he did not know of many other gay people. It was a closeted environment, he remembers. "We couldn't contact each other [openly]. That world . . . was a very isolated place." Joe remembers that the only outlet was a gay bar called Rube's, located in Allentown: "That was important for me, to find people who were actually gay, because you could trust them." That kind of trust was impossible for Joe to find elsewhere in the area. Outside the bar, "you had to establish by various means that somebody was gay, that you could talk to them, or you could come out to them." It was a "very difficult process."

Even under these circumstances, Joe was motivated and decided to join the Mattachine Society, even though he was not living in New York. He eventually made it to New York and met Dick Leitsch, who was then the executive director of the society. He was inspired not only by his meeting with Leitsch but also by the larger mission of the organization. Joe reminisces about the message of the Mattachine Society: "It was something [like] 'We are putting ourselves forward as a light, to light a candle, so that those who follow us in the dark, or immersed in the dark, . . . [will] have somebody holding their hand.' And that was so important to me, to feel that there was somebody out there, and that's all I wanted to be. I just wanted to be the person who, if you had to reach [out], I was going to be there." Joe also attended meetings of the Mattachine Society in Philadelphia, where he became familiar with the lesbian activist Barbara Gittings. A major news story had just run on her in the *Philadelphia Inquirer*, as an out lesbian, which left a life-changing impression on Joe. He recalls, "I just thought, 'Oh my God, if she can do that, I can do that.' So that's when I came out. That's when I decided that's what I was going to do—[and] whatever else, I was not going to hide anymore. If she could do it, then I had enough strength to do it." In 2016, the Pennsylvania Historical and Museum Commission, the commonwealth's official state history agency, erected and dedicated a state historical marker honoring Gitting's contributions at her former residence in Philadelphia for her role as "the mother of the LGBT civil rights movement."

In March 1969, Joe received a letter from the Mattachine Society that informed him that someone in his area wanted to form a group, and they would be in contact. Shortly thereafter, Ron Seeds contacted Joe from the mailing list provided by the society. Ron had just founded the group Le-Hi-Ho, the Lehigh Valley Homophile Organization, and Joe soon met with Ron and the four other members of the fledging group.

The group of six quickly grew to thirteen members, meeting in various remote locations in Bethlehem. They were fearful at first, concerned for their safety, but they realized they were dealing with very important issues about coming out, taking a stand, and helping other gay people deal with issues of discrimination and harassment. They felt a responsibility to be examples to other gay men and women. Joe, among all others, was not afraid. He was inspired by Stonewall and the protest movements against Vietnam War and the draft. "At that time [1969], the very special question that we wanted to organize around was 'Do you check the box, or not?'" For those facing the draft, the question was "[whether] you want to check the box and say I'm homosexual, because it has consequences about employment for the rest of your life. There's important consequences if you join the sevice and then are found out . . . you'll be thrown out of the service, and you can't get benefits, all kinds of things. It was a very important question. And lots of people were asking." To answer these questions and others like it, Le-Hi-Ho started a newsletter, which Joe eventually took over as editor.

Le-Hi-Ho began to host discussion groups and convened various social gatherings, sponsoring movies and other events. Joe recalls, "The social hour [was] a very, very important thing. Most guys just loved to come and they would do any program. . . . Wonderful programs, and they would sit through them, and then they would go walk by themselves and have this great time. But they were there for the conversation; they were there because it was the alternative to bars. It was the way you can meet people . . . [and] talk to them about sensible things." In addition, he had amassed a library for the group that contained more than 150 books spanning fiction and nonfiction on the subject of homosexuality, which he allowed anyone to borrow.

In early 1970, Joe returned to New York City and went to the Oscar Wilde Memorial Bookshop near Sheridan Square, the country's first gay bookstore, to acquire more books for his library. While there, he overheard the store's owner, Craig Rodwell, making plans for a Christopher Street Liberation Day March in remembrance of the Stonewall riots—essentially the nation's first Gay Pride parade. The march was being supported by new activist groups, such as the Gay Liberation Front (GLF), Gay Activists Alliance (GAA), and the East Coast Homophile Organization (ECHO), as well as the Mattachine Society. Joe was excited and brought the news of the march back to the members of

Le-Hi-Ho. He wanted the group to support the march and attend, but reaction was mixed. After much discussion and debate, Joe and two other members (his partner, Ricky, and Fred Reed) decided they would travel to New York City in late June to participate and represent Le-Hi-Ho in the historic march, lending their voices to the burgeoning gay liberation movement.

On June 28, 1970, the three members of Le-Hi-Ho set off for New York City. They soon arrived at Sheridan Square and found themselves in the midst of several hundred people milling around, waiting for the march to begin. A young woman happened to see the sign they were carrying and recognized that they had come from the Bethlehem area. She came up to them and said, "I'm from Bethlehem, too." She decided to stay with Joe and the others. Now the group from Le-Hi-Ho had four representatives.

The groups were carrying signs to identify themselves—GLF and GAA, among others—and soon the march began. Joe estimates that there were just a few hundred people marching. They marched up the street, chanting "Gay Power" and "Off the sidewalks and into the streets!" He recalls one particular chant: "'Two, four, six, eight: How do you know your husband's straight?' That's one that I especially appreciated, and we went past the New Yorker Hotel and all these rich people are out there with their limousines . . . and there we are walking by like, 'Two, four, six, eight: How do you know your husband's straight?' Just really enjoying ourselves. Same when we got to [St. Patrick's] Cathedral. Now, [we changed it to] 'How do you know your priest is straight?'"

As the march began, the crowd was only a block long. "We just fit in that the traffic lane, . . . and people kept coming along the sidewalk and joining us." People continued to arrive. "I got out of line [to get a drink], and realized all of a sudden that now we're five blocks long. Just that many more people. And I think I did it again, and then we were eight blocks long. And it was just so exciting." The parade eventually made its way to Sheep Meadow in Central Park, where the crowd numbered more than two thousand people. There were no speakers or organized protests, just thousands of people celebrating the birth of gay liberation. "It was just so amazing. And I always talk about that as the beginning of the movement. That's how we knew how successful we were." In Central Park, "with nothing else to do, [we] had our 'gay-in' for hours. . . . I held Ricky's hand, and we kissed when we wanted to and liberated the park." The experience remains powerful. "That's an amazing feeling walking down with a press of people like that. . . . The love and the support [are] just so incredible."

Fig. 22 The Le-Hi-Ho contingent with their sign, marching in the Christopher Street Liberation Day March in New York City, June 28, 1970. (This photograph is not the one that appeared in the *Advocate*.) Photo: Diana Davies. © Manuscripts and Archives Division, The New York Public Library.

The parade received widespread media coverage from all outlets, including the *Advocate*, the country's first national gay newspaper. One of the *Advocate*'s photographs is a picture of four marchers—Joe, Ricky, Fred, and the woman from Bethlehem—holding a sign from Le-Hi-Ho. Joe and Le-Hi-Ho are now immortalized as part of a defining moment in gay history.

CHAPTER 3

Awakening

The Stonewall uprising also caused a surge of gay activism that spread across college and university campuses throughout the United States. By the early 1970s, campuses saw more than 150 groups begin to appear under various names, such as the Gay Liberation Front (GLF), Gay Activists Alliance (GAA), Student Homophile League, the Radicalesbians, and names that had special significance for a specific group. Some groups focused on political issues, while others concerned themselves more with convening students around social activities. By 1972, student campus groups were beginning to organize regional and national conferences around issues of sexuality and coming out at Rutgers University (the State University of New Jersey), the University of Minnesota in Minneapolis, the University of Texas in Austin, and the University of Nebraska in Lincoln.[1]

In the early years, college and university administrators denied official recognition to some of the groups. Such was the case at Sacramento and San Jose State Universities in California, Florida State University, the University of Kansas, and the University of Texas. The reasons given by university administrators for their denial were twofold. The chancellor of the California State University system explained that the Gay Liberation Front could not receive official recognition because "the effect of recognition by the college . . . could conceivably be to endorse or promote homosexual behavior, to attract homosexuals to the campus, and to expose minors to homosexual advocacy and practices." Moreover, he argued that "the proposed Front created too great a risk for students—a risk which might lead students to engage in illegal homosexual behavior." The vast majority of the gay and lesbian student organizations would flourish on most campuses and continue their role in activism, raising awareness and creating social networks on their campuses and in their communities, sometimes even influencing local and state politics.[2] This activist movement would eventually arrive at Penn State University.

The Pennsylvania State University is one of the very few iconic institutions strongly associated with the Commonwealth of Pennsylvania's culture. Founded in 1855, Penn State grew from a rural farmers' high school to a state college to a major university in just under a century. By the twentieth century, its graduates worked throughout the state, the country, and the world.[3] In the late 1960s and early 1970s, change was in the air, as college students became more like community activists, advocating for and against various social and political causes. How would the conservative administration of a major institution of higher learning in central Pennsylvania deal with this change?

At Penn State, beginning with the winter semester of 1971, a course was offered in what was referred to as the Free University, a chartered student organization that sponsored noncredit courses that could be initiated by anyone who wanted to study or instruct on any topic. That semester, one of the courses offered was Homosexuality: A Growing Subculture. By the end of the semester, approximately forty students had registered and were attending the class. From this group of students emerged the idea to create the first gay student organization on the campus.[4] The group formed a steering committee and submitted an application to be chartered as an official student organization by the Undergraduate Student Government Association.[5]

The official name on the charter was "The Other Vision: Homophiles of Penn State," but the group was more commonly referred to as Homophiles of Penn State or by its acronym, HOPS.[6] Bruce Miller served as its first president and Joe Acanfora as its treasurer. On April 20, 1971, the Penn State Undergraduate Student Supreme Court rendered a unanimous decision to award a charter to the new group, granting it such privileges as using college facilities for meetings and events and applying for and receiving funding for its activities.[7]

Excited to receive the group's charter, students began publicizing the existence of their new organization around campus and planning meetings and events. But within weeks of receiving its charter, Raymond O. Murphy, acting vice president for Student Affairs, "informed HOPS that its privileges had been suspended pending the results of an arbitrary investigation of the organization's 'legality.'"[8] Administrators immediately tore down the group's bulletin board in the Hetzel Union Building and the flyers that had been posted throughout the campus. The members of HOPS were outraged. In town that weekend was Barbara Gittings of the Homophile Action League of

Fig. 23 Demonstration by members and supporters of Homophiles of Penn State on the campus of Penn State University, circa 1971. "Demonstrations (B&W), 1970," Students, 1855–Present (1190), Photographic Vertical Files. Used with permission from the Eberly Family Special Collections Library, Penn State University Libraries, University Park, Pennsylvania.

Philadelphia and Frank Kameny, a warrior in the gay liberation movement. Kameny had founded the Washington, DC, chapter of the Mattachine Society and was a member of the American Civil Liberties Union (ACLU). He waged a continual battle against discrimination against homosexuals by the federal government and in private industry. Both were in State College to conduct a colloquy on homosexuality and to lend moral support to HOPS.

As reported in the *Daily Collegian*, on May 14, Kameny "incurred the displeasure of two important Pennsylvanians, Gov. Milton J. Shapp and University President John W. Oswald," when, unannounced, he took over the speaker's podium after the governor's address at Old Main, the administration building on the Penn State campus. Kameny demanded that the university reverse its decision to temporarily suspend the HOPS charter: "In sharp, angry tones he denounced Raymond O. Murphy, acting vice president for student affairs, as a 'benighted bigot,' and later called him a 'sick man who should be put on compulsory sick leave.'"[9]

Protests continued when, on May 20, representatives from approximately twenty-five chartered student organizations picketed Old Main to demand restoration of HOPS's privileges. Murphy's only response was that the investigation had not yet been completed. Finally, on September 1, the administration

AWAKENING

released its decision to revoke the HOPS charter. The university's statement regarding the decision was strident. "We are advised that, based upon sound psychological and psychiatric opinion, the chartering of your organization would create a substantial conflict with the counseling and psychiatric services the University provides to its students, and that such conflict would be harmful to the best interests of the students of the University."[10]

HOPS responded that the administration's position was "a bold but typical act of repression." The conflict may have stemmed from the fact that the American Psychiatric Association did not remove homosexuality from its official *Diagnostic and Statistical Manual of Mental Disorders* until 1973. The aggressive choice of words in the HOPS newsletter speaks to a growing confrontationalism, as students grew exasperated with the conservative university administration. Still, the students were encouraged to know that so many of their peers supported the creation of HOPS and had protested the withdrawal of their charter. Undaunted, HOPS leaders continued to plan and hold events on and off campus. They organized group consciousness-raising meetings, workshops, parties, dances, movies, and rap sessions. Before long, membership increased to more than sixty members.[11]

Within several months of the university's decision, HOPS decided to fight back. Four students from the group filed suit against the administration in February 1972, naming John W. Oswald and Raymond O. Murphy as defendants. The suit, filed by attorney Leonard Sharon of the Pittsburgh Law Collective on behalf of HOPS, cited the First and the Fourteenth Amendments to the US Constitution as the basis for their challenge.[12] The First Amendment guarantees the freedom of speech and the right to peacefully assemble. The Fourteenth Amendment guarantees that no one will be deprived of life, liberty, and property without due process and grants all citizens the right of equal protection under the law. According to the suit, in dealing with HOPS, the university had violated both of these amendments. HOPS eventually prevailed and regained its charter in an out-of-court settlement announced on January 24, 1973.[13]

Another Battle

The fight for HOPS reinstatement would take a dramatic toll on one its members, Joe Acanfora, one of the plaintiffs in the lawsuit. It would be an arduous journey that would involve an injunction and two court trials, eventually leading to the Supreme Court. It would also garner intense statewide and national media coverage.

At the time the lawsuit was filed for HOPS reinstatement, Joe Acanfora was in the midst of his student-teaching assignment. With the publicity surrounding the HOPS controversy, administrators at the school where Acanfora was teaching and at Penn State wanted him out of the classroom because of his admitted homosexuality and membership in HOPS.[14] School officials commented to the *Pennsylvania Mirror*, "[There was] no question as to [Acanfora's] performance as a student teacher." But, they said, HOPS objectives "are not compatible with the educational policies of the public school."[15]

Acanfora took immediate legal action to finish his student-teaching assignment and received a court injunction to return to the classroom.[16] Because of the publicity surrounding his reinstatement fight, controversy within the commonwealth was occurring on whether gays and lesbians should be allowed to be teachers.[17]

After Acanfora finished his student-teaching assignment, his next step was to file for his teaching certificate. His application was sent to the University Teacher Certification Council of Penn State in May 1972. Because Acanfora was an admitted homosexual, the issue before the council was whether he had the required "good moral character" to be granted the needed recommendation. The council met several times but could not reach a decision on whether to grant Acanfora his teaching certificate. They brought him in for an interview, which was more like an interrogation. They asked, "What homosexual acts do you prefer to engage in or are you willing to engage in?" Acanfora responded, "Well, there's a certain tradition of respect for privacy in our country, and especially in an academic community, and I would think that I would ask you to withdraw that question with respect to that." The questions soon ended. The council voted and was

Fig. 24 Joe Acanfora, with "Gay Is Proud" sign, at an early 1970s Gay Pride celebration. Courtesy of Joe Acanfora.

deadlocked on the question of "good moral character." They sent the matter to the Pennsylvania secretary of education for a decision.[18]

Knowing that his certificate to teach in Pennsylvania was pending, Acanfora decided to apply for teaching positions in Maryland. Each of the applications required a list of all the organizations and extracurricular activities that the applicants were involved with in college. Acanfora did not cite his affiliation with HOPS on any of the applications. In August, he received an offer from Parkland Junior High School in Montgomery County, Maryland, to teach earth science. In late September the Pennsylvania secretary of education held a press conference announcing his decision to award Joe Acanfora his teacher's certificate.[19]

After the press conference, Acanfora thought the best course of action would be to inform the officials at Parkland that the controversy and news over this newly awarded teaching certificate might reach Montgomery County. He was right: his story was big news. It was picked up by newspapers such as the *New York Times*, the *Philadelphia Inquirer*, *Asbury Park Press*, and the *Washington Evening Star-News*.[20]

The intense media coverage was too much for school officials in Montgomery County. They informed Acanfora that he was being removed from the classroom and being placed in a position in the school's administration offices. In an attempt to reverse the school board's decision, Acanfora sought and gained support from the Montgomery County Education Association and the National Education Association. In addition to this backing, petitions were presented from some of his fellow teachers and students from Parkland. These efforts failed to convince the school board to return Acanfora to the classroom, forcing him to take the next step and file suit in federal court.[21]

Public interest began to intensify about Acanfora's case, with more articles appearing in the *New York Times*, the *Washington Post*, and local papers.[22] Acanfora also appeared on numerous radio and television programs, including CBS's *60 Minutes*, which aired a twenty-minute segment on his case. In all these appearances, he stated that "employment discrimination against homosexuals was unjust, that he would never discuss his sexual orientation with students in or out of school, and that he hoped that greater public understanding of homosexuals would develop."[23]

The case went to trial in April 1973. Both sides used expert witnesses to present their arguments. The experts on each side all agreed that in general there was no danger in homosexuals teaching in public schools. But the county school board experts asserted that having Acanfora return to the classroom would be dangerous for two reasons: "(1) as a result of the publicity, his students would be aware of his homosexuality, and (2) he taught at a grade level in which students were entering adolescence."[24] In addition, the county presented its rationale for giving Acanfora a different job and removing him from the classroom. They felt that his "public statements forfeited any protection, and Acanfora had withheld relevant information on his employment application."[25]

Acanfora brought in expert witnesses to counter the county's arguments. He testified on his own behalf, stating, "I never did discuss my own private sexual beliefs or feelings, or I never discussed sexuality at any level with any student in or out of the classroom." Regarding withholding information on HOPS, Acanfora explained,

> It was based primarily on the experience I just had with the State College School District. I realized I had just completed four years of training to become a teacher and was judged perfectly qualified; and I realized had I put down the Homophiles of Penn State as an organization . . . that I would not be given a chance to even go through the normal application process for a teaching job; that I would not be considered on an equal par with all other applicants and, in fact, [it] would guarantee that I would not receive any sort of teaching job.[26]

Montgomery County Public School superintendent Homer O. Elseroad testified that he opposed the reinstatement of Acanfora "because teachers have a tremendous impact on students and it is not possible to separate where a teacher stops being a teacher and acts as a counselor, chaperone at social functions, or as a coach." The county's expert witness, a professor of child health, stated at trial that "returning Joe to the classroom would be a 'hazard' to their development and deny them 'free choice' of their sexuality."[27]

The transcript of the *60 Minutes* telecast was presented in Acanfora's defense. His attorney stated, "It is being offered in response to the School Board's position that he is an active, militant homosexual, as reflected on his television and radio appearances. We want the court to have the record before it, as what was said on those occasions." Acanfora's expert witness, a psychologist and sex counselor, presented evidence that "Joe's presence in the classroom would help in 'breaking down homosexual stereotypes' and 'affirm the self-image' of students who were gay."[28]

After days of testimony, the trial ended. The federal court issued its decision and denied Joe's return to the classroom. In his decision, the judge did find that the county had "transferred him without any prior investigation or hearing . . . and he was denied procedural due process." Despite this ruling, the court found that Joe Acanfora was entitled to "no relief" and that his appearances on radio and television "were not reasonably necessary for self-defense, and would likely spark unnecessary controversy regarding the subject of homosexuality and the classroom."[29]

Acanfora immediately filed an appeal with the Fourth Circuit Court of Appeals. In August he received notice that the Montgomery County Board of Education had voted unanimously not to renew his contract because they had eliminated his job.[30]

In February 1974 the circuit court upheld the district court's ruling, but its reasons were based on the fact that Acanfora "is not entitled to relief because of material omissions in application for a teaching position." They did affirm that Acanfora's public appearances and statements were protected by the First Amendment, and "they do not justify either the action taken by the school system or the dismissal of his suit."[31] Based on this reversal of reasoning, Acanfora decided to take his case to the Supreme Court. He was supported by the National Education Association's DuShane Foundation and defended by the Lambda Legal Defense and Education Fund.[32] In the autumn, the court denied certiorari, upholding the lower court's decision and refusing to reinstate Acanfora to his teaching position.[33]

He never pursed teaching again: "I was not motivated to fight another uphill battle trying to secure another teaching position." With his long battle over, Joe Acanfora moved on with his life. He relocated to California, where he embarked on a successful career with the University of California in contract and grant administration and later in technology, retiring in 2003.[34]

HOPS Continues

While HOPS was battling with Penn State's administration over its charter and right to exist, it continued to sponsor many programs and events. The spring of 1972 was an active time for HOPS. In April, supporters participated in the university's colloquy, sponsoring a panel discussion, cabaret, dance, workshop, and gay sensitivity session.[35] In May, they sponsored a conference for lesbians, with an open house, workshops, and a party. Members of HOPS also traveled to Indiana University of Pennsylvania to speak to classes.[36] Throughout this time HOPS was denied on-campus meeting facilities by the university

Fig. 25 Homophiles of Penn State banner, advertising a mixer on the campus of Penn State University, circa 1971. During the time the university administration pulled the charter of HOPS, the group had to rely on other organizations to sponsor its events (in this case, the Undergraduate Student Government Association). "Special Interest, LGBSA (B&W), Undated," Students, 1855–Present (1190), Photographic Vertical Files. Used with permission from the Eberly Family Special Collections Library, Penn State University Libraries, University Park, Pennsylvania.

administration but still held weekly meetings at an off-campus building called the Shelter, located at 400 Prospect Avenue.[37]

In June 1972, HOPS took on its most ambitious project to date, sponsoring a Gay Liberation Festival at an undisclosed off-campus location. This is probably the first occurrence of any type of Gay Pride event in central Pennsylvania. A mimeographed flyer promoted the event as a "48 Hour Gay Weekend—A Complete Liberation Experience." The festival was held "at a rustic hide-away lodge located on private property a mere five miles from the University Park campus." The event kicked off on Friday evening, June 2, with a movie and a party. On Saturday, there were workshops and a picnic capped off by another party that night; the following Sunday there were more workshops, another picnic, and swimming. HOPS employed the illustrative words of "food, beer, sun, people and nature" to describe the picnics, and the picturesque words of "music, dancing, beer, people, fun and love," for the parties.[38] To young gay college students just coming out, this event symbolized the new era of gay

Fig. 26 The crowd at the Philadelphia Gay Pride Parade, with a banner by Homophiles of Penn State, 1972. Photo: Kay Tobin. Philadelphia Gay Pride Rally and March, June 11, 1972, Professional and Archivist Photography, Barbara Gittings and Kay Tobin Lahusen Gay History Papers and Photographs. © Manuscripts and Archives Division, New York Public Library.

liberation, an opportunity to be out and be with others, a gay liberation festival where they could celebrate with other like-minded souls.

HOPS continued to grow and develop as an organization. Leaders maintained their focus on sponsoring a variety of social activities as well as service and educational functions for its members, the university, and the State College–area community.

Anthony "Tony" Silvestre arrived on campus as a graduate student in 1971 and recalled the lawsuit to try to reinstate HOPS's charter and Joe Acanfora's fight to obtain his teaching credentials. This was Silvestre's first exposure to gay rights activism, and he immediately became active in HOPS, eventually becoming president of the organization during his years at Penn State. He recalls becoming very involved in the programs with HOPS: "Because of my association in the organization I had a lot of opportunity to interact with people. So, we organized a hotline, which is a very common way of starting in many rural areas. . . . we had a lot of verbal interaction with people from Pennsylvania and it didn't take much to get our address, so we were also doing written communication with people who themselves were coming out or who wanted information."[39]

Once HOPS's charter was finally reinstated in January 1973, members now had full privileges and the use of the university facilities for their programs. "Having the resources of the university, like free rooms and so on, meeting rooms, we became a natural place [as a] crossroads, for other activists going across the state," Silvestre recalls. "We would bring speakers in from Philly or Pittsburgh. Many of our own members would leave, graduate Penn State and go down to Philly or Pittsburgh and get active locally. So . . . already we were building networks with these other communities."[40]

The record of HOPS is sporadic through the rest of the decade. It is not known whether HOPS kept sponsoring Gay Pride events after its first in 1972, but in May 1979 it held a Gay Awareness Festival on campus, primarily in the Hetzel Union Building, that included a women's coffeehouse, lectures, workshops, films, dance, and a religious service provided by the Metropolitan Community Church.[41]

By the early 1980s, HOPS ceased operation. It would be replaced by a succession of gay student organizations under different names over the ensuing years. But HOPS had secured its place in history as a pioneering gay student organization. Its activist members fought and won the right to its very existence and the right to shout the famous cheer, "We are Penn State!"

The Lesbian Connection

Women living in State College in the late 1970s also faced the same problem as Lorraine Kujawa and her friends in the Harrisburg area. Mary Margaret Hart and Lynn Daniels, both graduate students at Penn State, had just started dating in 1979. The My-Oh-My club (which catered to both a straight and gay crowd) had just closed, and the only other gay bar was the Scorpion Lounge. There were scant opportunities and places to meet and socialize with other like-minded women. According to Daniels, "I developed a kind of circle of friends that—most of them were connected to the university, and some of them were professors or teachers and some of them weren't. We found there was no way to meet people, really. . . . It was hard work. And so three or four of us got together and said, 'Let's do something about it,' and that was the TLC that developed—The Lesbian Connection."[42]

The TLC was not a newsletter, and it was not an organization. It was a network. "It was amazing. . . . There was a real need for people who weren't into the bars, particularly, where it could be university people but also . . .

community people," Hart remembers. "The way it ended up evolving was that it was a phone list, which had first names and phone numbers and no description on top of it, so that if somebody found a phone list somewhere, they wouldn't know what it was."

Members of the TLC would meet once a month, moving from home to home of various women who volunteered to facilitate a meeting. "It was specifically designed to be not political or activist," Hart recalls. "This is a social group where you're not committed to anything. There are no officers. What we did was each month [was] planned things that people wanted to do that month—and so there'd be events . . . [and] potlucks, and we even had a volleyball team once."

Soon the network had grown to more than one hundred women. Besides the potlucks, the women were planning bike rides and camping and hiking trips, along with other activities. The women formed subgroups, planning various activities that would go on the calendar. If a member did not want to attend an event, there was no commitment to do anything. The calendar of events was communicated through a telephone tree. Each member had a list of five or six women to call and detail to their designated listener the planned events for the upcoming month.

It was a diverse group of women, consisting of university people and town residents, with all levels of education and backgrounds. The ages ranged from women in their twenties to their late fifties. TLC continued on through the 1980s and 1990s, existing under the same structure. With the advent of the internet, their communication transitioned to an email list, but the group continues to thrive to this day. The original founding group has held various reunion gatherings, celebrating, remembering, and catching up.

Mary Margaret Hart and Lynn Daniels made a remarkable contribution for women living in the State College area. Like Lorraine Kujawa, they helped initiate a vehicle in which women could connect. They were trailblazers. Mary and Lynn were married in 2014, after being together for thirty-five years. They have remained active in the lesbian and gay community.

The Fear of Coming Out

Vehicles like the *Lavender Letter* and the TLC were essential for women living in central Pennsylvania during the late 1970s and 1980s, when bars for women were scant and other alternatives for social networking were rare. But this challenge remained throughout the balance of the century.

In the small conservative communities that punctuate central Pennsylvania, coming out was difficult for many gays and lesbians. In her 2001 book, *You're Not from Around Here, Are You? A Lesbian in Small-Town America*, Louise A. Blum, a professor of English at Mansfield University of Pennsylvania in Tioga County, wrote about the challenges she faced. She tells of wanting to start a women's political activist group in their small community by hosting a lesbian potluck at the home she shared with her wife, Connie. On the day of potluck, they began to receive telephone calls, with women cancelling. When asked why they didn't want to come, the women said they were afraid of running into other women they might meet on the street after the potluck, and they felt they couldn't risk public exposure—they, after all, had family in the area. "Why were they all so scared all the time?" Blum asked herself. "'Get over it!' I wanted to say. Get real! Connie and I had come out. We'd survived. Nothing bad had happened to us. Somehow I'd thought everybody would just come out after us, as if we'd dug a trail out from underground and liberated the burrow in which we'd all been hiding."[43] The fear of exposure for many living or working in remote areas of Pennsylvania was too daunting.

Profile

DAN MANEVAL

Born in the small town of Williamsport in the late 1940s, Dan Maneval grew up as an only child of a father who was a "jack-of-all-trades" and a stay-at-home mother. Their small family was poor. Dan's father scraped together enough money from all of his odd jobs to enable him to purchase a home for the family. "[I] led a sheltered life, [and] we were very poor," Dan remembers. "I had health problems . . . and I was sick all the time with asthma."[44] Growing up was difficult for Dan. Because of his health problems, he was on medications that stunted his growth, making him a target for others to pick on. "It didn't have anything to do with [being] 'gay,' you know, and I was a scrawny little kid," Dan recalls. Nonetheless, he knew that something was different about him. "When I played with my cousins, the boys would be in the room watching football, and the girls would be in the room playing with dolls—I'd be in that room with them, playing with dolls. . . . I didn't know what it was, and I know there were kids in my high school graduating class that were gay and out, even then, but I didn't . . . I was too afraid. . . . I hadn't been exposed to it at all."

Dan's world abruptly changed during his senior year of high school, when his mother died of cancer. Dan soldiered on, entering Lycoming College in Williamsport, where he pursued a bachelor's degree in elementary education. Immediately after Dan graduated, on Easter Sunday, his father had a sudden stroke and died. As Dan recounts, "So at twenty-one I was an orphan, if you can be an orphan at twenty-one, you know. . . . I was not ready to be alone in the world. But it was the beginning of the change in my life." The first big change was his career in education. He tried teaching, but Dan realized that he was not good at it, and it was not as rewarding as he thought it would be. He eventually went to work in an office environment as an auditor and bookkeeper.

The next change that occurred dealt with his sexuality. Dan decided to "come out" and ventured to a gay beach in Atlantic City, New Jersey. "A man picked me up. And I was thrilled to death, you know. I felt dirty afterwards—I took two showers [after the experience]. But that was the beginning, and I knew something about it was right." After that Dan started going to the few gay bars that existed in Williamsport. Gay bars in the small remote town did not usually last long. They were either straight bars that would tolerate a gay crowd for a short period or gay bars that would eventually turn straight. For the most part, gays and lesbians living in Williamsport would have to travel long distances to Harrisburg and Lancaster to go to a strictly gay bar.

Eventually Dan made his way to a gay bar in Cresson, in eastern Cambria County, a town two and half hours away from Williamsport. As luck would have it, he happened to meet Gary Norton, another resident of Williamsport, who lived several houses away from Dan. The two got to talking, and Gary informed Dan that he was starting a gay activist/social group in Williamsport. Dan was eager to join.

Dan had one earlier experience with an activist group. He had attended several meetings of the Susquehanna Valley Gays United (SVGU) in Northumberland, Northumberland County. "I went an hour down to Northumberland to go to my first gay meetings, and that thrilled me to death that I met gay people . . . SVGU was my first exposure to gay groups, and I really liked it, I really liked getting to know people through that non-bar atmosphere. . . . [SVGU] was somewhat political in nature, and that floored me, that there was a whole political scene that I didn't know anything about."

After Dan met Gary, they formed their own group in Williamsport. Motivated by other homophile groups such as HOPS and the Lehigh Valley

Homophile Organization (Le-Hi-Ho), they named their group Homophiles of Williamsport (HOW). According to Dan, "HOW was pretty successful for a while, anyway. Our purposes were educational and social more than political. People didn't want to be political, they didn't want to be 'out there.' . . . They didn't want to expose themselves to the general public, because in Williamsport . . . it was very, very backward then. I mean, the gay movement was just getting under way, really, and it really wasn't getting under way in Williamsport at all." Because of this, members of HOW needed an outlet to meet up with one another socially in a non-bar environment. Dan's major focus was education: "I wanted to educate both the gay and the straight [communities] about what our lives are like and how hard the coming-out process can be."

To facilitate this, the group began holding monthly meetings in various members' homes, but mainly in Dan's, holding both social events and discussion sessions. The topics at the discussions would range from religion, bisexuality, and coming out to rap sessions. The social events included parties, dances, and dinners. Many of the meetings were held in public places such as church basements and the local library. Lutheran and Methodist churches were the most accepting, and their congregations were not opposed to renting space to this small gay group.

Dan's focus on education and gay activism soon led him to speaking engagements in various colleges and universities in the area. Dan would give a lecture and then hold a question-and-answer session afterward. He was always welcomed in the classrooms in which he spoke. But one time at the Pennsylvania College of Technology, where he had been invited to speak numerous times, the professor walked Dan out to his car after the lecture. Curious, Dan turned to her and asked, "Why did you come out with me? You never did that before." The professor looked at Dan and replied, "'Cause one of the students, I heard them say after class, threatened your life." As Dan remembers, "That was a rude awakening to what kind of negativity was out there toward me and toward my kind of people. That was from a college classroom in the '70s. . . . But that didn't stop me. It was shocking, but I still spoke a few times after that, but not as often."

Things changed dramatically for Dan and HOW in 1978, when Anita Bryant came to the Bloomsburg Fair (the oldest fair in the Keystone State, founded in the mid-1850s), approximately forty-five miles from Williamsport. Bryant was coming to the fair as part of her antigay Protect America's Children campaign, which she had initiated in Dade County, Florida. After the county legislators passed an ordinance that prohibited discrimination based

Fig. 27 Demonstrators marching at the Bloomsburg fairgrounds in protest of an appearance by entertainer and antigay crusader Anita Bryant, 1978. *Campus Voice*, September 27, 1978, 1. Bloomsburg University Archives, Bloomsburg, Pennsylvania.

on sexual orientation, Bryant used her notoriety to organize a petition drive to place a repeal on the ballot for the next election. The repeal of gay and lesbian rights was passed by an overwhelming two-to-one margin. Emboldened by this success, Bryant now decided to take her antigay campaign national with the aim, as historian Tina Fetner describes it, "to save America from lesbian and gay activists, whom [Bryant] claimed were predatory homosexuals bent on recruiting children into their sinful lifestyle."[45]

As the Protect America's Children campaign continued, it became a clarion call for the gay community to organize and fight for their civil rights. Angry protests against Bryant broke out across the county. As one activist predicted, "I thought it was the first great opportunity nationally to mobilize the gay community with a political consciousness. I hoped that gay rights would mature into a major civil rights issue on the national agenda." Bryant's campaign, as gay historian Amin Ghaziani notes, "placed gay issues on the table of national media and public opinion" and, ironically, helped mobilize the community that she was demonizing to defend their dignity.[46]

With Bryant bringing her nationwide campaign to the Bloomsburg Fair in rural Columbia County, Dan and the members of HOW were alarmed and felt that they had to do something. Along with Gary Norton, Dan contacted the local Williamsport chapter of the National Organization for Women, and together they organized a rally against Bryant's appearance at the fair and invited the Pennsylvania Rural Gay Caucus to participate. They invited speakers opposing Bryant's agenda to Town Park in Bloomsburg. They then marched in protest at the fairgrounds and proceeded to march around the fairgrounds grandstand oval on the day of Bryant's appearance and concert.

At Town Park, Dan was one of the first speakers. "There were TV cameras there . . . from Channel 16 or Channel 28, one of the Wilkes-Barre/Scranton stations. And they televised a part of my speech on the evening news that night as to what was going on and what was there. [On Channel 16 they had been reporting] there was going to be a rally in Bloomsburg in [protest of] Anita Bryant, they were talking about that for days and days and days before it happened. So, naturally, they were going to go there and cover it. So my speech made the airwaves."

The resulting media coverage was devastating for Dan. As Dan remembers, "There was a teenage gang in my neighborhood at home that didn't like . . . the fact that I was on TV and they didn't like the fact that I was gay, and they didn't like the fact that I was living there in their neighborhood." Within days of the broadcast, the gang vandalized Dan's house. First, they threw tomatoes onto Dan's porch. Soon the tomatoes became stones, and the stones eventually became bricks. Ultimately, every window in Dan's home had been shattered.

Dan called the police after every attack:

> They did very little . . . every time there was damage, yes, I called them, yes, they wrote it down, they wrote it up. I had no proof, I had no witnesses, but I knew who it was. And they didn't—I don't know what they did. But some of them were more receptive in taking down the information than others. Some of them, you could tell, were sympathetic to what was going on, and some of them weren't. But eventually . . . I had to move. My life could have been over. Attacks could have happened. I could have been hurt. So I moved. . . . This was my family home, I inherited it from my mother and my father, and I was an only child, so I lived there. It was my home, and so I had to give it up.

Dan was forced to sell his family home and leave Williamsport. He moved into a small trailer in the town of Linden, just west of Williamsport. There he lived for the next five years until he felt it was safe enough to return to Williamsport. Dan's departure also signaled the demise of HOW. People were now fearful to go to Dan's or anyone else's home and, because of this fear, the group disbanded.

During his five years away in Linden, and with HOW no longer in existence, Dan founded another group, the Susquehanna Lambda. This organization in turn led to the founding of the Gay and Lesbian Switchboard of North Central Pennsylvania. The Switchboard was a vital referral source and helpline for a number of years, especially during the AIDS crisis. Dan healed from his traumatic experience, but the scars remained.

CHAPTER 4

Convergence

The Stonewall uprising, combined with the unparalleled social and political upheavals occurring in the United States in the 1960s and 1970s, galvanized and dramatically altered lesbian and gay activists' strategies in their quest for civil liberties. As gay activists harnessed lessons from their past, new organizations began to form across the United States. The increased visibility and awareness of the lesbian and gay community helped propel the movement forward as it entered the new decade of the 1970s.[1]

The activist movement that erupted after the Stonewall uprising found its way into various small cities and towns in central Pennsylvania. Gay activists began focusing on creating organizations, services, and activities where they lived. In some cases, they had heard of similar organizations being created in other places in central Pennsylvania, but most of these activists had never met. It would take a heterosexual Jewish businessman from Cleveland, Ohio, to help them connect with one another and to create a more cohesive force in gay political activism in Pennsylvania.

That visionary individual was Milton Jerrold Shapiro, who moved from Cleveland to Pennsylvania in 1936. Although he was forthright about his religious affiliation, his fears about anti-Semitism prompted him to change his last name to Shapp. In a few years, he founded the Jerrold Electronics Company, which pioneered the development of the cable television industry by bringing television to mountain-locked communities across the nation—and his company took off. Even in those early years, Shapp employed a diverse workforce. The *Philadelphia Bulletin* described his labor pool as a "little United Nations." Shapp eventually made a fortune when he sold the company for $50 million in 1966, or $395 million in today's dollars.[2]

Shapp entered politics in 1960 by campaigning for Democratic presidential candidate John F. Kennedy. He also devised the concept of the Peace Corps.

Shapp served in the Kennedy administration as consultant to the then secretary of commerce, Luther H. Hodges Sr., and helped organize the Area Redevelopment Administration to combat unemployment in the nation's less developed regions. After an unsuccessful run for governor in 1966, he won the 1970 Pennsylvania gubernatorial election against his Republican opponent by more than five hundred thousand votes. He was the first governor elected who was allowed to serve two terms and was Pennsylvania's first Jewish chief executive.[3]

Shapp took a businesslike approach to government but was always aware of his constituents. His belief that government must serve as an advocate for all people, along with his liberal policies and diverse staff, made him enormously popular. He was an individual on whom one could take a chance—and that is precisely what gay activist Mark A. Segal, a Philadelphia native, did.

Segal had participated in the Stonewall riots and became active in the Gay Liberation Front in New York (GLF-NY). As Segal grew in his activist role, he, along with friend Harry Langhorne, had formed a new gay activist organization, the Gay Raiders, whose primary purpose was to bring attention to the gay rights movement. He believed the newly emerging gay liberation movement was invisible to the general public. What little the public did know about the movement and about gay people was mainly negative, fed by distortions in the media. To combat these misperceptions, the Gay Raiders would use "zaps." A zap was a nonviolent but highly disruptive protest designed to gain media attention. They aimed to break down false stereotypes and to promote the legitimacy of gay rights.[4]

Segal launched his first zap in 1972 by handcuffing himself to the rail above the Liberty Bell at Independence National Historical Park in Philadelphia. The moment he did, television cameras focused on him. He immediately started yelling, "Independence for gay people! We want nondiscrimination!" Segal stayed handcuffed for barely ten minutes before he was taken to jail. Local media coverage was swift. He continued doing zaps at other public places and meetings that year, including at a national United Way meeting and at a fundraiser for President Richard Nixon.[5]

His biggest and most famous zap came when he burst onto the set of the *CBS Evening News* with Walter Cronkite in December 1973. Segal and Langhorne posed as Temple University media students in order to be allowed into the CBS studio. At fourteen minutes into the broadcast, Segal rushed onto the set, right in front of Cronkite, holding a sign and shouting the message printed on it: "Gays protest CBS prejudice!" CBS shut down the cameras, and screens across the nation went blank. Mark was hauled off. When the show returned to the air, Cronkite reported on the incident and the disruption of his show. This marked the first report on a gay demonstration by CBS News. Segal's message was heard and seen by millions of Americans.[6]

His reputation as an activist was growing, and so was his courage. He brought these urgent feelings of activism back home to Philadelphia, and now he wanted to do more politically:

> Up to that point in American history, you will not find an elected official anywhere that had ever mentioned gay, lesbian, homosexual, homophile, what have you. You must remember what the condition of gay people was at that point in history. We were fighting to allow lawyers to pass the bar. . . . If a doctor became known as a gay person, he might've not gotten his license, he wouldn't have gotten into a hospital; governments would fire you; people who had [a] liquor license might lose their liquor license if they served gay people. Things were not very good for us. . . . If you were gay, you were immoral to the religious society, you were illegal to the criminal justice system, . . . [and] to the medical industry, you were psychologically ill. We were the bottom rung of American society.[7]

During his first run for governor in 1966, Milton Shapp had met with the Homophile Action League (HAL) of Philadelphia, a newly formed gay activist group. They told Shapp they wanted to "change society's legal, social, and scientific attitudes toward the homosexual in order to achieve justified recognition of the homosexual as a first-class citizen and a first-class human being." Shapp listened attentively, and, though he lost his bid that year, HAL's persistence left its mark.[8]

But when Shapp secured the office in 1970, Mark Segal decided to gamble on the governor. "Governor Shapp had a reputation for being a progressive," Segal says. "What we were doing was obviously out of the box. There were no rules—no one knew what to do." In 1974, Segal sent him a letter requesting a meeting. "Up to that point, no governor anywhere in the nation had met with LGBT activists. If anything, if they saw a gay person coming towards them, they would've run the other way."[9] To Segal's surprise, he received a letter stating that the governor would be glad to meet with him. Later that day, he received a telephone call from the governor's office, informing him that he was going to be in the Montgomery County seat of Norristown the following day, and if Segal could make it, they could meet then.

Segal was elated. "When a dog hears a very strange sound and he just tilts his head—that's how I felt. It was like, wow, the man is actually going to meet with us! And then I thought, does he realize what this means? And then, my third thought was, basically, oh, it's in Norristown, he doesn't want anyone in Harrisburg in the press corps to see this so we're doing it in Norristown."[10]

As it turned out, there were no strategic machinations on Governor Shapp's part. He was on a statewide tour, which was why the meeting was scheduled for Norristown. The next day, when Segal and Langhorne walked into the room, the governor immediately walked over to Segal with his hand extended and said, smiling, "I've seen you on TV." When Segal did not seem to understand, the governor added, "Cronkite seemed to be surprised to meet you, but I'm not." Segal was completely disarmed and felt quickly comfortable with Shapp. They talked for a while, and the governor, rather than asking what Segal could do for him, instead asked what he could do to help Segal's cause. According to Segal, "I always go for the brass ring, so I said 'Governor, gay men and lesbians are discriminated against in almost every part of the state government.'" Shapp immediately responded, "How can we change that?" Segal replied, "Create a commission to explore these problems and find solutions." Shapp immediately responded, "Let me consider the options and get back to you."[11]

Segal thought he was having a private, off-the-record meeting, but to his surprise the governor turned to his assistant and said, "Bring them in." Segal remembers, "They [opened] the doors, and the entire Pennsylvania press corps came into the room and photographed the governor and I. *He* decided he wanted it on the record. . . . Those photographs are the first photographs of any governor in America meeting with gay activists. That was his decision, not ours. And that was in every newspaper in the state of Pennsylvania the following morning." When the press arrived, questions were thrown at the governor, too many to answer. Shapp responded by saying, "We had a good meeting," and added, "It's a start." Segal at the time was probably the best-known gay activist in the nation because of his famous television zaps and the headlines he garnered from the activities of the Gay Raiders. He had also made guest appearances on many of the country's televised talk shows, including the *Phil Donahue Show*.[12] Governor Shapp's decision to meet with Mark Segal was a groundbreaking event. What happened next was even more important.

In late 1974, Shapp convened a task force to study issues of importance to the gay community. On November 21, 1974, the first meeting was held with the governor's staff and a select group of gay community activists. Terry Dellmuth, Shapp's special assistant for human services, presided over the meeting. Barry D. Kohn of the Community Advocate Unit in the Department of Justice took an active staff role. They decided to continue the meetings, and, within a few

Fig. 28 Gov. Milton J. Shapp, Mark Segal, and unknown individual. Photo: Harry Eberlin. MS Coll. 25, Tommi Avicolli Mecca Collection, 1967–92, John J. Wilcox Jr. Archives, William Way LGBT Community Center, Philadelphia.

months, more activists heard about the task force. The number of participants grew with each meeting. Sam Deetz, who lived in Northumberland, recalls,

> Gay rights task force meetings were starting to take place in the governor's office in the capitol in Harrisburg. . . . This was a task force in the gay and lesbian community. Friends, people who were interested, were invited into the governor's office. He had a huge conference room. . . . But the room would get so crowded with the participants and the people who were assigned to assess this gathering that people would come and stand along and line the walls. So we were coming from every part of the state, and this gave me even more opportunity to meet even people from all the rural areas.[13]

One of the first requests the gay and lesbian activists made was to ban discrimination in employment on the basis of sexual orientation. Governor Shapp was powerless to do that on behalf of the entire commonwealth without the state legislature passing legislation. He knew that it would be an impossible fight. As governor, however, he did have administrative control over policies in state government. On April 23, 1975, Governor Shapp made history by issuing a landmark executive order:

In furtherance of my commitment to provide leadership in the effort to obtain equal rights for all persons in Pennsylvania, I am committing this administration to work towards ending discrimination against persons solely because of their affectional or sexual preference.

Terry Dellmuth, my Special Assistant for Human Services, and Barry Kohn, Director, Community Advocate Unit, Pennsylvania Department of Justice, are hereby assigned to review and monitor this effort. They will work with state agencies and private groups to further define the problem and make recommendations for further action.

State departments and agencies are instructed to fully cooperate within the effort to end this type of discrimination.[14]

With the single stroke of a pen, Governor Shapp signed the first antidiscrimination order for sexual minorities in the nation. No other state or governor had made such a bold move for gay and lesbian equal rights.[15] The effect of this executive order was especially significant for central Pennsylvania, where the state government was one of the largest employers, especially in the Harrisburg area. Gay and lesbian state employees were the first in the commonwealth to receive such protections. The executive order made many of them more comfortable about coming out and made it easier and acceptable for the community to establish viable organizations, services, and programs. The order also likely attracted more gays and lesbians to state employment, now that they knew that they had equal protection under the law.

The executive order made headlines nationally. It was released by United Press International, which announced, "Shapp Orders Homosexual Equal Rights." The article reported that Shapp was the first governor in the nation to issue such an order and quoted Richard Duran, Shapp's top aide: "We would never force anyone to hire people with different sexual preferences. But if someone is extremely well qualified, even for the state police, then they should not be denied employment."[16]

On February 12, 1976, Governor Shapp formalized the task force by issuing another executive order creating the Pennsylvania Council for Sexual Minorities. He ordered each department to appoint a top official to be a member or liaison to the council. The cities of Philadelphia and Pittsburgh were to have six gay activist members each, and the rural areas of the state were to have two members. Within months, representation from the rural areas was expanded to six members. The council now had a total of eighteen gay and lesbian activist members.[17]

Fig. 29 Gov. Milton J. Shapp (*left*) with Tony Silvestre at a meeting at the governor's mansion in Harrisburg just prior to the governor appointing Silvestre as chair of the Pennsylvania Council for Sexual Minorities, 1976. Image: Neg. 10, *Governor Shapp Meets with Gay Liberation Group at Governor's Residence-Mansion*, file 1198, Governor's File of Photographs and Negatives, 1971–87, RG-52.28, Records of the Department of Transportation, Pennsylvania State Archives, Harrisburg.

Mark Segal's bold vision had come to fruition. He wanted to lead the commission, but the governor's choice was instead rooted in a savvy assessment of political reality. The governor called Segal into his office and told him, "Mark, you're too much of a firebrand, and if I allowed you to chair the commission, it would get nowhere, and we both want it to make change, you understand." Segal was disappointed, but he understood. He knew his reputation and knew it would take a different type of personality to chair the council and work with the various levels of state government. Shapp appointed Segal to two subcommittees, prisons and insurance. Tony Silvestre, former president of Homophiles of Penn State, would chair the council, and Barry Kohn was appointed liaison to the governor.[18]

The council immediately went to work, and for the next two years it made major progress toward ending discrimination in the commonwealth for agencies under the governor's jurisdiction. On September 19, 1978, an amended executive order was issued authorizing the council to work with state agencies and firms that contracted with the commonwealth to end discrimination against people based solely on their sexual orientation. They started working with these agencies, focusing on educating employees, examining hiring practices, providing speakers, and hosting educational seminars when necessary.[19]

The council issued a policy with respect to sexual orientation to the twenty-seven state agencies that prevented discrimination in hiring, employment, housing, credit, or any related matters. All but three of the agencies agreed to the policy, the exceptions being the Pennsylvania State Police, Game Commission, and Fish Commission (renamed the Fish and Boat Commission in 1991). Those three agencies would finally consent to this policy years later.[20]

In 1978, in a groundbreaking decision, the commonwealth's attorney general agreed that the definition of sexual orientation included transgender and transsexual people. This redefinition was years before anyone in the gay and lesbian community nationally took up the fight for transgender rights. Another breakthrough occurred when the council mandated that the commonwealth's colleges and universities revise their policy to include not only their employees but their students as well. In the last year of Governor Shapp's term, the council was able to get three labor unions, representing nurses, college professors, and social workers, to adhere to the policy.[21]

The council and the governor quickly encountered opposition to their work. Shortly after the council was created, State Senator Thomas M. Nolan (D), majority leader, immediately began introducing legislation to revoke Shapp's executive order. This failed to pass. He continued by introducing legislation that would forbid the hiring of people known to be gay in jobs that involved interacting with children, specifically in education. Nolan introduced Senate Bill 83, which would have denied employment as a police officer or prison guard or in juvenile or mental institutions to anyone convicted of admitting to deviant sexual intercourse as defined by state law. The law passed both houses of the state legislature but was vetoed by the governor. The bill was aimed at homosexuals but could easily have applied to heterosexuals. Had the bill been signed into law, it would not likely have withstood a constitutional challenge because it violated the equal-protection guarantee of the Fourteenth Amendment.[22] Nolan's bill prompted a reaction from the gay community, resulting in the first gay rights demonstration ever held in Harrisburg in 1977.

"He didn't get anywhere with his bills, except really to alienate the other legislators," says Tony Silvestre. "They found themselves getting lobbied both from our people and from the other side. And it put them in very uncomfortable positions to have to talk about these issues back in their home towns, issues that they didn't really think were relevant since there was nothing happening in the public that was generating all this legislation." As a result of this pressure, Nolan was eventually voted out of his majority leader position. It

Fig. 30 First gay rights demonstration held in Harrisburg, protesting antigay legislation introduced into the Pennsylvania legislature, 1977. Photo: Bari Weaver. Courtesy of the LGBT Center of Central PA History Project, Archives and Special Collections, Dickinson College, Carlisle, Pennsylvania.

became more difficult for his allies in the Democratic Party to align themselves with him on these issues. "People were much happier to just turn away and not pay any attention to it. It was a no-win for them, in their view. No matter what they did," Silvestre adds.[23]

Not long after the council was created, Ethel D. Allen, a highly respected member of the Philadelphia City Council (and the first African American woman elected to it), made a special request of the governor to issue a proclamation in support for Gay Pride Week in June 1976. The governor did so, and the reaction was swift and vociferous. The state legislature immediately issued a rebuke to his proclamation. A resolution was offered in Pennsylvania's House of Representatives that put lawmakers on record as opposed to Shapp's proclamation because it was "contrary to the morality and laws of the Commonwealth."[24] According to Silvestre, "Some people . . . found it much easier to accept the notion that [the governor] supported civil rights, but not that he would support Pride. It was sort of a new idea for many people and [many] saw it as a kind of proselytizing or a level of approval that they thought was not appropriate for a governor." He adds that Shapp was "one of the few politicians . . . that I can recall who were so outspoken on this issue. . . . A lot of the governors [on the East and West Coasts] were more used to being openly supportive of LGBT people, but it was very rare for a governor to be so outspoken. And it brought a lot of attention to the issue and it helped us develop our own understanding of what the state could or could not do in terms of LGBT people."[25]

By the time he left office in January 1979, Shapp's legacy had been solidified. His successor, Republican governor Richard "Dick" T. Thornburgh, initially wanted to dismantle the council but was widely advised against such a move. Under Thornburgh, the council became inactive for a short time, lacking his administrative support and backing. But when the AIDS crisis suddenly emerged, the commonwealth and the governor turned to the council. Maria A. Keating, an aide to the governor, reached out to the council to help write the commonwealth's policy for the Pennsylvania Department of Education on AIDS education and training in schools as well as policies for the Pennsylvania Department of Public Welfare (DPW).

When AIDS diagnoses started to appear, the disease was first labeled "gay-related immune deficiency" (GRID). No one knew what to do. "There were so few resources on which to draw. No one knew anything about it," recalls Carol Rankin, a member of the council representing the DPW. "The only organizations in the country that were dealing with it were the Gay Men's Health Crisis in New York and a group in San Francisco. We had to find out about the disease and what to do about it ourselves. We turned to the gay community for answers. They were the ones who knew the most about the disease and medical treatments available." The council formed an AIDS Advisory Committee, made up not only of members from the DPW and the medical profession but also of people with HIV. "It was a rough time in the beginning. Some of the members were dying within six months."[26]

Within its first few years, the advisory committee had established statewide public and private AIDS education and prevention training. It increased statewide AIDS funding, making Pennsylvania one of the nation's leading states in the fight against the disease. The council established statewide AIDS policies on welfare, education, training, and benefits. It also worked to establish a fund for a grant for the drug AZT, the first drug developed to fight the AIDS virus, for pharmacy distribution through DPW. The council's work during the AIDS crisis also created delivery services for the gay and lesbian community. Because of the new urgency surrounding AIDS, major administrative advances were made against discrimination in children and youth, drug and alcohol, mental health, antiviolence, aging, and homeless service agencies.

This progress ensured that critical services were available to gays and lesbians and that these agencies were competent to deal with sexual minorities.[27] In addition to the work with AIDS policies, the council worked with Governor Thornburgh to get the Pennsylvania State Police, Game Commission, and Fish Commission to adopt the nondiscrimination policy in state employment, thus making it consistent throughout all agencies.[28]

When the council began in 1976, many people were skeptical. Sam Deetz remembers that at the time, gay people "lived two lives. They had one life that they lived on weekends and holidays and so forth—that's when they met socially and interacted with people that they were comfortable with, where they didn't have to worry about how they said something or what pronoun they used and so forth. During the week, of course, it was going to work and acting like anybody else, monitoring how they spoke, who they spoke about, and how they spoke of friendships. . . . The folks who were living that way and were accustomed to it, a lot of them didn't see any hope, any chance for a change."[29] Others, like Deetz himself, were excited and believed that change could happen. Governor Shapp's executive orders and the Pennsylvania Council for Sexual Minorities were landmark beginnings of change for the commonwealth and for the nation.

The Pennsylvania Rural Gay Caucus

By the summer of 1975, many gay activists living in rural areas and small cities began caucusing after the governor's task force meetings. They realized that they shared similar experiences and problems and found their discussions particularly helpful. The rural representatives decided that it would be efficient and useful to join forces to address the concerns left off the agenda because they weren't priorities in urban settings. Pittsburgh and Philadelphia had their organizations, so why not rural areas? A recommendation was made to meet each month. A vote was taken, and it passed unanimously. Members of the group decided to call themselves the Pennsylvania Rural Gay Caucus, describing themselves as surrounded by large areas of "rural" lands rather than "being from the larger cities."[30]

The Pennsylvania Rural Gay Caucus was originally composed of the Lehigh Valley Homophile Organization (or Le-Hi-Ho), Allentown-Bethlehem; Gay Coordinating Society of Berks County, Reading; Gays United, Lancaster; Gay Community Services, Harrisburg; Homophiles of Penn State, State College;

94

Fig. 31 A meeting of the Pennsylvania Rural Gay Caucus in Wilkes-Barre, April 10, 1976. Photo: Thomas F. Schmidt of Fay Broody Studios, Shavertown, Pennsylvania. Courtesy of the LGBT Center of Central PA History Project, Archives and Special Collections, Dickinson College, Carlisle, Pennsylvania.

Susquehanna Valley Gays United, Northumberland-Sunbury; Northeast Pennsylvania Gay Association, Wilkes-Barre; Homophiles of Williamsport; Shippensburg Gays United; Gay League of Lebanon; Gay League of Edinboro (Edinboro State College); Gay Students at West Chester (West Chester State College); Dignity/Central PA; and unaffiliated individuals.

In the beginning membership was informal; any individual who attended and participated in discussions was considered a member. The caucus primarily consisted of working-class adults and students who shared similar concerns and goals. The first elected chairs were Ray Stickles, Lancaster, and Ruth Steck, Sunbury. The chairs, along with the caucus members, decided that there would be no dues. Travel arrangements and expenses would be made and paid for by the individual members. The goal was to use the group's ideas and discussions to work together for the good of the gay and lesbian communities. The caucus would meet at different members' locations around the state to discuss issues, solve problems, make decisions, and plan events to improve the future of the gays and lesbians living in nonmetropolitan areas of the commonwealth.[31]

OUT IN CENTRAL PENNSYLVANIA

The inaugural project undertaken by the caucus was to organize the first statewide conference on gay issues. Held in conjunction with a meeting of the governor's task force, the Pennsylvania State Gay Conference was held in Harrisburg on October 17 and 18, 1975. The conference held its opening and closing plenary sessions in the auditorium of the William Penn Memorial Museum (now the State Museum of Pennsylvania) and offered workshops on a variety of gay rights topics at the Society of Friends Meeting House on Herr Street. To conclude the conference, a buffet dinner was held at the Neptune Lounge, a popular gay bar opposite the museum, followed by a disco dance at the Central Dauphin Democratic Club on Walnut Street.[32]

The next major effort the caucus launched was Gay Education Day, a day of lobbying Pennsylvania's state legislature. Planning began in October 1975, and the date of March 23, 1976, was chosen for lobbying. The goal was to educate legislators about the need for gay rights, antidiscrimination laws, and the repeal of the sodomy laws. The repeal of the sodomy laws was initially the focus, and Pennsylvania had a voluntary deviate sexual intercourse law. Sodomy laws classified intercourse between persons of the same sex as a criminal offense. Gays or lesbians convicted of this offense could be denied employment and housing. In the 1970s, prejudice was insinuating its way into antigay bills in the legislature. Various bills were introduced that would prevent employment in state government, education, or the medical profession if a person had admitted to or had committed acts of so-called deviate sexual behavior based on the current sodomy laws.[33] Mary Nancarrow, caucus member, remembers, "If you were lesbian or gay or accused of being such, you could not be a nurse, you could not work in day care, you could not teach, you could not be a doctor, could not be a youth group leader—*nothing*—because the prejudice was that lesbians and gays were child molesters. . . . [They were] creating these bills and putting them into committees, and we were trying to stop them from coming to the floor to be voted on. . . . We would be lobbying throughout the existence of the Rural Gay Caucus."[34]

After months of planning by the caucus, education day arrived. More than a hundred gay activists from across the commonwealth, traveling by buses, trains, and automobiles, arrived in Harrisburg and gathered at the Society of Friends Meeting House. There, caucus leaders gave them instructions, along with a list of state senators and representatives to lobby. They were also given ID tags and an upside-down Pink Triangle badge on a black background. "We loved the pink triangle," remembers Sam Deetz. "A lot of us really took that

Fig. 32 Members of the Pennsylvania Rural Gay Caucus in State College in 1976. *Left to right*: Pam Erdly, Sam Deetz, Jonathan Smith-Cousins, and Tony Silvestre. Photo: Bari Weaver. Courtesy of the LGBT Center of Central PA History Project, Archives and Special Collections, Dickinson College, Carlisle, Pennsylvania.

to heart. We had all read about the situation in Germany before World War II and just kind of felt a kinship with that, this symbol."[35]

Activists paired up and walked to the State Capitol to meet with legislators. It was a long day, but they did not deviate from their mission. "There were states that had legislatures that were rescinding it [the sodomy statute], but Pennsylvania was not to be one of them. . . . [We] already had [antidiscrimination in] the employment and housing situations on our list, but the top of our list was repeal of the sodomy statute," Deetz explains. "When I talked to the legislators about that, that was the first thing I brought up, and they really didn't have any answer. Their best answer usually was, 'Well, we don't have the votes for that. Most of the legislators are elected by people who feel that that is wrong. That is contrary to God's work.'"[36]

Tony Silvestre, chair of the Pennsylvania Council for Sexual Minorities, was present that day to lobby, helping educate legislators on all the issues about which the caucus and council were concerned. He was paired with Spencer Cox, head of the American Civil Liberties Union (ACLU) in Philadelphia, an unrelenting supporter of gay and lesbian rights and an expert in dealing

Fig. 33 Back page from an issue of the *Gay Era* newspaper, showing photographs from the first Gay Education Day in 1976. Photos: Bari Weaver. Courtesy of the LGBT Center of Central PA History Project, Archives and Special Collections, Dickinson College, Carlisle, Pennsylvania.

with legislators, who died at the age of forty-four from complications due to AIDS. "No matter how rural or conservative the district," Silvestre recalls, "the members of the legislature [we] would talk to—or their aides—were always very responsive and supportive. . . . By that time there was a lot of movement in the country and even in the state, in support of various commissions and issues related to feminism and even gay rights so we didn't surprise them— they weren't surprised by us and they seemed to be very receptive in what we had to discuss."[37]

At the close of the day, the activists gathered on the grounds of the State Capitol for an announced news conference. Along with affiliates from major television networks were reporters for daily newspapers in Philadelphia, Pittsburgh, Harrisburg, and Allentown, as well as smaller regional papers. Tony Silvestre and Ray Stickles, chair of the Rural Gay Caucus, conducted television interviews. Newspapers sought out activists from their areas, and in many cases the story was front-page news the following day. The stories reported on what the gay activists were doing in Harrisburg that day and their objectives,

CONVERGENCE

concerns, and goals. The caucus made inroads that day in educating not only the legislature but also the public.[38]

In 1977, the caucus held a Human Rights Day at the State Capitol in protest of Senate Bill 531, which would have strengthened existing sodomy laws and other antigay legislation. Garnering support from the ACLU and the National Organization for Women (NOW), the caucus printed and distributed five thousand flyers to rally support against the bill.[39]

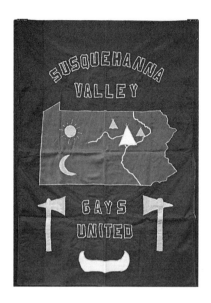

Fig. 34 Handmade fabric banner for the Susquehanna Valley Gays United. Photo: Don Giles. Pennsylvania Historical and Museum Commission. Courtesy of the LGBT Center of Central PA History Project, Archives and Special Collections, Dickinson College, Carlisle, Pennsylvania.

In 1978, the Rural Gay Caucus launched a second day of lobbying legislators, again called Gay Education Day. The major focus remained the repeal of the state's sodomy laws. It would take until 1980 for the state legislature to repeal the statute.[40]

The next large event the caucus undertook was the organization of a second statewide conference for gay activism and gay rights. Gay and lesbian organizations and activists from all corners of the Keystone State were invited. Under the leadership of newly elected cochairs Joe Burns and Mary Nancarrow, the conference was scheduled for January 1978 in Allentown. In the fall of 1977, organizers made arrangements with the management of the historic Americus Hotel to host the event, titled Pride '78. The keynote speakers chosen for the conference were Bruce R. Voeller, founder and director of the National Gay and Lesbian Task Force (NGLTF); Elaine Noble, democratic state representative from Massachusetts, the second openly gay politician elected to public office in the country; and Tony Silvestre.[41] The choice of Bruce Voeller was especially significant to the Rural Gay Caucus, since the NGLTF was founded to coordinate the more than eight hundred gay organizations in the country, something of a model for the caucus.[42]

Allentown seemed the perfect choice: the city's Human Relations Commission had recommended an ordinance that would ban discrimination against gays. The recommendation had been submitted to the city council. But controversy began swelling. Local elections were scheduled in the near future, and, according to the *Gay Era* newspaper, "Mayor Joseph S. Daddona and city council members seem acutely aware of the policy's potential impact in an election." Robert Manley, the Human Relations Commission's executive director, reported, "It will take two months to transmit the recommendation to city hall." He then acknowledged, "In view of the national publicity, nobody wants to touch it." Council member Watson W. Skinner added, "There's no support for it. Most council members hope the issue will just go away."[43]

Even the logistics of holding the conference proved daunting. In a sudden reversal of its commitment, the Americus Hotel refused to accommodate the conference scheduled for January because it was being sponsored by the Pennsylvania Council for Sexual Minorities and the Pennsylvania Rural Gay Caucus. The decision was made by Albert Moffa, the hotel's owner, not by the manager who had originally agreed to the event (but was no longer employed by the hotel).[44]

The controversy over the antidiscrimination ordinance had impacted the hotel's decision. Joe Burns, caucus chair, issued a strident statement: "It is without doubt the most open and glaring example of discrimination against gays we can document in the state. Under private, unincorporated ownership, without the existence of a written contract and without a gay rights amendment in local or state governments, their discrimination is legal."[45] The conference was now in jeopardy. In the two months since the hotel reversed its decision, many of the alternative sites had already been booked. The caucus was forced to look for not only other venues but also at other dates.

A solution was eventually found and the conference was held in April 1978 at the Howard Johnson's Motor Lodge at Delaware Water Gap in Monroe County on the Pennsylvania–New Jersey border. Hundreds of gay activists attended and were greeted by a supportive letter from Governor Shapp.

> Dear Friends:
>
> As you know, I am deeply committed to the cause of minority rights. The work you and other minority activists in the Commonwealth are doing is sorely needed and I am happy to see that you all remain dedicated in the face of strong opposition. Courage for this generation can be defined by your actions. I want to extend my sincerest wishes to all of you for a most successful conference.[46]

The conference featured numerous workshops and seminars on coming out, bisexuals and married gays, relationships, grassroots organizing, feminism, gay rights, minorities within the gay and lesbian movement, and gays and religion. At its conclusion, it adopted a series of resolutions that emerged

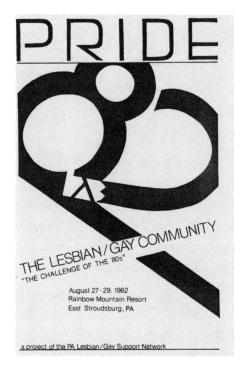

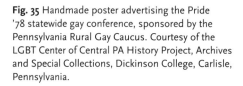

Fig. 35 Handmade poster advertising the Pride '78 statewide gay conference, sponsored by the Pennsylvania Rural Gay Caucus. Courtesy of the LGBT Center of Central PA History Project, Archives and Special Collections, Dickinson College, Carlisle, Pennsylvania.

Fig. 36 Program for the Pride '82 statewide gay conference, sponsored by the PA Lesbian/Gay Support Network , successor organization to the Pennsylvania Rural Gay Caucus. Courtesy of the LGBT Center of Central PA History Project, Archives and Special Collections, Dickinson College, Carlisle, Pennsylvania.

from discussions during the event. The resolutions dealt with commitments to endorse the following: the formation of a statewide support group, the organization of a statewide association of gay switchboards, the founding of support and self-help groups for gay youth, approval and affirmation of the Equal Rights Amendment, participation of racial and sexual minorities within the gay community, and emphasis on serving those with special needs within the gay community.[47]

The caucus went on to hold statewide conferences in Pittsburgh in 1979 and Harrisburg in 1980. At each venue they continued to expand their fight for gay rights activism and education, giving support and laying the ground-work for the inclusion of antidiscrimination bills in various communities and towns throughout the commonwealth.

In the autumn of 1976 a tragedy struck that reverberated through the gay and lesbian community. A young high school student, Kenneth Myers of Leba-non, Lebanon County, committed suicide after being bullied because he was gay. The caucus immediately met with John C. Pittenger, the secretary of the Pennsylvania Department of Education, to organize sensitivity training workshops with its staff. The caucus also created a book fund to place books about homosexuality in schools and colleges in the commonwealth.[48]

Statewide elections were held in 1978, and the caucus helped to mobilize the gay vote. It appointed regional coordinators and assembled a sizeable volunteer network to increase voter registration and distribute information on candidates to local gays and lesbians. The caucus sent a questionnaire to survey candidates for the governor's office and legislative seats regarding their positions on gay rights. From this survey, caucus members developed a strategy pertaining to which candidates to support and which voters to target in November. Not every candidate it endorsed was victorious. But this effort was the first major mobilization of the rural gay vote.[49]

The caucus, much like the Pennsylvania Council for Sexual Minorities, proved to be highly effective during the last years of Governor Shapp's administration. After Governor Thornburgh took office on January 16, 1979, the caucus became relatively inactive, eventually dissolving sometime after a new organization was created called the Pennsylvania Lesbian/Gay Support Network in July 1978.[50] Its short existence notwithstanding, the caucus was a powerful political force in gay activism in the commonwealth between 1975 and 1978. Combining the voices of about a dozen small groups from the rural areas of Pennsylvania turned out to be as powerful as activist efforts in Philadelphia and Pittsburgh. Members of the caucus created change not only in broad strokes across the commonwealth but also at a local level in their own communities.

Profiles

TONY SILVESTRE

Born in 1946 in the Bronx, New York, Tony Silvestre grew up in a working-class Italian neighborhood. By the time he had reached the age of thirteen, he knew he was gay. "I went through high school knowing I was gay but not doing anything about it or talking to anyone about it," he says. "I really got familiar with the closet and the woes and problems that arise from that closet and I think that has somewhat informed my development, centered my interest in the gay movement, since then."[51]

After graduating from high school, Tony entered a religious community near Boston, the Holy Cross Brothers of the Catholic Church. After three years, Tony left out of disillusionment about the church. He entered King's College in Wilkes-Barre, Luzerne County, to complete his undergraduate degree. His path took him to Penn State, where he would not only embark on his master's and doctoral degrees but also be introduced and become actively involved in the struggle for gay and lesbian rights.

Tony entered Penn State at the time the student membership of the Homophiles of Penn State (HOPS) was suing the university for its charter, concurrent with the case of Joe Acanfora's denial of his teacher's certificate because he was gay. These simultaneous actions inspired Tony to get involved, and soon he was standing at a table collecting signatures on Acanfora's behalf. "And then I became active in the organization Homophiles of Penn State."

Tony became president of HOPS and was instrumental in moving the organization forward. By the early 1970s, HOPS had become the crossroads activist organization in the commonwealth between the large urban centers of Pittsburgh and Philadelphia. Because of the high-profile lawsuits in which HOPS had been involved, Tony knew many of the activists in the state, and he brought them to Penn State. Individuals such as Barbara Gittings, founder of the New York chapter of the Daughters of Bilitis and editor of its newspaper, the *Ladder*; Mark Segal, founder of the Gay Raiders; and Randy Forrester, founder of the first gay and lesbian rights group in western Pennsylvania (affiliated with the Mattachine Society), presented lectures or seminars at Penn State.

Because of Tony's leadership and involvement with HOPS, he was invited to Harrisburg to discuss the possibility of developing the governor's task force. Tony met with Terry Dellmuth, an aide to Governor Shapp, and Barry Kohn, of the Attorney's Advocate Unit, who arranged for him to meet with the governor. Tony recalls his first meeting with Shapp: "I met him in the current governor's mansion [with Dellmuth and Kohn]. . . . I remember we had breakfast together. And he was a very quiet-spoken man. Intense man. And in our conversation it became clear that he was very progressive in all of his political views. He formed the first Women's Commission about that time and was amenable and probably by then had already agreed to form the council on the urging of Terry and Barry." Tony's level head and leadership skills did not go unnoticed in that meeting by Governor Shapp, which led to his appointment as chair of the Pennsylvania Council for Sexual Minorities.

As council chair, Tony was responsible for all its committees. "A lot of my work was making sure that each committee was functioning appropriately and had resources and [was] reporting back to the whole council [on their implementation of the governor's policy]. . . . At the time, I spent a good deal of energy making sure that the various state departments and agencies were represented on the council." According to Tony,

> I tried to move the different state agencies . . . one way or another [on gay-rights issues]. . . . We were always looking for opportunities to add our language into their contracts and into their policies. And we were pretty successful. At one point, all of the state agencies were required to notify us of any discrimination complaints that were [raised] in their agencies around LGBT issues. And that had a major effect in terms of letting people know that this was a serious issue, that these [complaints] had to be recorded and that reports had to be generated if these complaints came in. And bureaucrats know that when you have to generate a report, that business is serious, and I think it had a lot of impact . . . [it] gave notice that these kinds of complaints were not welcome and that actions would be taken to remedy them.

Tony's and the council's actions helped change the whole attitude of the governmental bureaucracy. The Pennsylvania Council for Sexual Minorities commanded the same attention as the Governor's Commission for Women and his Latino Council, in addition to the other programs Shapp supported.

In reflecting back on the achievements of the council, Tony says, "I don't think we ever really fully understood the potential for change that could be generated through state government. Most of the focus of the community at that time was on getting rid of sodomy laws and supporting federal efforts from GRNL, Gay Rights National Lobby, to get a statewide antidiscrimination bill passed. . . . It was very unusual to look at other ways that one could bring about change, and Shapp gave us an opportunity to focus on county government and the counties as providers of services." Tony further explains,

> We did that in a couple of places. Both in Philadelphia and Pittsburgh, there was movement in their children and youth agencies to support sensible placements for gay foster kids, and so there were attempts to find foster parents who would support these kids so that [they] could be placed in healthy environments. And this is important because there [were] thousands of children in the children's and youth services throughout Pennsylvania, many of whom were there because they were LGBT, and maybe had come from homes which weren't accepting of them. So finding homes in support for these young people was

very important. It was Shapp's executive order which showed us how one can move county governments and therefore move county programs around jails, around children and youth services, around services for the aged, services for disabled populations, all of these services that served millions of people around the country could all be moved to better serve LGBT people in their populations. And so this became more and more evident to us as a council, and we began to do more and more outreach, even nationally . . . to try and move people on these kinds of issues.

"I have to say, even to this day, I don't think people appreciate the importance of moving the bureaucrats who run government services to include proper policies and programs for LGBT people," Tony continues.

We still have most programs in this country operating with the assumption that their clients are straight people. Whether it's nursing homes, whether it's hospitals, whether it's group [homes] for kids. Most of them run with the assumption that people receiving these services are straight, and we know that's not true. And because of that assumption, these other populations, non-straight populations, are being shortchanged. They're not getting services that are culturally appropriate. So I think this was the major, probably the most significant, finding, or position, that the council developed and tried to export as far as we could, even throughout Pennsylvania and then beyond Pennsylvania, outside the state. . . . It's the county commissioners who often develop the agenda for the Democratic or Republican Party in their state. The county commissioners often choose [or] have a lot to say about who [will become] members of Congress and who [will become] the nominees for the Senate as well as the governor.

And it's the county commissioners who hire and fire the various heads of health departments, welfare departments, and so on. . . . It's those county commissioners who really have a lot of authority and power to be able to move systems to be more accessible to LGBT people. And so that became our clarion cry, and hopefully it's something that might still yet inspire people to pay more attention to county government and county services, because they affect our most vulnerable populations.

Tony's attitude reflects the payoff of allying with government to effect systemic change.

Looking back on his years as an activist, Tony recalls,

Any of the progress we've made has really been due to the efforts of lots and lots of people. I could, in [a] very few minutes, come up with a list of a hundred people who made all these things happen. . . . But the activism in this state was . . . generated by lots of interesting and heroic people. I know activists in Pennsylvania who have been shot at, have been threatened, who've been attacked one way or another, who've been pressured by their employers and so on. But even in the face of that, [they] kept being active with not much reward.

After Tony's years on the council, he went on to the University of Pittsburgh, where he currently serves as a professor of infectious diseases and microbiology. Since 1983, he has been the coinvestigator for the Pitt Men's Study, which has characterized the natural history of AIDS in gay and bisexual men. In addition, he directs the HIV Care and Prevention Project, which is studying HIV-prevention knowledge, attitudes, and access to services of people at risk of HIV infection and of HIV experts throughout the commonwealth. The study, funded by the Centers for Disease Control and Prevention (CDC) and the Pennsylvania Department of Health, is being deployed to develop an HIV-prevention plan for the Keystone State.[52]

MARY NANCARROW

Mary Nancarrow was born in Penbrook, a small suburb southeast of Harrisburg, in 1951. Her parents divorced when she was six years old, but even though her mother retained custody of Mary, along with her twin brother and older sister, she saw her father every week. Growing up in the 1960s, however, the turbulent events of the time began to have their effect on her. In Mary's last year of high school, her sister enlisted in the US Air Force and was soon sent to Vietnam. When Mary and her brother graduated, instead of going to college, her brother also enlisted in the Air Force and was also deployed to Vietnam.[53]

Mary enrolled at Shippensburg State College (now Shippensburg University of Pennsylvania) but was consumed with fear about her siblings. "I was reading everything I could about why we were in Vietnam. . . . I thought, from what I had read, [that] we shouldn't have been there. I was very worried about my sister and my brother, and I wanted them to come back in one piece. I couldn't abide all the death that was happening to thousands of guys in the war and the people of Vietnam." Mary's activist beginnings took hold, and she began attending antiwar demonstrations in Harrisburg, Washington, DC, and other cities. At one of the marches on Washington to protest the war, she and her friends were teargassed. She remembers, "We were at the Washington Monument after the march. . . . And without even saying, 'You need to disperse,' [the Mounted National Park Service Police came] on horseback towards us to disperse the crowd, running into us, thousands of people. And of course, we ran. When you see a huge animal coming at you, you run. They also did the tear gas. So we were running through the streeets of Washington, trying to escape the tear gas."

This was a difficult time for Mary, who at the time was trying to come to terms with her sexuality. "I was coming out to myself. I was in counseling, because I was having trouble in school, and I was just a troubled young person," she says. Mary disclosed to her counselor that she was attracted to women. He responded by saying, "Well, I think that's nothing more than mutual masturbation." Mary was dumbfounded by his ignorant response, particularly because the person discounting her feelings and identity held professional credentials.

Mary tried to sort out her feelings, and a turning point came when she attended a press conference in Harrisburg that the Pennsylvania chapter of NOW had called to issue a plea for nondiscrimination legislation against lesbians and gays. It was led by a high school student, Rachel McLaughlin, from Mechanicsburg, Cumberland County, a NOW member and a lesbian. Mary was moved: "I thought, 'Well, if she can do it, I can do it!' I was already [twenty-three] at the time." Visiting each parent separately, Mary told them that she would be on the news—and that she was a lesbian. They were "upset and angry," Mary recalls. "It just didn't fit their vision or their dreams for me." But over the next few years, Mary and her parents reconciled, and her parents eventually became very supportive.

After Mary came out, she became active in Shippensburg Gays United. She began speaking in various classes on gay and lesbian issues at Shippensburg State College. She also became a featured guest on a radio talk show that aired in York County. "[These were] some of the few first ways that lesbians and gays became visible, especially in rural areas," Mary comments.

When the governor's task force was created, Mary was one of the at-large members who attended the meetings. Eventually, the Rural Gay Caucus was formed, and Mary and Shippensburg Gays United were among the founding members. Mary played an active role in the caucus, ultimately becoming one of its cochairs. She was also concurrently involved in the Pennsylvania chapter of NOW. Many of the gay and lesbian activists that Mary had worked with were also NOW members and active in the women's movement. Mary, along

Fig. 37 Mary Nancarrow, speaking at the first Community Recognition banquet, at Miss Garbo's Tea Room in Carlisle, circa 1992. Courtesy of the LGBT Center of Central PA History Project, Archives and Special Collections, Dickinson College, Carlisle, Pennsylvania.

with the caucus and NOW, worked with the Pennsylvania Human Relations Commission to support the inclusion of sexual orientation in the Human Relations Act recommended by the commission. The state legislature, however, never approved the inclusions.

By the mid-1970s, Mary was an active member of NOW. "In the late '60s and very early '70s, national NOW had its problems accepting lesbian women, especially as leaders," Mary remembers. "However, they sorted that out in the first four to five years of NOW." By the time the first national conference convention was held, she adds, "it had reconciled." NOW became a leader in seeking lesbian rights and formed a National Committee for Lesbian Rights.

Mary was a leading voice in the battle for the ERA and traveled to Washington, DC, for the hearings on the extension for the amendment's ratification. When she returned home to Pennsylvania, Mary continued the fight. "We would take actions on the courthouse steps in Chambersburg . . . for the Equal Rights Amendment. We organized ERA walkathons [in Harrisburg]." In fact, during the years of the Thornburgh administration, "Ginny Thornburgh, the First Lady, walked with us during the Equal Rights Amendment walkathons, because she was a NOW member and a feminist and [supported] the Equal Rights Amendment."

In addition to the ERA, Mary and the Harrisburg NOW chapter were instrumental in the creation of the Pennsylvania Coalition Against Domestic

Violence and the Pennsylvania Coalition Against Rape. "We had a lot of domestic violence demonstrations and actions in the '70s and '80s. Lesbian women were very much involved with feminism and vice versa. We were writing articles in the *Harrisburg Area Women's News*, and the *Lavender Letter* would include all of the women's events. . . . NOW was very much involved with lobbying for lesbian rights in the legislature, and they started it, actually, before even the Rural Gay Caucus was born."

In 1982, Mary and the Harrisburg NOW chapter embarked on a groundbreaking campaign to ensure the passage of an ordinance proposed by the Harrisburg Human Relations Commission that would protect its citizens from discrimination based on sexual orientation and gender identity. Taking advice from the national NOW organization, Mary solicited local unions for their support of the bill. She also organized campaigns in ethnic neighborhoods and in the gay and lesbian community. Mary garnered support from Dignity/Central PA and the Gay and Lesbian Switchboard as well. "We [leaders] would meet with the individual city council members and with the leader on the council." Mary's efforts paid off. In June 1983 Harrisburg passed the ordinance, becoming only the second city in Pennsylvania to pass an antidiscrimination law. Philadelphia was the first, passing its own ordinance in 1982. It would take another seven years before Pittsburgh followed suit.

After her victory in Harrisburg, Mary took a month off and went to Florida so that she could campaign with NOW for the passage of the ERA. While there, she was approached by NOW board member Gloria Sackman Reed to run for the presidency of the Pennsylvania chapter of NOW. Mary agreed and was elected. She went right to work. There were more than ten thousand members statewide, and she formed a Political Action Committee. "We worked on the [presidential] campaign for Mondale-Ferrraro. We had a PAC that we raised money for—a Political Action Committee, and we were supporting twenty some women candidates—[in] both parties. . . . We hired two campaign advisors and placed them in campaigns for women legislators to be elected [throughout the state]." The phone banks were not only for these candidates but also for other issues NOW was working on, such as reproductive rights, the marital rape bill, and funding for the Pennsylvania Coalition Against Domestic Violence. In addition, Mary was overseeing the publication of a monthly newsletter, the *Pennsylvania NOW Times*; holding monthly board meetings; recruiting new members; and fundraising for the chapter.

Mary's most overwhelming experience as president of the Pennsylvania chapter of NOW was spearheading the passage of the marital rape law. "We were also fighting for marital rape legislation, . . . [which is] rape by a boyfriend or husband. No [district attorney] was taking these cases, because it was not seen as rape. It was more or less [an environment in which] the man is entitled to sex with his girlfriend or his wife and that harkened back to women as property. And so untold numbers of victims could not have any justice or protection from the police." The bill was introduced by a NOW member from northeast Philadelphia who had been physically and emotionally abused by her alcoholic husband and had been raped in front of her children. In 1983, the bill was introduced in the state legislature but was stalled in the judiciary committee.

> We met continually with the judiciary committees in both houses and particularly in the Senate, which was Republican controlled, and lobbied individual legislators . . . especially those on the committees and in leadership for their caucuses. . . . They finally saw from our personal stories that [these issues] touched their own families. I mean, one of the senators had a daughter who had been in an abusive relationship—marriage. That was never known or disclosed, but he confided to me that that was why he was going to vote for [the legislation], and it finally passed on the last night of the session . . . [at] three o'clock in the morning."

Mary and the NOW chapter had prevailed on the leadership to bring the bill forward, and history was made: "It was on the books."

Mary continued as NOW president until 1986 and then took a much-needed and well-deserved rest. She continued her activism with gay and lesbian causes, working with the Switchboard in Harrisburg and later with the Central Pennsylvania Women's Chorus, a lesbian-feminist choral group. Mary eventually retired from her job as a supervisor with the Pennsylvania Human Relations Commission in Harrisburg in 2013.

CHAPTER 5

Turbulence

Fueling an unprecedented wave of gay activism, the Stonewall uprising also unleashed an exhilarating sense of sexual liberation. For many men, being gay in the 1970s meant casual, anonymous, promiscuous sex. Like magnets, gay communities in Philadelphia, New York, and Washington, DC, drew men from central Pennsylvania to experience the myriad of gay bars, discos, bathhouses, and cruising areas. What they did not know was that a horrific viral seed had been transmitted that would soon devastate the community.

In June 1981, the Centers for Disease Control and Prevention (CDC) published an article in its newsletter *Morbidity and Mortality Weekly Report* titled, "Pneumocystis Pneumonia—Los Angeles," detailing the sudden outbreak of cases among gay men. The article was picked up by both the *New York Times* and the *Los Angeles Times*, which reported on this new cancer that was mysteriously striking gay men. The *New York Times* ran with the headline "Rare Cancer Seen in 41 Homosexuals."[1] Cases of Kaposi's sarcoma and pneumocystis pneumonia were spreading rapidly among homosexual men. Because of the association with gay men, this strange disease was first labeled "gay-related immune deficiency" (GRID). It was renamed "acquired immune deficiency syndrome" (AIDS) in July 1982 by the CDC, which identified four risk factors: male homosexuality, intravenous drug abuse, Haitian origin, and hemophilia A.[2]

By the end of 1982, there were 771 cases of AIDS nationally, with Pennsylvania reporting 7 instances. By 1984 the number soared to 7,239 nationally, with 143 in Pennsylvania. By the end of 1990, there would be 160,969 cases nationally, with 4,437 in Pennsylvania, of which 526 were in central Pennsylvania. By 1995 there would be more than 500,000 cases nationally, with 15,000 cases in Pennsylvania and 1,700 in central Pennsylvania.[3]

As the cases increased, so did the fear among the public.[4] These attitudes sealed gay people's fate as outsiders in society, deplored for their sexuality, with gay men stereotyped as having and transmitting AIDS. Political and religious conservatives fueled the fire of this hatred and prejudice.[5] With the onset of the epidemic, discrimination and prejudice against gay men and lesbians intensified.

Because of the widespread belief that AIDS was strictly a gay disease, the federal government did not allocate any additional funds for prevention or research.[6] The lesbian and gay community faced a troubling situation. The disease seemed to be striking gay men in particular, which reinforced the anti-gay rhetoric that linked the disease to gay identity and gay sex to death. With the lack of government support, victims of the disease were forced to take measures to care for themselves. A grassroots effort of service organizations mobilized to care for the sick and dying, even as they sought to educate the broader community.[7] As the nation's gay community responded to the crisis, so did the gay community in central Pennsylvania.

The Epidemic Strikes Central Pennsylvania

By 1982, the first AIDS cases were reported in central Pennsylvania. By then, Harrisburg residents Frank Pizzoli and Rodger L. Beatty had anticipated the forthcoming devastation. Although he never formally lived in New York City, Pizzoli was a frequent visitor and had studied dance there in 1978 at the Merce Cunningham Studio. He recognized firsthand what was being reported in the *New York Times* article. He had seen many friends succumb to the strange, new "gay cancer." Based on information collected by the Gay Men's Health Crisis in New York, which had been founded by Larry Kramer and others, he knew the disease was contracted through sexual contact and that it would swiftly spread. Beatty was also aware of these facts. Both men were acutely concerned about the lack of medical knowledge about the disease. Education for prevention and services to help those afflicted were severely deficient.[8] Federal and state governments were turning a blind eye to the burgeoning epidemic. Pizzoli and Beatty knew something needed to be done as AIDS made its way into central Pennsylvania.

In late 1983, Beatty and several others began meeting at the Strawberry Inn, a gay bar in downtown Harrisburg, to discuss how they could help those affected by the disease. Their objectives were daunting: educating the medical community as well as the public, along with caring for the sick, both physically and financially, if necessary. When fire destroyed the Strawberry Inn in

January 1984, the group moved to Beatty's home. At the same time, Pizzoli had begun convening a group in his apartment with the same agenda. Pizzoli's group was already caring for one of the first cases in central Pennsylvania, a young man who lived three stories above Pizzoli. One of the members of Pizzoli's group, Robert ("Bob") L. Sevensky, a member of the teaching staff at the Hershey Medical Center, told him about Beatty's group and suggested the two of them work together. Pizzoli called Beatty, and they discussed their mutual passion and mission. Beatty had a larger group, so they agreed that the two groups should merge and work together for better efficiency and greater impact.

It was an all-volunteer group in the beginning, meeting in Beatty's living room, where members gathered to discuss and determine priorities and needs. Early on, they decided to bring in someone suffering from AIDS, so the group could fully understand what that individual had to deal with and experience. They brought in an African American man who had been an IV-drug user since he was a teenager. He explained the drugs he was on and their side effects and how his body was being ravaged by AIDS. He spoke of the poor treatment he had received not only from the medical community but also from his family and friends. It was a turning point for the volunteers and reinforced the urgency and necessity of their work. After that man courageously spoke, a collection was taken up and quietly presented to him as he left. Afterward the group resolved that any funds raised would benefit individuals with AIDS regardless of their circumstances—gay, IV-drug user, African American, hemophiliac, Haitian, or any combination of demographics. It was about the virus, not the person.

To raise money in those early days, Beatty donned a bear costume and, accompanied by Pizzoli, visited local gay bars. "This was at the height of disco, and it was dance season," Pizzoli says. "The music would stop, the lights would come up, and we'd have a basket of condoms and lube. We would say, 'Excuse me. Put this on. If you don't, you are going to die.' We would pass the basket around, and we would collect six [hundred] to eight hundred dollars." With the money they raised, they were able to print educational brochures, buy wheelchairs, and purchase much-needed supplies to help those for whom they were caring.

By the end of 1985, with more than forty-three cases of AIDS in central Pennsylvania, the group decided to organize the South Central AIDS Assistance Network (SCAAN). On February 25, 1986, SCAAN officially registered with the commonwealth as a nonprofit organization and hired Peg Dierkers

Fig. 38 Peg Dierkers (*left*), gathering with volunteers at the South Central AIDS Assistance Network (SCAAN) AIDS Walk, circa 1990. Peg was the first executive director of the organization. Courtesy of the LGBT Center of Central PA History Project, Archives and Special Collections, Dickinson College, Carlisle, Pennsylvania.

as its first director in 1988, the only paid staff member. SCAAN opened its first office in the basement of the Planned Parenthood building on Second Street in Harrisburg in 1989.[9] With AIDS cases reaching more than five hundred in central Pennsylvania, SCAAN had its work cut out for it.[10]

"I worked at SCAAN [from] late '88 until early 1994," remembers Dierkers. "From the time we started to see pretty systematic treatment of AIDS and actually even moving from focusing on AIDS to HIV, and then, also really seeing the migration of the disease from primarily gay men to intravenous drug users and heterosexuals. So [I was] very excited [and] worked to really build the organization. I was the first paid staff, and the volunteers were very supportive and remained very supportive [and] involved. And we wrote about medical treatment, helped people pay for their housing, attended a lot of funerals—a lot of funerals, [and] worked with families."[11]

SCAAN was a vital human service organization helping those suffering from AIDS. They were there helping those who could not pay their electric bills or buy groceries. They provided volunteer attorneys who would work with people with HIV/AIDS, drawing up powers of attorney, living wills, and last wills and testaments. Dierkers recalls, "There was so much discrimination and prejudice still going on in families and folks at the time. We would use any tool necessary to legally protect our clients and their partners when they passed and make sure their wishes were honored to the extent that they could."[12]

By January 1992, with AIDS cases totaling more than eight hundred in central Pennsylvania, SCAAN hired more employees. In addition to Peg Dierkers, there were four paid caseworkers, a receptionist, an education director, and a part-time bookkeeper. Deb Fulham-Winston, hired as director of development, remembers, "We had a boatload of volunteers, many of whom would come in and out at odd times. . . . They'd come in and stuff envelopes, and make photocopies, and get the street packets ready for people, which were little plastic bags, little Ziploc bags, and there was a condom, a sterile wipe, . . . [and] lube [in them]. . . . Maybe [an educational] booklet of some kind. We handed out hundreds of these things to people."[13]

With the caseload growing, caseworkers and the volunteers had their hands full. Their major function in the early years of the crisis was trying to help people live longer. "A fair number of our clients were IV-drug users; their systems were already affected by the drug taking, so their immune systems were already [pretty damaged] before they got infected. So, for those folks, it was a real struggle to stay healthy . . . they were dealing with multiple things. Maybe they had hepatitis, maybe they'd *had* hepatitis C. There could have been other whacks to their immune system before [contracting] HIV, so they were always in a delicate balance about what sort of meds might work, what meds don't work," Fulham-Winston recalls. In addition, there was a homelessness problem. Many landlords, upon finding out their tenants were sick with HIV/AIDS, forced them out, and many families kicked their own children out of their homes. The caseworkers and volunteers spent hours on the telephone trying to make sure that patients were comfortably settled, safe, and secure.[14]

After counseling many HIV/AIDS patients in Lancaster, Betty Finney, a psychologist, noticed this dramatic increase of homelessness. In 1988, she presented this problem to her church community and organized a committee to meet the needs of this population. From this grassroots effort evolved the Betty Finney House Corporation. With a staff of twenty volunteers, the organization administered several programs assisting those living with AIDS in Lancaster County by providing housing or financial assistance.[15]

The Betty Finney House Corporation developed a four-unit apartment building along with a group home project. The project met the housing needs of up to three individuals per group home. In addition, the project provided permanent housing for people diagnosed with HIV/AIDS who were currently living in shelters or on the streets.[16] Jerre Freiberg, director of the corporation for seven years, remembers Betty Finney's enormous impact. "I had seventy-two clients [in] apartments all over the city. And if anything [was] needed, I called Betty, and she'd be sitting with that client. She was wonderful. . . . When I was director of the Betty Finney House, [we] had federal funding, which was pretty nice, but it was never enough. So we had to have [fundraisers]. . . . One time we had a hangar out at the airport and we had live bands set up. Well, Betty got up there. You could hear a pin drop. And boy, checks flew. You know, she was really wonderful to the HIV community."[17]

In 1987, the Gathering Place (TGP) was opened in Lancaster to help support and care for the homeless and the disadvantaged living with AIDS. The services TGP provided were similar to those of the Betty Finney House. By 2002, the house had closed its doors and merged its services with TGP. According to the Reverend Robert Lewis, executive director of TGP, "I think the Betty Finney House directors saw that it just seemed to make the circle complete if everything was done by one agency."[18]

AIDS education was critical during this time. Deb Fulham-Winston remembers SCAAN's prevention educator: "She would speak anywhere—churches, schools, fire halls—anywhere she could actually get somebody to let her in. . . . She knew her stuff inside and out. So she was often very good at getting people to kind of open their [minds] a little bit about what was going on."[19] That indefatigable individual was Martha "Marty" R. Tornblom, a member of SCAAN's board of directors, who eventually joined the staff as the prevention educator. "I did a lot of public speaking, as did my volunteers," she says.[20] "We also had an AIDS fact-line that was supported, paid for, by the [Pennsylvania] Department of Health. . . . It was a fact-line, not a hotline," she emphasizes, "where people could call and get information and be directed to services. It was both for those affected and not, affected or infected, and we had volunteers staffing that. . . . Ours was the agency that operated the fact-line and handled the phones for it. That was a vital link to the community."

Tornblom and her volunteers were speaking everywhere:

> [We would go to] prisons and schools and so forth, but anywhere that we were invited. So it might be civic clubs; it might be a PTA. . . . Corporate staff would ask us to do training, but the public speaking was any organization at all. There wasn't a place I wouldn't go. Sometimes people in the outlying communities and counties other than Dauphin would wonder why I would be willing to come, and I was thrilled to come. I loved to go out into the hinterlands, so to speak,

because my mission was . . . number one, to talk about prevention, but number two, to try to bridge the gap between the outlying community and those infected, so that they would be less fearful and more accepting and more supportive of the kinds of legislation that would bring the protections that were needed for confidentiality and for preventing harassment and discrimination, particularly. That was the serious issue.

As the prevention educator for SCAAN, Marty Tornblom relentlessly lobbied the state legislature on nondiscrimination bills for persons with AIDS, for additional funding for organizations dealing with AIDS-related issues, and for safety in the workplace to guarantee anonymity for those infected with HIV/AIDS.

Integral to SCAAN's services was a buddy program staffed by volunteers. "There were so many individuals who didn't have family support," Tornblom recalls. "There was a need just to have people who could do the simple tasks like driving back and forth to the doctor, or to other services, or laundry, or bringing food in, or helping with food. Maybe spending time at the bedside or just being a friend, because it was a lonely, lonely place to be [for those who were sick]."[21] As Deb Fulham-Winston recollects, "The caseworkers were always trying to get people settled and safe in some place, any place. . . . There were only two hospice houses at that point [York House Hospice and Hospice of Central Pennsylvania]. . . . They were active very early on and took people in when no one was doing very much at all, and [they] gave people a quiet and warm and peaceful place to die."[22]

To fund the organization, SCAAN began hosting an annual AIDS Walk in the fall, raising $80,000 to $90,000 each year. In 1990, the federal government passed the Ryan White Act, which finally released more than $200 million to fund AIDS care and treatment. (The act was named for a teenager, a hemophiliac living in Kokomo, Indiana, who learned he was infected with AIDS at the age of thirteen by a blood transfusion. White was expelled from middle school and Congress responded by enacting, on August 18, 1990, the act that remains the largest federally funded program in the United States for people living with AIDS.)[23] SCAAN secured a grant from the Greater Harrisburg Foundation and the Family Health Council, a subcontractor for the distribution for the monies from the federal government. "Those dollars really made a difference for a lot of those programs; people were being fed and housed," Deb Fulham-Winston says. The local community helped, too. "There would be small fund-raisers, often by church groups or family groups. Someone would

Fig. 39 The starting point and registration area of the SCAAN AIDS Walk, on City Island, Harrisburg, 1994. Courtesy of the LGBT Center of Central PA History Project, Archives and Special Collections, Dickinson College, Carlisle, Pennsylvania.

Fig. 40 Walkers along Riverfront Park in Harrisburg, participating in the SCAAN AIDS Walk in 1992. Courtesy of the LGBT Center of Central PA History Project, Archives and Special Collections, Dickinson College, Carlisle, Pennsylvania.

Fig. 41 Pin and red ribbon from the 1994 SCAAN AIDS Walk. Photo: Sue Blosser. Courtesy of the LGBT Center of Central PA History Project, Archives and Special Collections, Dickinson College, Carlisle, Pennsylvania.

have a birthday party where they [would] take up a collection and that kind of thing. And people would occasionally just appear on our door and say, 'Here, we did this over the weekend, and here's some money.' Great!"[24]

An unusual source of funding came from a Harrisburg drag troupe called Lily White and Company. Founded in the late 1980s by Harrisburg resident and professional theater costumer Paul R. Foltz, Lily White and Company was an assemblage of gay men who dressed in drag and performed to prerecorded songs. The high-spirited company staged shows at the Neptune Lounge and charged an admission fee, with all proceeds benefitting SCAAN. Performances had themes and were highly choreographed and painstakingly directed. They soon became immensely popular.

By the 1990s the shows had become major productions. The demand for tickets was so great that the show was moved to the ballroom of the Holiday Inn in downtown Harrisburg and other large venues throughout the region. As Lily White and Company's performances became massive undertakings, Foltz formed a board of directors to help manage logistics and fundraising. Dr. Eric W. Selvey, a Harrisburg optometrist who was a board member and performer, remembers, "I always had a goal: $10,000 [a show, after costs]." The shows were staged, costumed, and well rehearsed. Selvey adds, "We would have rehearsals two times a week. . . . Of course, when it got close to the show, we'd

Fig. 42 Paul Foltz, aka Lily White (*foreground*), and Tim Rhinehart, aka Kelly, from a production of Lily White and Company. Photo: Jack Radcliffe, with the collaboration of Joy Ufema and Barbara Ellen Wood. Courtesy of the LGBT Center of Central PA History Project, Archives and Special Collections, Dickinson College, Carlisle, Pennsylvania.

have them more often."[25] On the day of the show, they would start to set up at 5:30 a.m. with the lights, staging, and sound equipment, and at showtime it was a packed house. The board set a long-range goal of raising $100,000. It took ten years, but they raised $120,000, eventually distributed to SCAAN and other AIDS-related organizations.[26]

In addition to Lily White and Company, Foltz was also a founding member of the Harrisburg Men's Chorus, along with Bernie Pupo, one of the early volunteers with Frank Pizzoli's group helping the victims of AIDS. One of

Fig. 43 Lily White and Company performers. *Left to right*: Jackie, Cathy, and Grace gather before a performance of the drag troupe. Photo: Jack Radcliffe, with the collaboration of Joy Ufema and Barbara Ellen Wood. Courtesy of the LGBT Center of Central PA History Project, Archives and Special Collections, Dickinson College, Carlisle, Pennsylvania.

Fig. 44 Show program from Lily White and Company production, *Into the Woods and Out of the Bushes*, undated. Courtesy of the LGBT Center of Central PA History Project, Archives and Special Collections, Dickinson College, Carlisle, Pennsylvania.

Fig. 45 (opposite) *Lilybill* show program from the Lily White and Company production of *Lily "Unplugged,"* July 20, 1997. Courtesy of the LGBT Center of Central PA History Project, Archives and Special Collections, Dickinson College, Carlisle, Pennsylvania.

those whom Pizzoli's group was taking care of was Joe Tucci. Pupo, a hair-stylist, was asked to cut Tucci's hair because Tucci's stylist had refused to cut his hair when he found out that Tucci had AIDS. Tucci would come to Bernie Pupo's house—because he wanted to avoid going to the salon—to have lunch and get his hair cut. The two shared many personal things. As Pupo recalls, "I asked him one day, is there anything that you regret, that you may not be able to do in your life?" Without hesitation Joe Tucci responded, "The only thing I regret that I have always wanted to do is start . . . a gay men's chorus in the city, and I don't think that I'm going to be here long enough to do that." Tucci was a music direc-tor and organist at a church in Harrisburg and sang with local choral groups. "He had a beauti-ful voice," Pupo says. Pupo distinctly remembers Tucci making him promise that he would do just that. "I wanted to call it the Joe Tucci Memo-rial Men's Chorus, but they wouldn't let me do that once I got the board together to organize the chorus."[27]

Sunday, July 20, 1997
8:00 P.M.
Ramada Inn on Market Square
2nd & Chestnut Streets
Harrisburg, Pennsylvania

In 1987 the organization was founded and the board of directors finally approved the name: the Harrisburg Men's Chorus. "[We did not use] Gay Men's Chorus," Paul Foltz says. "There were times when we were not allowed to perform in certain places because of the nature of the group. . . . it was open to all men, because it was a men's chorus, but you had to be either gay or gay-supportive, at least." He adds, "We had our share of controversy over the years, places that we were denied perfor-mance[s], concerts that weren't covered [by the press] . . . there was a period of time where [getting press notice] was almost impossible." But, Foltz says, the chorus created "a public awareness of the growing LGBT community."[28] The group eventually did change its name and the Harrisburg Gay Men's Chorus is successfully performing today, founded on the dream of a young man dying from AIDS.

As the AIDS virus was spreading into central Pennsylvania in 1984, it also touched the city of Lancaster. Phil Wenger was a young gay man, born in Ethi-opia and a son of Mennonite missionaries, who had returned to Lancaster. With a strong religious background, Wenger had come to terms with his sexuality by the time he entered college. When he came out to his parents, his father

Fig. 46 The Harrisburg Men's Chorus, performing at a SCAAN AIDS Walk in 1991. Courtesy of the LGBT Center of Central PA History Project, Archives and Special Collections, Dickinson College, Carlisle, Pennsylvania.

said to him, "It's not what you believe but it's how you take what you learn and apply it in a set of beliefs that work for you. . . . As long as you know how to think and as long as you know how to process, you'll end up being fine." He took his father's words to heart when AIDS first appeared. In 1984, "HIV was just coming to the forefront," Wenger remembers. "We didn't know what it was, it was [the gay] cancer. We had some friends who were infected, and all of a sudden people were dying by the late '80s, and we needed to respond as a community."[29]

Wenger had already become a leader in the community, owning and operating a successful restaurant, Isaac's, which would eventually grow to nineteen locations throughout central Pennsylvania. "I hired several people who worked for me who were HIV positive, and everybody was like, 'What are we going to do about this? It's a death sentence, and we aren't organized.' And so there were a number of activists . . . who came together and wanted to form an organization where they could go out—like the Gay Men's Health Crisis in New York, they wanted to take care of the people in our community." Wenger recalls, "Families wouldn't want you there; there wasn't knowledge [of] whether or not you could be infected by blood or body fluids. There was a real fear that if you hugged somebody and kissed somebody or did any of those kinds of activities, that you were going to get infected. So people really got isolated. . . . When someone got sick, they had nobody but their friends to take care of them. And so there was a real compelling need to take care of people and to raise money to help provide that support structure." Because of these fears, not only within the gay community but within the greater community as a whole, Wenger founded the Lancaster AIDS Project (LAP).

Like SCAAN, the early days were difficult for LAP. "United Way wanted nothing to do with us," says Wenger.

> They wouldn't fund us, [and] we were pretty desperate. But I had office space in my company, and I basically said to them, as we formed the initial group, "You can have the office space and let's set up an organization. Let's actually go file [for] nonprofit status, because that way we can apply for grants, and that way we can funnel money into the organization." And then we set up committees to take care of different pieces of it. Some were on prevention, some were on taking care of people who were sick, and then some were in much more of the political activism.

During the first three years, the organization experienced many deaths:

> We had a whole host of people that died. I mean, I've been at the bedside of at least a dozen people when they took their last breath, and it will shape you for the rest of your life. It just burns right through you, because they are people your age and my age, people in their twenties. You just die for having sex, if you don't know better. It's very, very sad. I would say there was probably about six or eight years, between 1984 and 1990, that that was pretty much the focus of at least the men in the community. But most of the lesbians I knew, they came together and joined us. It was a time when we had to take care of our own rather than relying on other people to take care of us.

To help fund LAP, David Leas, at the time vice president of operations for Isaac's restaurants and a LAP volunteer, initiated a program that had proven successful in Philadelphia: Dine Out for Life. Leas knew other restaurant owners in the Lancaster area and persuaded eight of them to donate 20 percent of their profits from the night of dining to LAP. Volunteers would host tables on the selected evening at the participating restaurants and fill the restaurants. The program was successful and grew each year under the banner of Caring à la Carte. By the fourth year, the fundraiser had expanded to Harrisburg, helping raise money for SCAAN.[30]

Fig. 47 Pin from the 1995 Arts Against AIDS fundraiser for the Lancaster AIDS Project. Photo: Sue Blosser. Courtesy of the LGBT Center of Central PA History Project, Archives and Special Collections, Dickinson College, Carlisle, Pennsylvania.

By the end of 1995, the number of AIDS cases in Pennsylvania had reached 15,000, with more than 1,700 cases reported in central Pennsylvania alone. By this point, SCAAN and LAP were doing identical work. Both organizations agreed that the community would be better served if they joined forces and expanded their services. By the late nineties, the two groups had merged and adopted the name AIDS Community Alliance (ACA).[31] ACA would continue gradually expanding its services until 2010, when it officially changed its named to Alder Health Services, offering fully comprehensive and integrated care for its clients in central Pennsylvania. Expanded services now include behavioral health, case management, education and wellness, primary care, and trans health services for people with HIV/AIDS.[32]

The Introduction of AZT

By the mid-1980s, the gargantuan pharmaceutical company Burroughs Wellcome had developed azidothymidine (AZT), determined to be the first drug effective in the prevention and treatment of AIDS. In 1987, the US Food and Drug Administration approved the use of the drug to prolong the lives of AIDS patients. With this approval, the federal government issued a block grant to the states of $30 million for the distribution of AZT.[33] The federal government's only requirement was that the state was to match fifty cents on each dollar allocated to fund the program for the drug. Gov. Robert P. Casey turned the program over to the Pennsylvania Department of Welfare, which established the position of AZT director to coordinate the program. This would be a high-level Pennsylvania State Civil Service Commission position, and thirty-nine individuals were applying for the job.[34]

John Folby, a former visual merchandising director for Pittsburgh's venerable Kaufmann's Department Store, had just moved to Harrisburg. He was distressed over the many friends in Pittsburgh and New York who were coming down with AIDS. "I started getting really angry," Folby says. "I wanted to know, what was the government doing? I came home and said to my partner [who worked for state government] one night, 'What's the commonwealth of Pennsylvania doing about all these people who are dying from GRID?' And he said, 'Well, as a matter of fact, they're going to start an AZT program.' . . . So I said, 'How do I get that job? I want that job. I want to do that. I want to be the AZT guy.'"

Folby researched the name of the person to see, Suzanne Love, and went to the State Capitol in Harrisburg, made an appointment, and applied in person for the job. In his first interview, Folby said, "I heard about this AZT program. I want the job. I think it will be my way of helping the community, by being a gay person on the inside . . . in the government agency that's going to give them drugs." Love explained to Folby that it was a Civil Service Commission position, and he would be required to officially apply for it, have his application notarized, and then be called back for another interview.

Folby complied with the procedures and was called back three weeks later. Suzanne Love told him that she would really like to hire him, but others had experience in state government as well as seniority, which gave them an edge over him. She also said, "The thing you have going for you is you are the only person out of all them that wanted the job for what it is, not because it was a promotion." She went on to explain that the other applicants could file grievances if she were to fill the position with a less qualified candidate. Folby responded, "Fine. If you don't hire me, I'll file a grievance and say you didn't hire me because I'm gay. . . . Really, if you want, I'll be real flamboyant about it. I'll put on a feather boa and some chandelier earrings and paint my nails, and I will go with you to [the] Civil Service [Commission] and file a complaint." Love laughed, but she was impressed with Folby and asked him to give her time to work it out. Love had extensive notes from every single interview with the applicants and took them to the head of Civil Service. She argued that out of all the people, Folby was the only one who wanted the job for what it was intended. Within three weeks, John Folby was named Pennsylvania's AZT coordinator.

AZT was expensive—more than $8,000 a year for treatment. Under the federal program Folby administered, people with income below certain levels were given either a blue or green card entitling them to obtain the drug at no cost. Most states labeled their initiative the AIDS Drug Assistance Program, but in Pennsylvania it was the Special Pharmaceutical Benefits Program to avoid the stigma against people living with AIDS. The cards were accepted in every pharmacy in the commonwealth, and people were no longer afraid to go in, present their cards, and have their prescriptions filled. Folby also mandated that pharmacies no longer call out patients' names when announcing that AZT prescriptions were ready for pickup.

In the beginning, it was only Folby staffing the office of the AZT program. At Pride events, he distributed a flyer that bore the message "Free AZT, call this number." Folby went to the Gay Pride festivals in Harrisburg and handed out pamphlets anywhere he could to advocate for the program. In 1990, when Congress passed the Ryan White Act, additional monies were allocated, and the program and Folby's staff expanded. As other lifesaving drugs came on the market, such as pentamidine and interferon, they also were included in the program. John Folby became the voice of various AIDS service organizations that lobbied the state legislature and the governor for the treatment, care, and housing of AIDS patients as well as AIDS education and prevention. Folby continued this work for the commonwealth for the next twenty-four years, until he retired in 2011.

With the onset of the AIDS epidemic, the gay community found itself literally fighting for its own life. With no immediate help coming from the medical community or the state or federal government, the lesbian and gay community was forced to come together to take care of its own. In central Pennsylvania, as the number of victims began to mount, grassroots organizations formed to come to their rescue. The heroic work done by the dedicated staff and volunteers of SCAAN, LAP, the Betty Finney House, the Gathering Place, York House Hospice, and Hospice of Central Pennsylvania exemplified the dogged dedication to curb the suffering. The local community pulled together to fund these organizations, whether through private fundraisers, AIDS walks, or elaborate drag shows staged by creative groups such as Lily White and Company.

As disjointed as the community was at the beginning of the epidemic, by the mid-nineties it had begun to unify. Grassroots organizations that sprang up in central Pennsylvania during the early days of the AIDS crisis further brought the lesbian and gay community together. Activists' warnings that the gay community needed to pull together to fight for their civil liberties now ing for their lives, now wanted more. And more change was on the way.

Profiles

JOY UFEMA

Some people go their entire lives without a direction or passion for their life's work. Joy Ufema found her passion, caring for the dying, at the age of twen-ty-nine while working as an LPN at what was then Harrisburg Hospital, but only after a rocky start.

By her own account, Joy had an idyllic childhood in Altoona, Blair County, one of two girls raised by a stay-at-home mother and a father who worked for the railroad. Looking back, Joy comments, "It was very stable and secure. Very predictable . . . it was a pretty delightful childhood."[35] Joy believes this environment helped build self-esteem, self-worth, and confidence in a tradi-tional, old-fashioned type of neighborhood with mothers around lending a watchful eye.

But for girls back in the fifties and sixties, when it came time to choose a career, there were only two options: "You're going to be either a teacher or a nurse. There was no option, like you could be a physician—that was not in the works." So Joy chose the nursing route and was accepted into the nurs-ing school at Altoona Hospital, a three-year program. Joy was excited to leave home, move into a dormitory, and live with other young women. She found herself spending time playing Ping-Pong and shooting pool with the others and also discovered her same-sex attraction to them. She soon became so distracted by her new surroundings and feelings that she failed to study and, within five months, failed out of school.

Feeling discredited and disgraced, Joy returned home. Her parents challenged Joy to understand why she failed, so that she might regain her commitment. Joy refocused and was accepted at Lewistown Hospital in Miff-lin County, another three-year program. Steadfast in her studies, Joy continued to battle her attraction to women. According to Joy, there was "a lot of pres-sure from my parents, church, society that this is way wrong, and 'You're not okay.' . . . But I knew inside there was this other whole part of me that was great." Feeling the pressure, Joy started dating a man she met at a birthday party, and soon she became pregnant. "And then we had to get married, and it was just awful. I had two daughters, and it was just—I was going to kill myself because this is—I couldn't quite put in [words] how to escape and what would the ramifications be, because I had these two little children, but I knew that mentally and physically I can't do this. So I ran away." Joy fled to Steelton, Dauphin County, and began working at Holy Spirit Hospital in Camp Hill as an LPN, where she took the boards and passed.

After some time had lapsed, Joy, still unsettled, left and moved to Jamestown, New York, where she found work at the Warren State Hospital, a mental institution just across the Pennsylvania border, and became involved in an ill-fated relationship with a nurse who was conflicted about her own sexuality. The nurse, remorseful about her own feelings, reported the relationship to her supervisors, resulting in Joy's termination. This set the wheels in motion for Joy to return to Harrisburg, where she enrolled at Harrisburg Area Community College to finish her schooling and earn her nursing degree. Joy eventually obtained a position as a nurse at Harrisburg Hospital, and then fate stepped in and she found her life's work.

Working as a urology nurse, Joy did an excellent job, but, as she jokingly recalls, "I spent more time talking with the patients than recording their bowel movements."[36] Upon hearing a speech by death-and-dying expert Elisabeth Kübler-Ross, Joy knew what her mission would be. "I had this affinity for dying patients," she says. "It was almost identification with suffering and pain and loss. And I created the job. First one in the country of a nurse specialist in death and dying. And the whole gay thing sort of just dissolved and I just focused on this. And I created an entire career out of it."[37]

For the next six years Joy treated and cared for terminally ill patients at Harrisburg Hospital, even granting some of them their last wishes. In Joy's own words, "I was aggressive with nurses who treated patients abysmally. I wouldn't take that crap that the patient was the doctor's property."[38] Joy always advocated for her patients. She began to write a monthly column for the *Nursing Journal* on death and dying, an assignment that would last for the next thirty years. In 2007, Joy published a book, *Insights on Death and Dying*, a selection of various articles written for the *Nursing Journal*.

Word began to spread about Joy's work. The *Washington Post* published a front-page story about her, and suddenly she was in demand on the national lecture circuit. In 1977, CBS called and wanted to do a television movie of the week about Joy's work, titled *A Matter of Life and Death*, starring Linda Lavin, known for her portrayal of the title character in the television sitcom *Alice*. This led to an appearance on the *Phil Donahue Show*.

Joy left Harrisburg Hospital and worked at a small hospital in Baltimore, where she could continue on the lecture circuit and still take referrals. In 1984, she wrote her first book on death and dying, *Brief Companions*. The hospital was taken over by Johns Hopkins Hospital, a nonprofit academic medical center, which eventually shuttered it. Without a hospital and death-and-dying work, Joy returned to her farm near York to determine her next move.

One day, when Joy was out on her farm, she was digging around in the dirt by one of her favorite pine trees when she unearthed a small kitchen magnet in the shape of the letter *A*. It was an aha moment for her: "It's AIDS, you're supposed to be working with AIDS." This was late 1989, at the height of the AIDS epidemic, and it all suddenly made sense. Joy Ufema was now off on yet another mission: to create the York House Hospice.

She searched around and found a comfortable three-bedroom brownstone on Duke Street in York that was owned by the city. It was suitable for a hospice that she intended to open. Joy quickly found some individuals that would compose her board of directors and solicited David Hawk, a renowned doctor in the field

York House Hospice
145 S. Duke Street
York, Pennsylvania 17403

Fig. 48 Drawing of the exterior of the York House Hospice for AIDS patients. Courtesy of the LGBT Center of Central PA History Project, Archives and Special Collections, Dickinson College, Carlisle, Pennsylvania.

of AIDS testing and education, to be her medical director. Armed with this backing, Joy went to the mayor of York and told him, "I am going to create a nonprofit [hospice]. . . . I have a board of directors, I have Dr. Hawk as our medical director, it's all up. But I need the building." The mayor was incredibly responsive. He told Joy she could have the building for the purchase price of only one dollar and that she only had to pay the annual property tax. Suddenly, Joy had her hospice. After that, everything fell into place. The students at the Art Institute of York took on the hospice as a volunteer project and designed and produced the wallpaper for all the rooms.

Joy launched vigorous fundraising efforts, not only in York but throughout the state. With only three rooms, the hospice did not qualify for Medicare reimbursement. Many of the nurses did not take a paycheck, and some of the patients would hand over their disability checks. But each month the hospice survived financially. News of her hospice spread, and Harford Community

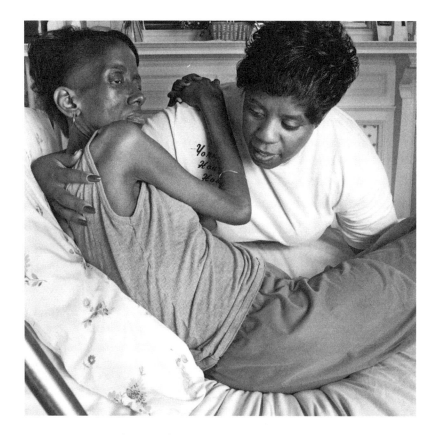

Fig. 49 Nurse Mimi with patient Sheila at York House Hospice. Photo: Jack Radcliffe, with the collaboration of Joy Ufema and Barbara Ellen Wood. Courtesy of the LGBT Center of Central PA History Project, Archives and Special Collections, Dickinson College, Carlisle, Pennsylvania.

College in Churchville, eastern Harford County, Maryland, assigned its photography class to undertake a relevant AIDS project, selecting Joy's hospice as the subject. Then the Corcoran Gallery in Washington, DC, and the National Hospice Foundation commissioned Jack Radcliffe to create a photo essay on the hospice, later to be displayed in their galleries. This became an exhibit that traveled to museums and galleries throughout the country. All the publicity helped Joy with her fundraising endeavors.

But the real work was being undertaken at the hospice in York. Joy's mission was to offer comfort and dignity to those who came. She describes how she imagined the hospice:

> We're going to use cotton sheets because these patients perspire profusely, and the cotton absorbs that. . . . We're going to use down comforters because these patients get chilled very badly and have tremors and shake. . . . We're going to have a tone in this hospice of love and acceptance and peace. And it's not going

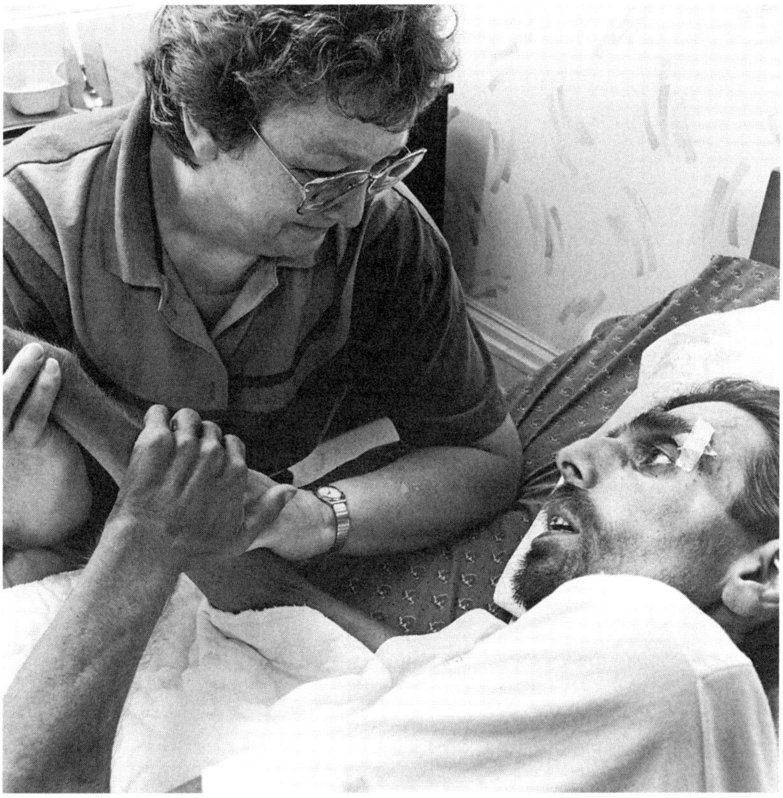

Fig. 50 Nurse Carolyn, fully present with a patient at York House Hospice. Photo: Jack Radcliffe, with the collaboration of Joy Ufema and Barbara Ellen Wood. Courtesy of the LGBT Center of Central PA History Project, Archives and Special Collections, Dickinson College, Carlisle, Pennsylvania.

to be clinical. I never had an oxygen tank at that hospice. If patients were getting short of breath, I gave them small doses of morphine, hand and foot massages, and a small fan blowing air which gave a sensation of air and calming. We didn't have an elevator. We carried our patients up those stairs as our brother. We had a cook so that patients could eat [when they wanted].

Joy would have televisions turned off during the dying phase of a patient, and a nurse would sit by the side of the patient's bed. The death of a patient was turned into a spiritual event, surrounded by peace and love.

The hospice functioned from 1990 until 1995, serving more than ninety-five patients. York had the third-highest number of AIDS cases in the common-wealth, following Philadelphia and Pittsburgh. During the AIDS crisis, grassroots organizations came together to battle prejudice, educate the public, and care for those afflicted with the disease. By 1995, progress was finally being made in AIDS research, and antiretroviral treatments were discovered. Their use began the decline of AIDS-related deaths. Joy's patient load began to drop as the success rate went up in the treatment of the AIDS virus. By the end of 1995, Joy decided to close the hospice. It was suggested that she turn the hospice into something else, such as a respite house for cancer patients, but, according to Joy, the hospice closed "because it was meant for AIDS patients. And there were a lot of respite programs and hospitals for cancer patients. . . . [AIDS] was what it was intended for."

In central Pennsylvania those ninety-five individuals who were patients at the York House Hospice felt the comforting and touching grace of Joy Ufema as they lay suffering and dying from this horrible epidemic. As the AIDS epidemic spread through central Pennsylvania, Joy Ufema was there to create a place for some to go to find peace, love, and acceptance as they faced death.

RICK SCHULZE

Rick Schulze grew up in Camp Hill, a picturesque suburban-style community in Cumberland County, across the Susquehanna River from Harrisburg. Rick and his older sister were raised by liberal, opened-minded parents who were both teachers (although his father later went to work for the FBI). His parents' attitude would be important when Rick was confronting his sexuality at the age of thirteen. He had seen a television special feature on homosexuality. The documentary focused on gay bathhouses and sexually transmitted diseases that many of the gay patrons suffered as a result of their visits. "It was a very dark and dismal documentary and very depressing. I remember watching and thinking, 'Oh my God! This is awful.'"[39] Rick says, "[I thought] all gay men were just having sex everywhere and spreading diseases; this is what they're doomed to [for] the rest of their lives." In his frustration, he went to his mother and told her that he was a homosexual. Her response was neutral. "[It] wasn't one way or the other," Rick contends. "It was just like, 'Do you have some questions about it? What can I [help you with]?'"

Rick's parents arranged for him to meet with their family doctor, who was also neutral. "[He] asked me what I was upset about, and I said I had seen this documentary. I was upset. I thought this is what's going to happen to me. . . . I don't think [he] understood what to say." The doctor asked Rick if he wanted antidepressants, but Rick declined. "So, that was that in eighth grade."

By the time Rick was sixteen, he wanted to meet other gay people. Not realizing there were gay bars in the area, and not old enough to go in anyway, the only place available to Rick was a heavily patronized cruising area on State Street, near the State Capitol. When he told his mother that he was going over there, she asked him why. "I do have to give her credit for [her reaction]. . . . [If] I was in her place, I would've been very upset that my son was going to a cruising area. I told her I was going to meet people." Rick's mother was calm. She said, "I'm not happy you're doing it, but if that's what you're going to do, [I can't stop you].'" Rick explained to her, "'Well, I have no idea where else I'm supposed to meet people.' It's not as if we had gay groups in high school."

A few months later, Rick was reading the local newspaper, the *Harrisburg Patriot-News*, and in its Metro West section was a notice that Tressler Lutheran Services had a social worker who was doing outreach with gay and lesbian people and their families. He passed the notice to his mother, and she decided to go to the meeting. At that time the group was called Parents of Gays and was run by a clinical social worker and former Lutheran minister. Rick's mother, Jackie, found the meeting to be a turning point. She and another mother, Hope Nancarrow, decided to organize their own group called Parents and Friends of Lesbians and Gays (PFLAG), which became a saving grace for her and Rick. "It really focused her energy on feeling like she was doing something for her family, and it was a saving grace for me because it helped educate her." Jackie and Hope's group became part of the national PFLAG organization.

Rick's parents did locate a psychiatrist who was affiliated with the Hershey Medical Center when Rick was seventeen. The psychiatrist's specialty was childhood sexuality, and Rick saw him for several sessions. "I said, 'You know, I'm pretty sure I'm gay, maybe I'm something bi, I have no idea.'" As Rick remembers, "His message was, 'Don't worry about it. It's all going to work out. You may be bi, you may be gay. Who knows [what is] going to happen? You're young.'" The psychiatrist recommended books "on sexuality and sexual development." He recalls that the doctor said, "You might be in a relationship, [or] you might not." Rick adds, "I mean, basically, he was telling me the truth."

When Rick entered Mansfield University of Pennsylvania in Tioga County, he was emboldened and in touch with his sexuality. He, along with a few friends, organized the university's first gay and lesbian group. Called the Mansfield Gay Alliance, it had only 7 members out of a total student population of 2,500. But it was the first recognized gay organization on the campus with a constitution and funded by the university. Some of the members were harassed, including Rick: "I got a few phone calls saying they were going to kill me." Others were spat on. One member had lighter fluid put under his dorm door and was lit on fire. "That was kind of a scary time for all of us up there." In conservative north-central Pennsylvania, the Mansfield Gay Alliance faced opposition within the school's student body for acceptance.

Rick graduated and decided to enter graduate school at Penn State University in the fall of 1982. By the spring, the specter of AIDS had reared its head, and one of Rick's mother's friends, Gary Norton, pastor of the Harrisburg Metropolitan Community Church, was dying from AIDS. "I was never really close to Gary, . . . [but] my mother knew him well, and that was pretty devastating. And then there were a few other people that kept getting closer and closer in our circle over a period of a few years, and both of us really felt we had had that calling that we had to do something, because there was nobody else." Both Rick and his mother became active in AIDS volunteer work.

Rick initially volunteered in the State College and Williamsport areas. "Some of the people were just being treated horribly by the hospitals and by the health-care professionals and by their families. I can remember one gentleman [who] came back from New York City. . . . He ended up in the Shippensburg Hospital or Chambersburg Hospital, south of Harrisburg. I remember going down to visit him, and they made me suit up in this almost space suit just to go in and chat by the bed. They had him in isolation. It was a horror."

During that period, as Rick recalls, "It wasn't just that hospital. It was just such a bad time, and eventually some of our dear friends who were very close ended up being diagnosed . . . and dying within a relatively short period of time. It was just horrible. [I did] buddy work, essentially, volunteer buddy work, going to the homes and either running errands or taking people to appointments." In 1989 Rick went to Williamsport and took a job with the Pennsylvania Department of Health performing HIV counseling and testing. "They didn't have anything for people with AIDS. There were two public health nurses [we] could call allies, who were just wonderful people, and so we organized a buddy program up in this area, Williamsport, Lock Haven, Bloomsburg, [and] Sunbury."

The buddy program functioned much like SCAAN's program. "We had several dozen people living with HIV/AIDS. Most at that time were pretty far along, because there was so little treatment. . . . We had quite a few, probably a couple dozen volunteers and they would do the things, go to the house, cook meals sometimes, run an errand, go to the pharmacy. A couple [patients] didn't have transportation so we'd take them to appointments at Geisinger [Medical Center in Danville, an hour from Williamsport]." It was difficult to find volunteers. There was the fear of contracting the disease. "I think [it was also] just general homophobia," Rick adds. "By that time it was also people in recovery from substance abuse, or [they] were active users. We would sometimes go out and do educational programs, and you would still . . . [hear people say] 'Well, they did this to themselves.'"

The negative attitudes even infiltrated the medical community that Rick encountered. As he recalls, "There was an infectious-disease specialist at Williamsport Hospital, . . . and the public health nurse and I went in and met with him 'cause he was seeing some of the patients. He wasn't real good with patient communication [and] interaction, and we were just trying to get a feel about him and offer whatever services we [could]. He was not real kind to us." The program put together "a guide for the families of people with AIDS about where to go in the region, who they can see, and who are friendly counselors, all that kind of [information]. We put this guide together, but on the back page we also added some national organizations, and one of them was the AIDS Law Project, out of Philly." The guide was distributed to all the area doctors. The infectious-disease specialist at the Williamsport Hospital called the public health nurse who had accompanied Rick on their earlier visit. The doctor was incensed and spoke harshly to the nurse: "Why would you [do this]? These people aren't entitled to any rights." According to Rick, he was terrible to the nurse over the telephone. "I just couldn't figure out why a physician, who is an ID [infectious-disease] specialist, would be so horrible about that. But he was the type of [person who would say], if you were gay, [that] God put this disease on you." Thankfully, he retired soon after that, but that was also a burden on patients. "It meant the patients in Williamsport then had to drive forty minutes to Geisinger Medical Center because they couldn't see [this man]. I mean, who would want to go to a doctor like that?"

In the early years of the AIDS crisis, many people diagnosed with HIV/AIDS living in rural Pennsylvania had a difficult time. "Nobody was having an easy time, but it was much harder for people in these rural counties. It's not as if they were in a gayborhood or something [like in the big cities] where there might be somebody around the corner. Their buddy—their volunteer—may be forty-five minutes away; their doctor [could be] an hour away." Rick, along with his volunteers, knew their mission was vital. They also were used to the isolation. They had all grown up in the area and knew what to expect.

In addition to the isolation in the rural counties, religion also played an important role in how communities responded to the epidemic. "Religion is very powerful up here, and some of the associated discrimination that can go with that. . . . [People] are even struggling with coming out because they come from very tiny towns or farms, and, except on the internet, they don't have any of that contact with other gay people. Church is everything in their community. If you didn't go to church on Sunday, your family isn't part of that community." Homophobia and guilt intensified the crisis for HIV/AIDS patients and continues today, according to Rick.

Rick and his mother also experienced a tragic consequence of their involvement with their AIDS work and related LGBT issues. Rick's older sister married a Christian fundamentalist and, when Rick and his mother became involved with SCAAN, his sister had just given birth to a son. Her husband was worried that Rick and his mother would transmit HIV to the baby. After a few heated discussions, the husband finally told them, "No more contact!" They were no longer allowed to visit. "They broke off all communication with us, her grandparents and everything," recalls Rick. "We haven't had any contact with them. My mother occasionally will send a card or try to talk to them on the phone, and I've sent my sister some letters, asking, 'What happened? Why you can't be in contact?' But I don't hear anything. . . . It's crushed my mother totally because she hasn't seen her grandson since '86." Communication was shut off because of the fear of AIDS, but how was that choice inflected by Rick's being gay or Jackie's involvement with PFLAG or his sister's husband's fundamentalist's beliefs? Rick and his mother don't know, but it is a tragic loss for both of them.

Rick continued with his AIDS work and the Pennsylvania Department of Health until 2000. He still raises funds for AIDS organizations in the region. After his public service ended, Rick settled into a career in academia, eventually becoming a professor of public health education at Lock Haven University in the Clinton County seat of Lock Haven.

CHAPTER 6

Battles

After experiencing the decade of the 1980s, which was dominated by AIDS, the lesbian and gay community entered the 1990s with increasing visibility. As the decade wore on, more celebrities began to come out, and in the arts, gay themes became more common in theater and films. Magazines and television specials were written and produced about the growing power and influence of lesbians and gay men.[1]

Gay men and lesbians were coming out in politics as well. By 1992, there would be more than fifty lesbians and gay men serving in various political offices in city, state, and federal government, including two Democratic members of Congress who were involuntarily outed.[2] Religious organizations began to address the issue of homosexuality, with some accepting gay clergy and supporting same-sex relationships. Scores of cities and towns, and four states, had begun to pass ordinances that protected gays and lesbians against discrimination. Most importantly, more and more gay men and lesbians were coming out.[3]

The 1992 presidential conventions would prove to be a defining point for gay rights. During his presidential campaign, Bill Clinton had openly sought support from the gay community, and at the Democratic Convention in New York City, he included them in his acceptance speech. When Patrick J. Buchanan addressed the Republican Convention in Houston, Texas, he spoke openly about his hostility toward homosexuals and called for a "culture war" against lesbians and gay men. Delegates at the convention held signs that read, "Family Rights Forever. 'Gay' Rights Never!"[4]

The culture war was on, and conservative members of the Republican Party and the Religious Right went on the attack. The fight for lesbian and gay civil rights would play out all across the country, with heated battles in cities and states such as Colorado and Oregon over the banning of all antidiscrimination laws.[5] The fight in Colorado would have a profound effect on the mayor of York, Pennsylvania. As gay and lesbian activists would soon learn through these fights, equal rights would have to be won one by one—with families, churches, schools, and local and state governments and in the courts. The activists faced an uphill struggle for their civil rights. They would find some people willing to listen and accept their position. They would also find many others who were adamantly opposed, based on their religious beliefs, to granting any such protections.[6]

The culture war eventually reached central Pennsylvania. The AIDS crisis had taught local lesbians and gay men that they were capable of quick and effective action and activism. Grassroots organizations formed during the AIDS epidemic in central Pennsylvania proved the community could take care of its own and successfully fight for what was necessary to combat the epidemic. Lesbians and gay men were now emboldened. More were willing to come out and lead initiatives and programs that not only would bring the gay community together but also guarantee their civil rights in the cities and towns in the region.

Fighting for Their Rights

The Keystone State broke new ground with Gov. Milton J. Shapp's executive order in 1975 that prohibited discrimination in state government based on sexual preference. Elsewhere in the commonwealth, however, there was little, if any, protection. Members of the lesbian and gay community were treated as second-class citizens, vulnerable to discrimination and the refusal of employment, services, and housing. In 1982, Philadelphia became the first city in Pennsylvania to break the barrier and pass an antidiscrimination ordinance to make it illegal for employers, housing providers, businesses, providers of public accommodations, and managers of city services to discriminate based on a person's sexual orientation.

In 1982, leaders of the Pennsylvania Rural Gay Caucus, along with members of local unions, working alongside Dignity/Central PA, Metropolitan Community Church of Harrisburg, and the Pennsylvania chapter of the National Organization for Women (NOW), lobbied the Harrisburg City Council to adopt an ordinance to forbid discrimination based on sexual orientation and gender identity (extraordinary for its time).

On March 9, 1983, in a meeting room with more than one hundred people, the Harrisburg City Council unanimously adopted the ordinance. Many

Fig. 51 The 1983 meeting of the Harrisburg City Council, when the nondiscrimination ordinance was approved unanimously. Jane Perkins, sponsor of the ordinance, is at the left end of the dais with city council members. Courtesy of the Historical Society of Dauphin County, Harrisburg, Pennsylvania.

attending the meeting saw an even larger issue at stake. Those supporting the ordinance argued it represented a protection of basic human rights. Opponents who surfaced for the first time publicly, according to the *Harrisburg Evening News*, "ardently believed the measure violated God's will and courted sin by condoning homosexuality."[7]

Rhetoric on both sides of the ordinance was intense. Before the vote, council member Jane Perkins, who sponsored the ordinance (which was seconded by all council members), said, "I am not going to discriminate against someone because he is or is not a sinner. That is not a good enough reason for me." Council president Earl F. Gohl Jr. said the issue was summed up in a letter he received from the Reverend Wallace E. Sawdy, a Roman Catholic priest. The letter read in part, "like everyone else, gay persons should not suffer from prejudice against their basic human rights." Gohl said, "I am very happy to see that the seven of us agree on that."[8]

Opponents argued that the Bible stated, "Homosexuality is a sin, and nondiscrimination against a homosexual can be likened to nondiscrimination against murderers, rapists, and thieves." Another contended, "We cannot legislate laws that are against God's laws."[9] One outspoken critic condemned proponents: "When you make yourself a friend of homosexuality, you make yourself an enemy of

God." Supporter Patricia Lichty, pastor of the Metropolitan Community Church, fired back, "We cannot use the name of God in place of reason; we cannot use the name of God in the place of justice." Other supporters of the ordinance argued the issue was a civil rights issue rather than a moral one: "To openly discriminate is to believe that people are not created equal before God."[10]

Jackie Schulze, a member of Parents and Friends of Lesbians and Gays (PFLAG), was an ally who testified before the city council in support of the ordinance and would soon experience the wrath of those who were opposed. The mother of a gay son, Rick Schulze, Jackie was living in a building containing three apartments and a dental office in Harrisburg. Within a short time after her testimony, someone entered the lobby to her building, laid a pile of religious tracts on the floor at the door to the stairway to the apartments, and set it on fire. Luckily, someone saw the fire before it got too large and called the fire department, and the blaze was quickly extinguished. No one was hurt, but it could have been disastrous for Jackie and her neighbors who lived in the building. The fire chief said that it is likely that the fire was the result of Jackie's appearance before the city council, because she had to give her address to verify that she was a city resident to give testimony at the public meeting. Rick, who was in graduate school at the time, said, "Surprisingly, I don't remember my mother being terribly upset by it, but maybe she was trying to appear stronger to me."[11]

The flawed religious arguments failed and justice prevailed. Harrisburg became the second city in the commonwealth to grant protection to gays and lesbians. Seven years passed before a third city in the state, Pittsburgh, provided such protection. By the 1990s, however, the conservative and the Religious Right movements were gaining force nationally. In Oregon, backed by the Religious Right, Measure 9 was on the voting ballot. This measure would have repealed the state's antidiscrimination laws. Furthermore, it mandated homosexuality be regarded as "abnormal, unnatural, and wrong" and treated this way in all public schools. Colorado's proposed Amendment 2 would nullify all existing protections for gays and lesbians and ban new ones from ever being passed. In Oregon, the measure was narrowly defeated, but in Colorado, the amendment passed.[12]

The Fight Moves to Lancaster

In the midst of this antihomosexual furor, gay and lesbian activists in Lancaster took up the fight for their rights. They had been experiencing troubling years in 1990 and 1991. There were numerous episodes of gay bashing outside the Tally Ho Tavern and the tragic suicide of a gay youth. Mary Merriman, pastor of the Vision of Hope Metropolitan Community Church, spares few details: "A young man had taken a shotgun and blown his head off." He was about twenty-three or twenty-four. Merriman recalls, "In his [suicide] note, [he] talked about being arrested and in one of the Justice of the Peace's offices, being back there a couple times, and the Justice harassing him, calling him names, making his life pretty difficult. . . . [His mother] just said, 'There's nothing we can do about it. He's gone. But I want you to know it.' I kept that for a long time. There was a lot of bloodshed that year in many different ways."[13]

Fig. 52 Pin for Pink Triangle Coalition of Lancaster. Photo: Sue Blosser. Courtesy of the LGBT Center of Central PA History Project, Archives and Special Collections, Dickinson College, Carlisle, Pennsylvania.

These events spurred people to action, including Mark T. Stoner, a young graphic designer, and Nancy Helm, owner of a short-lived gay bookstore. There were not any gay groups in Lancaster at that time other than the Lancaster AIDS Project and the Vision of Hope Metropolitan Community Church. Stoner and Helm formed a political action group, adopting the name Pink Triangle Coalition. "We chose the name Pink Triangle," says Stoner, "because of the Holocaust and the prisoners in concentration camps that were gay or lesbian."[14]

It became apparent that the lesbian and gay community in Lancaster needed legal protection, and people fought for an antidiscrimination ordinance. "Linda Martin was the president of [the Pennsylvania chapter of] NOW," says Mary Merriman, "and she had been doing some writing in the newspaper about gay and lesbian people not having protection under the law in public accommodations, housing, and education, and that people needed that kind of protection, that there was discrimination going on." Lancaster County had a Human Relations Commission, with a policy that protected people against discrimination based on race, color, creed, national origin, ancestry, sex, age, and disability, but it did not cover discrimination based on sexual orientation and marital status. The members of the Pink Triangle Coalition, along with Merriman, appealed to the Lancaster City Council to add sexual orientation and marital status to the ordinance.[15]

After several meetings the ordinance was introduced at the April 9, 1991, council meeting, but a motion to proceed was postponed. Finally, at the May 14 meeting of the council, before a crowd of 150 people, the ordinance was reconsidered. According to the city clerk's records, "All citizens speaking in support of the inclusion of 'sexual preference' and 'marital status' pointed out that the amendment is necessary to prevent discrimination as well as the violence that is directed at homosexual persons." Lancaster resident Laura Welliver opined, "The private life of an individual should not be a matter for public scrutiny, as we are a society that claims to be found upon the ideals of privacy, individual freedoms, civil liberties, and human rights."[16]

Those opposed to the amendment were also heard. "All of the citizens who spoke in opposition to the legislation specifically pointed out that the inclusion of 'sexual preference' is unwarranted, unnecessary, unfair, and contrary to good public policy. Furthermore, citizens believed the addition of 'sexual preference' to the list of protected classes would give special privileges to homosexuals and such a designation legitimizes what amounts to an immoral lifestyle that is detrimental to the family unit upon which our society depends so heavily."[17]

And then council member Jon Lyons spoke: "Government exists to include everyone, it exists to unite its people, it exists to teach us to tolerate each other, to co-exist." The president of the council stated that he "does not see this as an endorsement of a lifestyle but rather as a protection of some basic rights. Anyone who attempts to prevent this from happening is in fact discriminating against individuals."[18] The measure was approved by a unanimous roll-call voice vote. But the battle was far from over.

Bitter controversy still angrily swirled. The following day the Lancaster *Intelligencer Journal* reported, "Sexual Orientation Bias Banned in City." The newspaper quoted the Reverend Mary Merriman proclaiming that "the Council sent a message that there is finally hope for gay and lesbian people. We are finally starting to live." In an oppositional statement, Reverend Paul Armes of the Pilgrim Presbyterian Church of Strasburg minced no words: "The council had miserably failed their God," he said. "The city of Lancaster ought to be ashamed. The measure would encourage a homosexual lifestyle that breeds disease and is a practice more prone to violence."[19]

The Lancaster County Human Relations Commission, funded jointly by the City of Lancaster and the county (which was in charge of enforcement), now took issue with the ordinance. The commission, headed by R. H. "Bob" Brenneman, opposed the ordinance and argued that the language endorsed what they considered "a morally objectionable way of life and the city exceeded its legal authority in adding 'sexual preference' and 'marital status.'" They refused to enforce it. If the city wanted the new ordinance enforced, they would have to create their own commission. This was financially burdensome. The commission had the city backed into a corner. If the city refused to pay its fair share to fund the existing commission to finance their own, the county would withhold other funds due to the city for other services, such as transportation.[20]

By mid-August 1991, the city and county had resolved their differences by agreeing to split on their stand. Lancaster County dissolved the joint Human Relations Commission, and in its place county officials set up a new Human Relations Commission that was identical in all respects but one: the City of Lancaster was no longer a partner. This left the city powerless to enforce its ordinance. There was a heated discussion; supporters of the county praised the commissioners for their opposition to adding gays and unmarried people to the antidiscrimination law. Opponents of the commissioners attacked them for dissolving the joint Human Relations Commission and accused them of "self-righteous indignation" and "over inflated importance" of their own opinions and moral convictions.[21]

Because of the controversy fueled by the ordinance, members of the Invisible Empire, Knights of the Ku Klux Klan (KKK), announced that they were going to hold a march through the streets of Lancaster on August 24, 1991. The demonstration, according to the KKK's great titan Charles J. Juba, a charismatic nineteen-year-old who lived in Leola and worked in a Lancaster factory, was designed to protest homosexuality, drug dealing, and gang involvement. Given advance warning, authorities had "marshalled more than 350 local police officers and Pennsylvania State Police troopers to line the parade route on foot and on mounted horseback amidst rumors of possible violence."[22]

More than four thousand spectators crowded the streets corralled by plastic barricades. Many of the residents were apprehensive before the march. "These things can snowball," said Archer Morgan, who was on North Queen Street. "Someone hits someone and then someone gets a knife and then someone gets a gun. Pretty soon, out come the tanks." As the white crowns of the KKK marchers appeared, heckles from the onlooking crowd started to rise. At this point, the police suddenly reversed the parade route in hopes of avoiding confrontations.[23]

The onlookers began following the KKK marchers. According to Lancaster's *Sunday News*, "A throng of people followed—which included a few women and some unmasked men—along Chestnut Street, parrying the KKK's 'White

Fig. 53 Members of the Ku Klux Klan, marching on the streets of Lancaster in protest of the passage by the Lancaster City Council of an LGBT nondiscrimination ordinance. Courtesy of the Historical Society of Dauphin County, Harrisburg, Pennsylvania.

Fig. 54 Anti-KKK protesters, rallying on the street in Lancaster during the KKK march. Courtesy of the Historical Society of Dauphin County, Harrisburg, Pennsylvania.

Fig. 55 Members of Queer Nation, an organization with branches in major cities, marching with their banner in Lancaster to support the local LGBT community in opposition to the KKK march. Courtesy of the Historical Society of Dauphin County, Harrisburg, Pennsylvania.

Power!' chant and throwing their fists into the air. Across from the post office, someone held a banner that read 'Eat your Sheets.'" Confrontation did break out, and the police arrested seven people, including five county residents and the fifty-seven-year-old KKK imperial wizard J. W. Farrands. A large gay and mixed-race protest took place at the last minute, when at least one hundred demonstrators gathered on East Chestnut Street. Chanting, "We're together, yes we are," the group paused at the police station and then continued to County Park. After the march, the Klan held a rally on private property near Shrewsbury, in York County.[24]

In the end, Klan power was overshadowed by police power and a show of black, gay, and white solidarity. Officers from throughout the county, including the state police, bolstered the 125-member city force, reported Chief Walter T. Goeke, who added, "We weren't able to handle this ourselves." The cost of protecting Lancaster's citizens and their property that Saturday alone was estimated at more than $10,000.[25]

Members of the Pink Triangle and others continued to beseech Lancaster's first elected female mayor, Janice C. Stork, to establish a Human Relations Commission for the city, but they were unsuccessful in their efforts. It was not until 1998, when Republican Charles "Charlie" W. Smithgall was elected mayor and a new city council was organized, that their efforts began to pay off.

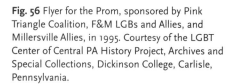

Fig. 56 Flyer for the Prom, sponsored by Pink Triangle Coalition, F&M LGBs and Allies, and Millersville Allies, in 1995. Courtesy of the LGBT Center of Central PA History Project, Archives and Special Collections, Dickinson College, Carlisle, Pennsylvania.

Fig. 57 Pin for the newly formed Lancaster City Human Relations Commission, circa 2003. Photo: Sue Blosser. Courtesy of the LGBT Center of Central PA History Project, Archives and Special Collections, Dickinson College, Carlisle, Pennsylvania.

On August 14, 2001, a motion was submitted before the council to create a Human Relations Commission. Three months later, on November 13, 2001, the motion passed. After a decade of work and fighting, the LGBT community in Lancaster was now fully legally protected by a commission whose decisions and actions were enforceable. It was the long-delayed culmination of activist efforts. The Pink Triangle Coalition was a persistent force for change in obtaining protection from discrimination while also providing services, programs, and social events for adults and youth for Lancaster's increasingly visible LGBT community.

Breakthrough in York

In the early 1990s, a small number of gay men and lesbians concerned about their civil rights mobilized and formed an alliance. "We were trying to figure out what to call ourselves," reminisces York resident Cindy Lou Mitzel. "At that time, you wouldn't have used 'lesbian' or 'gay' or anything, so we came up with . . . 'Lambda.'" The term was more inclusive. "We were a little more public at that point. It was a step."[26] Some members were leery about being out, given the city's conservativism.

York Area Lambda sent a letter to the mayor of York, Republican William J. Althaus, asking if he would support gay rights. The mayor's reply was noncommittal. By 1992, Mayor Althaus had a dramatic change of heart. He had been serving as the president of the US Conference of Mayors. In spring 1992, the conference, normally held in Colorado, moved the meeting out of the state in protest following Colorado's passage of Amendment 2. Althaus and other mayors were appalled by the blatant denial of rights to gays and lesbians by the Centennial State.[27]

Mayor Althaus soon became an advocate for gay and lesbian rights, appearing on ABC's *Nightline* with Ted Koppel to debate and defend his position. In January 1993, he announced that he was going to propose to the York City Council that an ordinance regarding discrimination be passed, handled through the Human Relations Commission, to include sexual orientation. There was opposition immediately, led by the Reverend James Grove, pastor of the Souls' Haven Baptist Temple in Loganville, a small hamlet in York County. Grove invited Paul D. Cameron of the Washington, DC–based Family Research Institute to York to help fight Mayor Althaus's proposed gay rights ordinance.[28] Cameron made his living traveling the country, speaking against gay rights, grounding antigay animus in religious arguments, and making unfounded psychological and sociological claims attacking homosexuality.

In January 1993, both Althaus and Grove had side-by-side op-eds in the *York Sunday News*. Althaus warned of coded phrases being used to instill fear and help people rationalize bigotry.

> Where the word-game comes in is the description of equal rights protection as "special rights." It is illegal throughout this country to discriminate against someone because he or she is a Christian. Is that a "special right" or is it a basic right, which is the foundation of our republic? When did the pursuit of justice and freedom from intolerance become an "agenda"? Is there a Christian "agenda"? Can we now discriminate against Jews? Against African-Americans? When in this land of tolerance and liberty, did we decide that morality is fixed for all by selective quotes from Scripture? Yet, for me, it is very much a moral issue. In my view, we are all God's children and should be treated fairly and equally. This round of argument was triggered by the passage of Amendment 2 in Colorado, which prohibits any municipality from affording equal protection to gays and lesbians.[29]

In his column, Grove warned that the ordinance was a threat to health, morals, and conscience, arguing that the passage of the bill would be a precedent-setting event for the whole nation and warning readers that the city was jumping on the "political correctness" bandwagon. "That the 'religious right' has seemingly become the proverbial enemy in the political arena," Grove wrote, "and at the expense of being labeled as such, I will attempt to set forth some of well-founded argument and concerns in opposition to such legislation."[30] Inspired by Cameron's provocative rhetoric, Grove contended that homosexuals should not be considered a minority. "Civil rights protection is extended to groups whose status is unchangeable. It is something a person is born with, such as race, national origin, gender, or a handicap. Homosexuality is a voluntary sexual practice. It can be resisted. Homosexuals are not born that way." Grove also made a "violation of conscience" argument: "Compelling people to hire homosexuals forces them to violate their own religious conscience, let alone moral conscience, that condemn such behavior. They would restrict a landlord's freedom to not rent to those who engage in what he or she believes is a sexual perversion." His final argument appealed to fears over health: "Homosexuals spread sexually transmitted diseases like wildfire. It is obvious that homosexual lifestyles create a biological swap meet."[31] Grove's claims that homosexuality is a voluntary choice and that gay intercourse is a "swap meet" were drawn straight out of Cameron's well-worn playbook.

In 1983, the American Psychological Association dropped Cameron from its membership rolls for violating the organization's preamble to the ethical principles of psychologists with his stance on homosexuality. The American Sociological Association two years later adopted a resolution condemning Cameron for consistently misinterpreting and misrepresenting sociological research on sexuality and homosexuality. The following year the association officially decreed that Cameron was "not a sociologist" and denounced his consistent misrepresentation of sociological research.[32] These facts were known at the time of Cameron's appearance in York, but they were not reported or publicized in the south-central Pennsylvania community.

Lambda and other supporters organized around Cameron's visit at the city council meeting. As Peg Welch remembers,

> We took out a full-page ad, and we asked people to help us pay for that ad. It was a signature ad, so we asked people in the community to state publicly that they supported the addition of sexual orientation to the ordinance. . . . [With Cameron's visit], we either had pink triangles or we had rainbow ribbons with

Fig. 58 Protesters against the passage of a local ordinance in York to protect LGBT people from discrimination, picketing outside the city council meeting. Courtesy of the York Daily Record/Sunday News.

pink triangles with a pin in them. There was a long line of people waiting to get into the city council meeting to state their opinion about whether or not that ordinance should be passed. So we went down that line and offered people our little pink triangle and our rainbow ribbon and said, 'By wearing this, you show support of the change in the ordinance.' So some people cursed at us, and some people accepted that and pinned it on, and it was a visible symbol of their support. . . . We really tried to do some things to move the community to understand that it was a good thing and a needed thing to be able to add sexual orientation protection to the human relations ordinance.[33]

On Tuesday, February 16, the city council met and, before a crowd of more than one hundred individuals, passed Mayor Althaus's ordinance, making York the third city in central Pennsylvania to ban discrimination against gays and lesbians in housing, employment, and public accommodations. After the vote, Mayor Althaus said, "I think it's fitting that in this, the first capital of the United States, the City Council has stood up and said hatred and discrimination are unacceptable."[34] Supporter Karen Lydon, a psychotherapist with Spring Garden Psychological Associates, stood up and gratefully proclaimed, "Thank you for having the courage of your convictions. To me this is an historic moment and it's an historic moment for thousands of people."[35]

Fig. 59 Mayor William Althaus (*left*) and members of the York City Council, deliberating at the meeting before approving a local ordinance to protect LGBT people from discrimination. Courtesy of the York Daily Record/ Sunday News.

Fig. 60 The Reverend James Grove, speaking at a meeting of the York City Council against the passage of a local ordinance to protect LGBT people from discrimination. Courtesy of the York Daily Record/Sunday News.

Opponents responded as well. The Reverend James Grove, the ordinance's fiercest opponent, retorted, "Welcome to Sodom. The Council was informed of the facts, and I believe they made an improper, immoral decision." Council member Helen Rohrbaugh read an unsigned, handwritten letter: "We know now that none of you people on the Council read your Bible. That's very plain—except for Mr. [Donald T.] Murphy [who voted against the ordinance] and God bless him for his stand."[36]

A year later, David Fleshler wrote a follow-up story for the *York Daily Record* on the aftermath of the passage of the ordinance. In the story Fleshler reported that the changes had not been dramatic a year after the passage of the law. "Most gays and lesbians remain in the closet, fearing harassment and the deep-seated attitudes that new laws can't change." In this environment, even the new president of the York Area Lambda, the organization that helped fight for the passage of the ordinance, still refused to allow her name to be published. The organization, however, remains active. They started a youth group and are about to start a new chapter of PFLAG. Doug Warner, the group's treasurer, says, "I guess what I really think is exciting is that the leaders of tomorrow will come out of these groups." Since the passage of the new law, only one complaint had been filed. But according to Fleshler, "Even if few complaints are ever filed, supporters say it's still important to have the law on the books, because discrimination is always possible."[37]

The article quotes Reverend Grove, who staunchly believed the lack of complaints proved the ordinance was unnecessary. "Discrimination, at any rate, that wasn't the issue. I was fighting against this because it does leave the perception that we allow immorality. It gives them the green light to perversion. Basically, what this allows them to do is promote their lifestyle. That's what they were after, to promote their lifestyle."[38]

Some of York's lesbians and gays felt empowered after enduring their trial by fire. When Doug Warner spoke at the council meeting the year before, he was worried that he would be shunned by his colleagues at Blue Cross in Harrisburg, where he worked as a systems analyst. Fortunately, that fear wasn't warranted. Warner spoke at another public meeting in February 1994, opposing a land-development application by the Cracker Barrel restaurant chain, which had reportedly fired gay employees. The company stated that it had rescinded its antigay policy. "It does happen," Warner said. "It happened with Cracker Barrel, and you have to use the court system to address it."[39]

Lambda membership remained relatively small—about one hundred members—partly because many people feared having their names on its mailing list, even though it was kept confidential.[40] According to Cindy Lou Mitzel, "It was always hard to talk about, . . . wanting people to come out. It's such a personal thing, and you couldn't insist." She adds, "The main fear is usually that you're going to lose your family. . . . I always say everything's a step. You have to take this step before you can take that step."[41]

Despite the outrage of many of the citizens of York, the mayor's proposed ordinance prevailed, and discrimination against gays and lesbians in York became illegal. Life for the gay community could now move forward. Mayor William Althaus was the primary driving force behind the legislation and the expanded fight for human rights in York. He, much like Governor Shapp before him, was a true trailblazer for gay rights.

A Safety Net for Young Gays and Lesbians

Sharon Potter was a married woman with six children, originally from Scranton, Lackawanna County, in northeastern Pennsylvania. She moved to Harrisburg to develop an early intervention program for children with disabilities for the Pennsylvania Department of Education. Barry A. Loveland, originally from Schenectady, New York, moved to Harrisburg to take a position as a historic-preservation architectural designer for the Pennsylvania Historical and Museum Commission. Loveland's and Potter's paths would soon cross, resulting in a critical lifeline for LGBT youth.

Barry Loveland had long been involved in gay activism. In his undergraduate years at Rensselaer Polytechnic Institute in Troy, New York, he was a founder of the first gay and lesbian organization at the school. Loveland continued his involvement with LGBT groups during his graduate years at Eastern Michigan University in Ypsilanti, Michigan. After obtaining his master of science degree in historic-preservation planning, Loveland moved to Montgomery, Alabama, to pursue his career. He continued his involvement with the LGBT community by helping to establish a Metropolitan Community Church in the city. In addition, Loveland was instrumental in organizing a gay men's chorus as well as a support/discussion group called Unique but United.

When he moved to Harrisburg, Loveland immediately became involved with the Metropolitan Community Church in Harrisburg and then later Dignity. "Dignity really was the only game in town in terms of non-bar activities for LGBT people," he recalls. "It was started in 1975 by Jerry Brennan, who

Fig. 61 Thurman Grossnickle with Barry Loveland (*right*), at the first Community Recognition banquet, at Miss Garbo's Tea Room in Carlisle, circa 1992. Courtesy of the LGBT Center of Central PA History Project, Archives and Special Collections, Dickinson College, Carlisle, Pennsylvania.

was active in the LGBT community. He was one of the first activists, really, in Harrisburg. . . . He got me interested enough to become president for a few years." Loveland also became part of the Gay and Lesbian Switchboard of Harrisburg. "That was a turning point in my activism, because I really got very involved in that. [I] became first codirector and then president of the Switchboard."[42]

During the early days of working with the Switchboard, Loveland remembers, "I'd volunteered first as a person on the phone. They had operated a phone line that was [staffed] in the evenings from six to ten, Monday through Friday, and you would get calls." Many of the calls, he says, were from people asking where the bars were or for other resources. "But we would get these calls from kids who were fourteen, fifteen, sixteen years old, and . . . your heart just breaks, because you can't—you don't know what to tell them, where to go, what to do. You can talk to them and say 'Look, your life is going to get better. Once you get old enough, you can do all these different things.'"[43] As the calls from young gays and lesbians continued, Loveland realized the growing need for a support system for this group.

The kids who called felt very much alone and thought they were the only ones who were gay. They didn't know what to do or where to go. Loveland wanted to tell them, "There is a support group that meets on Friday night," but he needed to find the right person to facilitate the group. Luckily for Loveland, that person would be Sharon Potter, wife of Tom Potter, an architect who worked for Loveland at the Pennsylvania Historical and Museum Commission.

Sharon Potter had just been appointed deputy director of the Pennsylvania Department of Education. She was testifying in front of the Pennsylvania House of Representatives Education Committee when a young man named Andy came to the microphone. He was in his early twenties, and he spoke to the committee about his experience in high school. He was a gay man who had survived being harassed and beaten. He had attempted suicide twice, and he asked the committee, "What are you doing now to protect kids who are in the schools?" Potter recalls, "They were kind of baffled. They weren't doing much of anything. I don't mean to say they didn't care. I think it wasn't on their radar, and it honestly wasn't on my radar, either. . . . When I heard this kid, I was very moved."[44] Sharon Potter went home that evening and spoke with her husband, Tom, about the experience and how she would like to do something for the gay community.

Tom spoke with Barry Loveland the following day and told him about Sharon's desire to become involved. Loveland recalls, "I said, 'Tom, she is the perfect person for this youth group. You know, I've been wanting to start this youth group for so long.'" Loveland and Sharon Potter met and developed an action plan. They sent out mailers to high school guidance counselors, private counselors, and psychologists in the greater Harrisburg area. They contacted youth resource organizations to let them know that there was now a resource for LGBT youth.[45]

There were just seven kids at the first meeting, but over time the group would grow to twenty or more attendees at the meetings. The kids came up with a name for the group, Bi-GLYAH, which stood for Bi Gay Lesbian Youth Association of Harrisburg. "They also referred to it as 'Big-LYA.' You Big-LYA! That was pretty funny, because many of them were lying," says Potter. "They would tell their parents they were going to a dance or a movie or whatever it was, and they would come to group."[46]

But the issues that brought them there or what they discussed were not always funny.

> One young man [came in and said], "This is the third time that I was at the door, and if I didn't make myself come into the room tonight, I was going to go to the

Bridge] and jump in the river." He came in in terrible pain, and he left laughing. . . . It was amazing, 'cause all they needed to do was feel they could be there, and it didn't matter, it was completely unconditional. . . . Like if a kid was going to come out to their parents, we always wanted them to know that they could call us, no matter what time it was. There were several times when kids were sleeping in their cars or sleeping on somebody's sofa, so they were homeless. So I would bring them home. We had six or seven families that were a safe house network that would take kids in at a moment's notice. So that was good. And often they reconciled with their own families, but sometimes not. They made their own families then.

There were also a few attempted suicides, but fortunately none was successful. Potter remembers one incident when one young man attempted suicide, and the family that was providing a temporary home for him called Potter after they called the ambulance. Potter raced to the emergency room, where she found the young man in a four-point restraint. The nurse told the young man, "I will let you out when you can prove you can behave." According to Potter, "He didn't want to behave, he wanted to die. . . . I had words with her [the nurse], and she told me I should leave. I told her I wasn't leaving, and she said, 'You're not even family, you shouldn't even be here.' And I said, 'So call security, because I'm not leaving. And besides, you need me here. . . . I'm the only one here that this young man trusts.'" Potter was allowed to stay, and the young man recovered.

Over time, the group developed programs and workshops for kids. "We always did safe-sex things. There was always something new going on around safe sex. . . . So we always did good sex education and boundaries and relationship stuff," says Potter. "Bob Coldren [a local pediatrician] talked about sexuality from sort of a clinical point of view. I also had a dear friend who was a transgender man . . . and he came down from the Scranton area and spoke to the kids."

Harassment and bullying at schools were major issues. If the group heard about an incident, one of the facilitators would be at that school within a few days. One school's solution was to accompany the youth to class. This infuriated Sharon Potter. "How about calling an assembly and saying, 'Under no circumstances is this going to happen in our school, and if you do it, you're out of here.' . . . It's not okay for someone to hit [a student]. So we did a lot of education." They also encouraged the formation of "allies" groups.

Fig. 62 The premiere screening of the documentary film *Jim in Bold* at the State Museum of Pennsylvania, Harrisburg, featuring a protest by members of the Westboro Baptist Church of Kansas and a counterrally and protest by about eight hundred supporters of the film. Courtesy of the LGBT Center of Central PA History Project, Archives and Special Collections, Dickinson College, Carlisle, Pennsylvania.

Potter worked with Bi-GLYAH for more than ten years. The youth group eventually changed its name to Common Roads, now with groups not only in Harrisburg but also in Carlisle and Lancaster. Reflecting back on her experience, Potter says, "You know, twenty years ago, people died. They jumped off the Forster Street Bridge, and they're not anymore, because [these groups] are here. That's pretty wonderful."

Jim Wheeler was nineteen in 1997, a gay teenager living in Lebanon, Pennsylvania. He suffered immense cruelty at the hands of his peers. He was harassed, bullied, pulled into the showers of his high school, and urinated on. Knowing no others like himself, he felt like he was the only gay person in the world. His isolation and loneliness led him to commit suicide shortly after his graduation from high school. There were no LGBT groups in Lebanon, twenty-six miles east of Harrisburg. Wheeler had no idea that Sharon Potter's group existed. If he had, perhaps Wheeler might be alive today.

Jim Wheeler's story was made into a documentary film in 2003, titled *Jim in Bold*. It recounts his troubled life through the memories and stories of his family and friends. The documentary has been screened at twenty-two film festivals on three continents, and its makers hope to turn it into a teaching tool for schools. At its September 28, 2003, premiere in central Pennsylvania, at the State Museum of Pennsylvania in Harrisburg, ten members of the Westboro Baptist Church, known for its extreme antigay views, showed up to protest. Because they announced their intentions to protest in advance, they were overwhelmed by eight hundred counterprotesters who declared the day Unity Day. The counterprotest was organized by the Pride Festival of Central PA and led by community organizer Reynaldo Lacaba.[47]

Jim Wheeler's mother, Susan Wheeler, was among the eight hundred people who came to watch the movie. "My message for Fred Phelps [pastor of the Westboro Baptist Church] is a message that everyone must hear: Homophobia is a killer. It is deadly," she said. "Our job as parents is to recognize our children for who they are and to respect and nourish and nurture and celebrate it. They're gifts from God, all of them."[48]

Sharon Potter could not agree more.

New Initiatives for Women

Born in 1958 in the small town of Willow Street, Pennsylvania, a small borough of Lancaster, Bobbi Carmitchell was destined to be a musician. After graduating from high school in 1977, she left home with the intention of going to Florida to pursue a career in music. However, Carmitchell got sidetracked and ended up going to the Blue Ridge Mountains to Skyline Drive in Shenandoah National Park, where she honed her musical skills as a singer and songwriter and came to terms with her own sexuality.

When she returned to Lancaster in 1980, some friends invited her to hear two women perform at a local tavern in Harrisburg. The women were Anne Billmyer and Deenie Hamacher, who had gained local fame from their appearances at Millersville University of Pennsylvania in Millersville, a borough in Lancaster County. Carmitchell was impressed with their performance and immediately went up to meet them. "I went up and I'm like, oh my God, an out lesbian! Anne Billmyer was the first out lesbian I'd ever met. She was out there. She didn't change her pronouns [in] the songs. She stayed with singing a love song for a woman. She didn't sing it about a man. . . . It was an absolutely amazing experience to have met them."[49]

The chemistry between the three women was immediate, and soon they joined together to form the group Wind and Wood. "It was the perfect storm of culture, the timing—the women's movement had picked up all this steam in the '70s. . . . All these factors combined to make this perfect pot of acceptance." Carmitchell describes the trio: "We had one big out lesbian [Anne]. And we had one big out straight woman [Deenie]. And we had me, just kind of staring at the floor playing bass [guitar], going, 'I think I'm a lesbian. I think I'm a lesbian.'"

The group began to play regularly, five nights a week, at the Midtown Tavern in Harrisburg. Wind and Wood gained popularity among all segments of society. "You'd look out [at the audience], and [there would be] straight women with their boyfriends, and there's no other table so the two gay guys are sitting with them that they've never met. Lesbians are over here. . . . It was like this total UN [United Nations] of culture, of who was sitting with who. It didn't matter. They were there for the music, and that was the common denominator. Everybody just grew up with each other in total acceptance. To have that be my first five years being a professional musician, it was just the best thing in the world."

It wasn't long before the group was playing at different clubs throughout central Pennsylvania, both gay and straight alike. At one point the comedian Rosie O'Donnell opened for Wind and Wood. "She was a friend of one of Anne's girlfriends. . . . She wasn't out at all at the time." In 1984, the group released their first and only studio record, *The Limo Is Waiting*, a collection of favorite songs from their central Pennsylvania fans.[50]

"It was an amazing time period," Carmitchell remembers of the first five years. "We met Maureen Reagan, who was doing an arthritis telethon, and we never hid . . . who we were. And she invited us down to play for her dad in '84, and we did." The draw wasn't necessarily Reagan himself, "the big freaking Republican, but it was a Susan B. Anthony celebration. So we're like, let's do this. That was good stuff, to have the small-town band go down [and perform]. . . . We busted through a lot of barriers."[51]

The group continued to perform, and when Harrisburg held its first Gay Pride festivals, Wind and Wood was lined up to perform. Tragedy struck in 1985, when Anne Billmyer committed suicide. It was an immense shock to all. "There were thousands of people that were just walking around going, 'What the hell—what just happened here?'" Carmitchell was forced to move on without the role model and music partner she so admired. She launched a solo career that would take her across the country, producing five more solo albums over the next ten years.[52] Carmitchell performed in different bars, clubs, and other venues, including women's music festivals throughout the country, but she always returned to Lancaster.

Fig. 63 Bobbi Carmitchell, performing at the SCAAN AIDS Walk, circa 1990. Courtesy of the LGBT Center of Central PA History Project, Archives and Special Collections, Dickinson College, Carlisle, Pennsylvania.

In the late 1990s, Carmitchell decided she wanted to do something meaningful to honor Anne Billmyer. She wanted to coordinate a music festival, but she needed a venue. She contacted Harrisburg mayor Stephen R. Reed and then the people that manage a state building in the Capitol Complex of Harrisburg, which houses the Pennsylvania Department of Education, the State Library of Pennsylvania, and a performance space capable of seating nearly 1,800 patrons—the Forum Auditorium, home to the Harrisburg Symphony Orchestra. According to Carmitchell, the people at the Forum "just gave me the building. The Harrisburg Symphony was supposed to rehearse that night. They had a performance on Sunday. . . . [But the guy who scheduled them said that] 'They're never here.' So he just crosses them off. And he's like, 'We'll do this for you 'cause you're doing it for Anne, because she needs to be honored.' [And] twenty years later, there are women musicians and there are lesbians playing, and it's because of her."[53]

The first women's concert was a huge success, with more than eight hundred people attending. "Lots of women who hadn't been in the area for a while came to support it. [It caused a resurgence in interest for] a lot of people in Harrisburg, going, 'Oh my God, where are the women musicians around here? We don't see them at the riverfront parks. We don't see them at Kipona [the annual festival held over Labor Day weekend in Harrisburg]. We don't see them anywhere." This motivated Bobbi Carmitchell to approach Harrisburg's Parks and Recreation Department, which gave her a grant of $1,500 to hold a reunion concert. Inspired, Carmitchell thought, "That's a good chunk of money. But how about we think a little bigger. Why don't I just break it up and stretch it out to nine hours—don't know what I was thinking—and do eight groups, and bring some of these women musicians in who are fifteen minutes away from Harrisburg, who live right here, and give them some exposure?"

HER STORY

WOMEN'S BOOKSTORE

BOOKS

CARDS

MUSIC

VIDEOS

COFFEE/TEA

INCENSE

JEWELRY

GIFTS

Summer Hours:
Mon.-Fri. 10-9
Sat. 9-9
Sun. 12-6

North Front Street
Wrightsville, Pennsylvania
17368

(717) 252-0188

Parks and Recreation had given Carmitchell one stipulation: she could not charge an entrance fee. That was fine by her. "They gave us the sound. They gave us the lights. So we had an eight-hour festival." To help with the expense of the festival, Carmitchell brought in women business vendors, who paid a fee for their vendor booths, which provided additional income. The primary expenses for the festival were the fees for the performers, so the money from the grant and the vendor income covered this cost.

Carmitchell had numerous television and radio interviews prior to the festival. Recalling those interviews, Carmitchell says, "What people wanted us to say was [that] it was a lesbian festival. [I just kept saying] it is a women's music festival. And they're like, 'Why don't you have men there? What do you have against men?' I'm like, oh my God. It's like they bait you because that's their job. They want one little line to say, 'Producer of festival hates men.' . . . And I never gave them that."

The Women's Music Festival continued on for another four years. According to Carmitchell, "We intentionally brought in straight women. We had the Sweet Adelines come in. They had a freaking riot hanging out with the big old lesbians [backstage]." She continues, "I could have called it the Central

Pennsylvania Music Festival . . . [and secretly thought] 'I'm going to stack it
with women musicians, and I'm not going to identify it as that.'"

Bobbi Carmitchell made an enormous contribution to the world of women's music, beginning with Wind and Wood, then her own solo career, then providing a vehicle like the Women's Music Festival to showcase the talents of other female musicians. She continued her visionary work for women later with the creation of the Women's Circle, a group to deal with issues directly affecting women.

The Women's Circle became important to Carmitchell. "One of the things that I really wanted to work on was to have a place for young women to go to realize they're not alone, whether it's their sexuality, whether it's their politics, or whatever. So the idea was to think about doing a women's center." That project seemed unsustainable, but an alternative was to form the Women's Circle. At first, they tried to plan monthly programs, but they were unable to find a location. Finally, the group decided to focus on doing one weekend a year and doing it really well.

The Women's Circle organized annual three-day retreats exclusively for women through the YMCA at Camp Shand in Lancaster County.

Fig. 64 (opposite) Bookmark from the Her Story women's bookstore in Wrightsville, York County. The store featured lesbian-themed books and gifts and hosted special events. Courtesy of the LGBT Center of Central PA History Project, Archives and Special Collections, Dickinson College, Carlisle, Pennsylvania.

Fig. 65 Matchbook from the Courtyard lesbian bar in Harrisburg. Photo: Sue Blosser. Courtesy of the LGBT Center of Central PA History Project, Archives and Special Collections, Dickinson College, Carlisle, Pennsylvania.

Every year they would select a theme and change the names of cabins in the camp to reflect the theme. During the retreat, planners offered workshops, programs, seminars, and mediation. The weekends were enormously successful. It was an empowering experience for women to attend these retreats.

Carmitchell made history with the Women's Music Festival, and she has continued to enrich the lives of women with her work with the Women's Circle. Building on this success, the women's music scene later expanded with the creation of the Central Pennsylvania Womyn's Chorus in 1994. All this was made possible by Bobbi Carmitchell, who broke barriers and changed lives.

The *Lavender Letter* continued to thrive and help women connect and create new opportunities and organizations for social interactions, education, and activism. New women's organizations formed, and new lesbian bars opened, such as The Courtyard and Beat-L's, both in Harrisburg. In Carlisle, a lesbian couple opened a restaurant called Miss Garbo's Tea Room. Her Story, a women's bookstore, opened in Wrightsville in York County, and Nancy Helm opened The Closet, an LGBT bookstore, in downtown Lancaster. The lesbian community in central Pennsylvania was becoming more visible.

Profiles

NANCY HELM

In the 1990s, Lancaster was a conservative bulwark. With its deep Amish roots and a tightly woven community, it was not a town openly affirmative to the LGBT community. Nancy Helm, who had been born and raised in Lancaster, had put down roots and decided to carve out a life and career here. After graduating from Manheim Township High School in 1981, she worked for a printing company and performed other small jobs before opening a hair salon in downtown Lancaster.[54]

The salon, however, left her unfulfilled. Her first love was books. Nancy would travel frequently to Philadelphia to visit Giovanni's Room, a gay and lesbian bookstore, where she would indulge in buying the latest gay and lesbian or feminist books. (The Pennsylvania Historical and Museum Commission installed, in 2011, a state historical marker honoring the bookshop's role as a "refuge" and "cultural center" during the birth of the modern lesbian, gay, bisexual, and transgender civil rights movement. More than four hundred celebrants, including Philadelphia's mayor Michael A. Nutter, attended the marker unveiling and dedication.) Tired of the drive to Philadelphia and her life in the salon, Nancy recalled, "I guess at the time I never felt fulfilled in anything. I always felt like I had more to do. . . . I would go to Philly to Giovanni's Room and I just loved that place. And I thought, we need something [like that] in Lancaster." It was at this point that Nancy embarked on a new journey. She began buying books, T-shirts, and gifts to stock her new store. She kept inventory at her salon until she had enough to open her very own bookshop.

Through a friend, Nancy was able to find the perfect location, a terrific storefront on Prince Street, the main thoroughfare, kitty-corner from her salon in downtown Lancaster. Nancy remembers, "I wanted the perfect location, and . . . I figured that if I was going to do it, it had to be full throttle out there. You know, and not hidden in some alley. . . . I wanted it to be right there where people had to deal with it. Because I just felt like, you know, things had to change, things had to get better. . . . And the bookstore was a gathering place as well as a bookstore." Nancy named her store The Closet, with a sign depicting a person coming out of the closet.

Inside The Closet, Nancy carried numerous gay and lesbian books such as *Lesbians at Midlife: The Creative Transition*; *Kindred Spirits: An Anthology of Gay and Lesbian Science Fiction Stories*; *The Gay Book of Lists*; and *Our World: International Gay Travel Magazine*. Nancy also carried books on AIDS, gay travel guides, and mainstream self-help books on alcoholism, bulimia, and anorexia. In addition to books, Nancy carried buttons and T-shirts emblazoned with slogans such as "Nobody Knows I'm Gay," "Nobody Knows I'm a Lesbian," and "Closets Are for Clothes." The Closet also served as a community calendar resource for gays and lesbians in addition to providing AIDS information. The bookstore posted events and newspaper articles pertaining to gays and lesbians. Nancy was quoted in the Lancaster *Intelligencer Journal*: "'I'm not dead-set on being any one kind of bookstore,' she said, citing a mixed clientele that included feminists as well as homosexuals. She plans to start carrying cassette tapes by gay musicians as well, and has been compiling a 'wish list' from customers."[55]

From opening day on May 15, 1991, Nancy had hundreds of customers, and, although most of the response was positive, she realized a violent reaction might be possible. As Nancy recalled in the Lancaster *Intelligencer Journal*, "I'm here to stay. If somebody shoots me, my friends will open for me tomorrow. I'm not putting my tail between my legs and running." Her response to those who would be upset by the bookstore's presence was, "If you don't want to see this, just walk by. Homosexuality is here to stay."[56] Nancy's notoriety had been enhanced by her involvement with the Pink Triangle Coalition.

The Pink Triangle Coalition was actively involved with the county commissioners and the city council of Lancaster, fighting for the ordinance that would protect lesbians and gays against discrimination. Nancy was a key spokesperson for the group. When the city council broke with the county commissioners and passed the ordinance for the city, Nancy was given much of the credit for the success. She was now well known in the city, not only as the owner of a gay bookstore but also as a gay activist.

Even with the new ordinance in Lancaster, widespread homophobia still existed. According to Nancy, "There was such a fear of being out and about here, at the time. And it wasn't unfounded. I mean, you could feel—you know, it was nothing to be walking down the road and have 'you fucking dyke' or whatever thrown at you." Nancy recalls the time when she was approached by a young woman in Rehoboth Beach, Delaware, and the woman asked, "Are you the girl that opened that bookstore in Lancaster?" When Nancy said that she was, the young woman responded, "Well, I'm gonna tell you right now, I'm never going to your damn bookstore. You put it on Prince Street."[57] As Nancy discovered, people were either on her side or not.

After the passage of the ordinance, two things began to occur: Nancy had numerous calls for interviews, and the police began to receive calls complaining that the bookstore was carrying pornography. The police would come in and inspect the bookstore, find nothing, and leave. "The first time they came in, they checked everything," Nancy remembers. "After that, they were like 'Psh, no big deal.' [They would] just come in; look around; leave. But people had this need to just harass to no end."[58] But the harassment soon came to a head early in the morning of June 24, when Nancy received a telephone call at one in the morning. The police called and told her that an explosive device had blown out the window of her bookstore. When Nancy arrived, there was the smell of gunpowder everywhere in the store. The front window had been blown out, but the explosion otherwise caused little damage.

A quarter stick of dynamite wrapped in cardboard was used in the blast, but no fingerprints were found. The police had no leads or motives, according to an official department incident report. Nancy was convinced it is was a combination of gay bashing and the result of the recent controversy over Lancaster City government's decision to ban discrimination based on sexual orientation and marital status. As far as the police were concerned, Capt. Joseph P. Geesey announced, "At this time we know of no motive."[59] So Nancy moved on, cleaned up her store, replaced the glass, and reopened. The police never reinvestigated the bombing.

During the following three months, threats and harassment intensified. The Ku Klux Klan came to Lancaster to protest its perceived acceptance of gays and lesbians. They held a protest parade, marching down Queen and Lemon Streets, the police steering them clear of Nancy's store on Prince Street. Soon, Nancy found that she was being followed by various people when she was driving her car. She went to the police, gave them a description of one of the cars following her, but, without a license plate to identify the vehicle, the police would do nothing. There was a threat of another bombing attempt when someone drove by and yelled, "We will throw the next bomb!"[60] Tension was building for Nancy. Everywhere she went she was recognized. She was frightened and angry. She was becoming a target of hatred.

Then, in August, a second bomb exploded. This time the bomber used four sticks of dynamite, taped the explosives together, and placed the bomb behind the brass rail of the antique door of the store. The force was so strong that it destroyed a chunk of the brick wall that was twenty feet back in the store. "It did a lot of damage," Nancy recounts. "I had an old candy case from way back when that I had a lot of my display in, and the glass shards scratched the entire front of it. It was like . . . a sunburst. My [gay] flag was burnt up."[61] This time a witness who lived a block from the bookstore saw two men run from the front of the bookstore just as the explosion went off. "It was two white males," the witness reported. "I couldn't get a really good description." Captain Geesey was again on the scene, confirming to press that it was an explosive device and that the police were continuing to investigate this and the first bombing. "My reaction is this time I don't want to see this buried," Nancy said. "I want the police to respond to this. I want this out." The following morning, Nancy stood outside the store with several friends and vowed to keep the bookshop open. "I'm going to fight until every gay and lesbian person has what they deserve in this town," she said. "Homophobia is Curable," read a sign placed over the broken door window.[62]

Nancy reopened within a month and was back in business. She kept following up with the police and their investigation but felt like she was getting the "runaround." "I felt like when I did inquire, I was just put off. . . . If it would have been anybody else's business, you know, would they have had that same attitude? They didn't look at [The Closet] as a legitimate business, that was the problem.. It was just a gay bookstore."[63] A detective was assigned to the case by the police, but he never had any answers.

From August until January, Nancy continued receiving many hate calls and drive-by threats with chants, "We are going to blow up your store again." Even after a successful Christmas sales season, Nancy received another threat in January and began to consider permanently closing the store. Once in a supermarket, a male shopper stopped her and said he wanted to "kick her ass." Walking down the streets, she was met with taunts of "There's that fucking dyke." According to Nancy, the comments were almost always negative. "Once in a blue moon there would be a positive [comment], but the majority of it was just hate and discontent."[64]

This began to weigh heavily on Nancy. Finally, it all came to a head when Nancy attended a local fair in the spring. Nancy was standing with a friend when one of the county commissioners with whom she had been at odds during the ordinance fight suddenly shoved her. The woman she was with wanted to confront the commissioner, but Nancy refused. As Nancy recalled, "I said, 'Don't feed him. He's an idiot.'" Her friend asked if she knew him, and Nancy explained that he was a county commissioner. "So you know if 'the top notch,' as they say, is willing to do ignorant things like that, what chance do you stand?" This started Nancy thinking. She had a great Christmas season at the bookstore, but then the threats started coming again, and she wondered, "What am I going to have to deal with this year? Who's going to get hurt this year? What's going to happen?" The police were not getting any resolution on finding the bombers. "It just felt like something was coming at me at all turns. I just kept thinking, . . . 'I don't know if I can do this anymore.'" Under all the pressure, stress, harassment, and fear, Nancy finally decided to close the bookstore, nearly a year to the day she opened it.[65]

Ironically, two weeks later, the police arrested five suspects in connection with the two bombings. Two adults and three juveniles were taken into custody after authorities confiscated enormous loads of explosives. More than 150 cases of class B and C fireworks and illegal explosive devices were seized, along with 30 cases of class B and C fireworks taken from another garage.[66] Nancy was stunned and angry. All this time the police had told her nothing, and a month after she had closed the bookstore they made the arrests. "Had I known that they were on the cusp of catching these people, I certainly would not have closed my store." But after the arrests, Nancy had to face the turmoil of testifying in court.[67]

When the case finally went to trial, of the two adults, Daniel J. VanAulen was charged with two counts of criminal conspiracy and one count of manufacturing, sale, and discharge of fireworks. He was found guilty and sentenced to a federal prison. The other adult, Linda A. Ward, was charged with two counts of arson and two counts of criminal conspiracy.[68] She was released because she had custody of her five children. The judge reprimanded her, saying, "If you ever end up in my courtroom again, you'll lose all five of those children and you'll never see them again."[69] The three juveniles arrested were turned over to juvenile court. Of the three juveniles, one was mentally impaired. He approached Nancy during the trial and apologized. Nancy gave the boy a hug and asked the judge to release him. The other two were sentenced to jail until they were eighteen.

Nancy stayed in Lancaster briefly, trying to blend in and not be noticed. Her notoriety made it impossible. She still received unfriendly comments and felt unwelcome, and so she left for twelve years, moving south to Tennessee. Nancy's home and roots were still in Lancaster, and in 2006, she moved back. Things are better now. People have forgotten. Nancy works at a local hospital and has made many new friends. Life is good. Still, the memories and pain of that horrible year in 1991 still linger. In looking at Lancaster now, Nancy remarks, "There's a lot more open-mindedness than there used to be. I mean you just didn't see that back in '91, and now it's like . . . wow! Totally different."[70] Nancy is happy to be home again.

DAN MILLER

Dan Miller was almost thirty years old when he came out in 1986.[71] Growing up in Harrisburg, he was active in school sports, playing on the tennis and basketball teams, and dated women throughout his high school and college years. He and his family went to a Methodist church every Sunday, with Dan eventually becoming head acolyte. Looking back on his youth, Dan says, "You know, I didn't have any sense of what being gay was. . . . Obviously, it was something—something wasn't right for me, you know. . . . I would have maybe a crush on some other boy, but it didn't really make sense." Dan continued to suppress his sexuality during college and graduate school.

There were times when Dan questioned his sexuality. When he was studying for his master's in business administration, he spent the summers working in Manhattan, living in the East Village. He never set foot in gay bars, nor did he have sex with another man. A male classmate who had become his best friend visited him in New York that summer, and Dan realized he had fallen in love with him. That fall, Dan felt close enough to tell him about his feelings, and, as Dan recounts, "It was really a disaster. . . . It just crushed me beyond belief that because I told this guy that I thought I was gay, he just never spoke to me again. And I can't tell you how devastating that was. I think that put me back into the closet." Dan went on to finish his MBA at Penn State in 1986 and returned to Harrisburg, due in large part to a woman he was dating.

Later that year, Dan and his girlfriend were shopping at a local supermarket when he happened to notice the current issue of *Newsweek* at the checkout counter. Flipping through the magazine, he came across an article titled "Growing Up Gay." He was entranced by the photographs of the men who looked just like him, with their arms around each other. Dan bought the magazine and read the article. As Dan remembers, it was about two men:

"One who had gone to college, . . . and he was gay. And he had his partner and they had an apartment, and it was like—it was just a normal life. But he was gay! It was like . . . 'Okay!' Now that was really the thing that got me to come out finally."

Dan's relationship with his girlfriend was deteriorating at the time. There was something missing. After reading the *Newsweek* article, he realized how he wanted to spend the rest of his life. Not knowing where to turn, Dan looked in the phone book and found a number for the Gay and Lesbian Switchboard of Harrisburg. Dan called it and found out that there was a gay volleyball game in Harrisburg every Tuesday and Friday. Apprehensive and nervous, he went nevertheless. There he met dozens of other gay men. After the game, they offered to take Dan to a gay bar. At the bar, he met a man that he made arrangements to go out with later that week. After that evening, Dan was "out" with a fury. He told not only his girlfriend but also his entire family that he was gay. His girlfriend was angry, but his family was accepting, with the exception of his sisters' conservative husbands, who were not welcoming of Dan's news. During the next four years, not only would Dan become actively involved in gay and lesbian politics and activism, but his career also took off.

At the time of his return to Harrisburg, Dan was hired by Donald DeMuth to work part-time as an accountant for Don's management consulting company. Dan was soon working more than forty hours a week, which resulted in an offer of a full-time position. With the offer came an agreement of employment for Dan to sign that stipulated, among other things, a noncompete clause. This seemed reasonable to Dan if he left on his own, but it bothered him that it might prevent him from making a living if he were fired. Dan asked DeMuth to define what the contract meant by "fired by cause." DeMuth then produced the definition of the provision: "Cause shall include, but is not limited to, moral turpitude, being charged with a felony, use of illicit drugs, intoxication while working, insulting employer's family and clients, not working, intentionally working slowly, intentionally losing clients, engaging in sexual activities in the office, and homosexuality."[72]

Dan was astonished when he saw the agreement, but at the time, he was still involved with his girlfriend and even contemplating marriage. He felt he had no choice but to sign. Dan had placed himself in a vulnerable position. In Camp Hill, Cumberland County, where DeMuth's offices were located, there were no laws protecting gays and lesbians from workplace discrimination. Just across the river from Camp Hill lay the city of Harrisburg, where such laws were in place.[73]

During the next four years, Dan excelled at work. He modernized the office with the introduction of computers, a knowledge and skill that he had and that DeMuth lacked. DeMuth was pleased, and so were their clients. Dan remembers, "I felt good about the job and was making very good progress. He wanted me to become a partner. So we talked about it. We had scheduled to become partners in the next year. And we were looking at buildings to purchase to move our practice to—it was growing. . . . And a building— we would both own part of it and be partners in the building and partners in the practice. So that was sort of the path." Although Dan continued to sign employment contracts in the first few years of their working relationship, in the last year, no contract was signed.

Concurrently, Dan's life as a gay man also blossomed. He met, fell in love, and moved in with another man, finally finding the love for which he had long been searching. He became a regular on the men's volleyball team and became active in the Gay and Lesbian Switchboard, eventually becoming its cochair and finally its chair. In the summer of 1990, during the height of the AIDS crisis, there were numerous gay bashings that occurred in Harrisburg. Many angry calls came into the Switchboard, protesting the violence. A meeting was scheduled at a local gay bar to discuss the situation, and Dan, in his capacity as chair, felt obligated to attend. The press was in attendance to cover the event. Even though the gay activists wanted the publicity, no one in the Harrisburg gay community was eager to be identified in the press. Not one person was willing to speak publicly. "We were afraid," Miller states. "We were asking victims of gay-bashings to go to police and speak out, but we couldn't even speak to the media." Dan finally stepped forward, and, though he was not willing to be filmed, he made a statement. He was quoted by name in the next day's issue of the *Harrisburg Patriot-News*.[74]

Luckily, DeMuth did not see the paper the next day. Dan was relieved. A month later, however, the Harrisburg City Council was scheduled to take up the issue of violence against gays and lesbians at its meeting. The matter was suddenly dropped from the agenda. Dan showed up at the council meeting to find out what was going on. The media was there to cover the event. With cameras rolling, a reporter put a microphone in front of Dan, and he spoke out. Dan simply advocated for more police protection for gays and lesbians. It was not a radical statement, and he did not identify himself as gay. But when he returned home and watched the news coverage, he found he was on every local broadcast, labeled "Daniel Miller, gay-rights activist." At that point, Dan recounts, "It was done, it was over. I knew what would happen the next day. I was scared."[75]

Dan did not get fired the next day when he went to work. DeMuth had not seen the news coverage. But when a client called DeMuth later that day, the client remarked, "I saw Dan on TV last night. He was on as a spokesman for the gay-lesbian coalition. He was talking about gay activism!" According to later testimony, DeMuth stated that he was floored and dumbfounded and felt betrayed. DeMuth then called his lawyer, and together they worked out a strategy for firing Dan. Miller was not fired that day, but rather two weeks later.[76] According to Dan, he was working on a project that only he could finish, and DeMuth wanted it wrapped up. On the morning of October 17, 1990, DeMuth called Dan into his office. When he entered, DeMuth looked at Dan and said, "Well, you know what this is about." It did not register immediately with Dan that he was being fired, for two weeks had passed. Then he asked Dan, "What do you want me to tell the clients?" Dan's interpretation of that was that Demuth thought Dan was embarrassed about being gay and that together they were going to make up a story, like "Dan left for health reasons." This line of questioning sent Dan over the edge, and Dan angrily responded, "Tell them the truth! Tell them you're firing me because I'm gay!"[77] And with that Dan got up and left the office.

Dan decided to start his own practice in Harrisburg. Things had now dramatically changed for him. Once Dan would never have considered telling his clients anything about his personal life; now he was open about having been fired because he was gay. To Dan's surprise, many of the clients he dealt with at DeMuth's consulting firm were now eager to follow him. Within a matter of days, one of DeMuth's largest clients, a medical group, called to inform Dan that they would be moving their account over to him. In a vindictive response to the loss of accounts, DeMuth sent off a letter to his account base; Dan found out about it when someone gave him a copy. In the letter, Dan says, DeMuth "talked about homosexuals and about how they get AIDS and die. And while he doesn't know my medical status, he assumes that . . . I would not be living for very long. And if my clients wanted to use me on some kind of long-term basis, they should be well aware of fact that I'm gay and probably have AIDS and I'm going to die soon."[78]

Within the year, with a thriving business, Dan had decided to give up on the idea of suing DeMuth over his termination. In November, he called his lawyer and told him to drop the matter. Two days later, when he arrived at work, he found a summons and complaint taped to his door. DeMuth had filed suit against *him*.[79]

The case of *DeMuth v. Miller* went to trial in June 1993 in Carlisle, Pennsylvania. DeMuth was suing for breach of contract and loss of business, and Dan countersued for wrongful termination and defamation of character. The lawyers for DeMuth argued that there was no signed contract, and he'd lost clients to Dan's firm. Before the jury could consider Dan's counterclaim of wrongful termination, the judge dismissed it, announcing, "The argument that a person is protected from either being a homosexual and announcing it in public may be the law someday. Someday the legislature may create such a set of legal principles. But as I understand the law to be at this point in time there is no such protection."[80] He then granted the motion by DeMuth's lawyer to dismiss Dan's claim.

When the jury went into deliberations, according to the judge, there were three points to consider: "whether Dan breached the contract that was in effect; whether Dan misappropriated any confidential information from DeMuth; and whether DeMuth defamed Dan by raising the AIDS issue in his letter." The jury deliberated for a day and a half and delivered their decision. They found in favor of DeMuth. Because the original contract allowed that homosexuality was a reason to be "fired by cause," and Dan was an admitted homosexual, and he had in fact taken clients from Demuth, he breached the contract. Also, the letter that was sent to clients never directly said that Dan had AIDS, thus invalidating the defamation of character claim. As a result, the jury awarded DeMuth a total of $126,648 in damages.[81]

After the trial, Dan was emotionally fatigued. It took five years out of his life and more than $200,000 to pay the fines and lawyers. Looking back, Dan sees Judge Hess as the impediment to his case: "He did not want this 'gay' issue in his courtroom. He did not want to make civil rights law for gays and lesbians. . . . You know the Pennsylvania constitution is really very liberal about this type of thing. And there would be a good way for us to argue it. He said we weren't allowed to do that. . . . When he gave the instructions to the jury, well, I knew we [had] lost."[82]

In retrospect, Dan feels that there were two defining moments in his life. The first was "in the room where everybody went around and nobody could speak to the press, and I had the courage to do that, because I didn't know what other choice there was." The second was the trial: "As a 50-some-year-old person you come to recognize how important integrity and honor and doing those things [are]. I did it for me. But I also realized I was doing it for so many other people. . . . Not everybody can do it. And I just happened to

Fig. 66 Pin for the (unsuccessful) candidacy of Dan Miller in 2013 for mayor of Harrisburg. Photo: Sue Blosser. Courtesy of the LGBT Center of Central PA History Project, Archives and Special Collections, Dickinson College, Carlisle, Pennsylvania.

be somebody at the wrong place (*laughing*) at the wrong time, but with the right fortitude to fight."[83]

Dan has moved on successfully with his life. He became Harrisburg's first openly gay city council member, serving from 2006 until 2010. In 2009, Dan was elected controller for the City of Harrisburg. In 2012, Dan married his longtime partner, Carl Bechdel. A year later, Dan decided to run for mayor but was defeated in the primary election. In 2016, he was appointed treasurer of the City of Harrisburg to fill a vacancy and was elected in 2017 to a full four-year term.

CHAPTER 7

Pride

On the night of June 28, 1969, the police raided the Stonewall Inn, a gay bar in New York's Greenwich Village. The routine raid suddenly turned into a violent protest as the bar's patrons began to resist and a crowd gathered on the street. When a police officer forcibly escorted the last person out of the bar, rioting erupted. The crowds and riots continued into the next few nights, with more than two thousand people gathering each night to protest and fight the police. Shouts of "Gay Power" could be heard.[1] Something dramatic and galvanizing had just happened in the gay community that changed it forever.

Word spread quickly about the confrontation, launching the gay movement across the country. On the first anniversary of the riot, Gay Pride marches were held in Los Angeles, Chicago, San Francisco, and New York, with participation in these cities exceeding hundreds of thousands of people. Gay Pride events would eventually spread across the nation and the globe, celebrating the event that triggered the gay rights revolution and ultimately the celebration of gay identity. The Stonewall uprising did not happen in a vacuum. By the mid-1960s, after enduring decades of oppression, discrimination, and police harassment, gay men and lesbians began to protest in various cities. As society was changing, so was the gay community.

In April 1965 in Philadelphia, underage gay teens were refused service at a local hangout, Dewey's Coffee Shop in Rittenhouse Square. They staged a sit-in and, when they refused to leave, were arrested for disorderly conduct. In response, the Janus Society (an early homophile activist organization founded in Philadelphia) protested for the next five days.[2] Annual reminder demonstrations were held at Independence Hall until 1969, when they were replaced with an annual event marking the anniversary of the Stonewall uprising.[3]

In New York, the State Liquor Authority had long told bar owners not to serve homosexuals. Dick Leitsch of the Mattachine Society, wanting to stop this harassment, arranged to have a photographer for the *Village Voice* in Julius's bar in May 1966, capturing the bartender covering Leitsch's glass to prevent him from taking a drink. Leitsch used the photograph in court to win his case against the State Liquor Authority, and bar owners were allowed to serve homosexuals. But the police harassment continued.[4]

A protest and riot broke out in the Tenderloin District of San Francisco in August 1966, when police tried to clear Compton's Cafeteria of unwanted gay customers. When a police officer asked a transgender woman for identification, she threw hot coffee in his face, and a riot ensued. The following day, gay men and lesbians gathered to protest police harassment.[5]

Protests broke out in Los Angeles in 1966 and again in 1968 over police harassment of gay men and lesbians arrested in gay bar raids. In Philadelphia, a raid on the lesbian bar Rusty's in 1968 led to a woman being arrested on charges of sodomy. The next day the charges were dropped. The purpose of the raid and arrest were to continue the harassment of gays and lesbians and hopefully discourage the continued patronage of gay and lesbian bars.[6]

These protest and riots were indicative of the rising anger and frustration in the gay community. Gay men and lesbians were reaching a boiling point. This pent-up anger would lead to the Stonewall uprising and ultimately unite the gay community.[7] Stonewall was the turning point for the fight for gay rights and identity—and the celebration of Gay Pride.

Pride Comes to Central Pennsylvania

It would take sixteen years before central Pennsylvania would establish its own Gay Pride celebration. Gay rights demonstrations had been held in Philadelphia since 1965, organized by the Janus Society and other organizations. After the Stonewall riots, events in Philadelphia had grown from several hundred marchers to more than a thousand by 1975. In central Pennsylvania, however, there was no celebration of Gay Pride during this period. The small gay community in Harrisburg had only three or four gay bars and just a few gay social groups. In this largely suppressed and closeted environment, the only avenues for those who wanted to celebrate their gay pride were in Philadelphia or New York.

In a bold move in 1976, however, Gov. Milton J. Shapp issued a proclamation declaring June 12–19 as Gay Pride Week in Pennsylvania. He was the nation's first governor to issue such a decree. In his unprecedented declaration, the governor proclaimed, "I hereby express my support for equal rights for all minority groups and for all those who seek social justice, and dedicate GAY PRIDE WEEK to those worthy goals."[8] Objection to the governor's action was intense, and the backlash was swift. Six days later, on June 15, the Pennsylvania House of Representatives passed a resolution rejecting Governor Shapp's proclamation of Gay Pride Week. Local outrage in Harrisburg over the proclamation was also quickly voiced. State representative George O. Wagner declared in the *Sunbury Daily Item*, "By setting aside a week to honor the Gay Movement, you have brought contempt upon the use of other proclamations from the Governor's office. I strongly disapprove of your use of your proclamation right to honor this group."[9] Joe Burns, a local gay activist and secretary of the Pennsylvania Rural Gay Caucus, sent a letter to members of the House of Representatives: "Never, in the annals of Pennsylvania history, have a people in peaceful pursuit of civil rights been so put down. We of the Pennsylvania Rural Gay Caucus have vowed to give our message to our legislature again and again and again. We have the pride, the strength, and the love to persevere."[10] Undaunted by the controversy, the city of Philadelphia continued with its Gay Pride observance that year.

Without a local venue in which to celebrate their gay pride, various groups from throughout the region, such as Dignity/Central PA, Gay Community Services, Susquehanna Valley Gays United, Gays United Lancaster, and others, decided to march under the banner of the Pennsylvania Rural Gay Caucus in Philadelphia's Gay Pride Parade. The caucus was represented by only a handful of brave lesbians and gay men who marched in Philadelphia that day in 1976. This was central Pennsylvania's first public effort to express gay pride. With the hostile reaction to the governor's proclamation, there was little local media coverage for the event, except for the *Sunbury Daily Item*, which reported, "The Susquehanna Valley Gays United would participate in the Gay Pride Parade in Philadelphia."[11]

By 1984 several local organizations, among them Dignity/Central PA, the Pennsmen, and the Metropolitan Community Church of the Spirit, had decided to finally organize their own Gay Pride event in Harrisburg. Given the animus and hostility that existed toward lesbians and gay men, the organizers feared that many people would be afraid to attend a Gay Pride celebration in a culturally conservative area such as Harrisburg. To encourage greater public participation, the organizers named the event the Open Air Festival, avoiding any reference to Gay Pride.

The festivals, staged from 1985 to 1987, were held at the Police Athletic League grounds on Linglestown Road in Susquehanna Township outside

Fig. 67 Members of the Pennsylvania Rural Gay Caucus, posing with their banner at Philadelphia's Gay Pride Parade, June 1976. Photo: Bari Weaver. Courtesy of the LGBT Center of Central PA History Project, Archives and Special Collections, Dickinson College, Carlisle, Pennsylvania.

Harrisburg (except for the last, which was held in a park outside Linglestown). It is ironic that the first gay festival would be held on police property, given the role the police had played in the suppression, entrapment, and legal prosecution of gays nationwide. The use of pink helium balloons served as the only markers to designate the gay festival's entrance. Over the course of the event, food, beverages, a simple crafts fair, and live entertainment were available. The few hundred people that attended carried rainbow flags, socialized, shared picnics, and played volleyball. It was a day of celebrating their gay pride and finding unity with others and in numbers. These festivals were a stark contrast to those in larger cities, where protests for equal rights, supporting gays in the military, and AIDS funding were mixed with the celebrations of pride. Local media ignored the event. Organizers of the Open Air Festivals intentionally avoided alerting the media in order to prevent hostile protests and derogatory coverage.

When the festival lapsed in 1988, the event was reimagined. In 1989, Nikki Knerr, a local businesswoman who owned a successful printing company in

Camp Hill, took charge. Knerr had become increasingly aghast at the AIDS epidemic. She and her friends grew concerned over the lack of awareness about the disease. They felt they should be doing something to help. While talking to her friends, one of whom was a doctor, Knerr found out that it was not only gay men falling victim to the disease. "We have droves of women coming in to the Carlisle Hospital," the physician told her. "They're not all prostitutes, they're not drug dealers, there's no needles—these are young girls, straight girls." Knerr realized that this was "not just a gay problem" but was everywhere.[12] She was compelled to act—and to raise money to help take care of people.

With support from her friends, Knerr took over the festival as a fundraiser for various AIDS organizations in central Pennsylvania. "I didn't want to call it Pride Festival," she said, "because I was developing the brochures, and my employees were all straight. So I was kind of worried about that." Bernie Pupo, Knerr's friend, suggested, "Why don't we just call it Unity?" Knerr embraced the name: "The point was, I was trying to unify everybody."[13] Since she didn't have the funds to support the festival herself, she held the event at her home on six acres of land in Mechanicsburg. Volunteers helped her. She arranged for vendors to display their arts and crafts, food, and, of course, T-shirts. Local musicians donated their entertainment. More than 750 people attended that first year, paying the $20 admission fee and ultimately raising more than $15,000 for AIDS causes.

Fig. 68 Flyer advertising the Open Air Festival, 1985. Courtesy of the LGBT Center of Central PA History Project, Archives and Special Collections, Dickinson College, Carlisle, Pennsylvania.

With the success of the festival, Knerr realized that it would only grow over time. She knew she needed a much larger venue. Her printing company was doing work for the local ski resort, Ski Roundtop, and in the summer the resort was completely vacant. She approached the owner and, as Knerr recalls, "they rented it to me. I couldn't believe it. I explained the whole situation; not a problem." With the expanded space, "I advertised [the event] in all the gay magazines, or newspapers, or anything that was gay-oriented. I just kept bringing in more people."[14]

Fig. 69 Unity Festival at Ski Roundtop, in Lewisberry, 1990. Courtesy of the LGBT Center of Central PA History Project, Archives and Special Collections, Dickinson College, Carlisle, Pennsylvania.

The following year, the Unity Festival became an all-day event, with attendance topping 1,500 people. Professionals appeared, including noted singer Bobbi Carmitchell and her group, Wind and Wood. Other local entertainers included Lily White and Company, the popular drag performance troupe. Tables were set up for gay and lesbian activists and political organizations, as well as for retail and craft booths. People sat on the hillside, listened to music, shared food, and socialized. By the third year, attendance soared to more than 2,000 people, making the event a totally inclusive festival reflecting the diversity of the LGBT community.

With the focus as an AIDS fundraiser, traditional media ignored the event. Peg Dierkers, executive director of the South Central AIDS Assistance Network (SCAAN), one of the AIDS agencies benefiting from the festival, commented, "This was at the height of the predominately white, gay, AIDS epidemic. People were dying every week. There was still much discrimination against gays and lesbians, so media coverage was tricky and not that welcome. Plus, the media wasn't all that interested and definitely not supportive."[15] This was evident in an editorial published in the *Lancaster New Era*: "Most addicts and gays know of the risks of their behavior by now. If their choice gets them in a bind, why is it that they expect everyone else to bail them out? It would appear to me that with Gay Pride parades and the recent demand of special privileges for gays that they are the ones bringing their bedroom activities out in the open to us! Not only are they bringing it to our attention, they are clobbering us over the head in order to get us to accept their behavior."[16]

After the third year, Nikki Knerr met again with the owner of Ski Round-top to place a deposit for the following year. He flatly told her he would not rent to her again. Knerr was shocked; the resort had previously made money during the event. The resort sold alcohol and memberships during the festival. When Knerr asked why, the owner responded, "Well, because this is a fami-ly-oriented business." Knerr didn't understand; she replied that there had been children at the festival. It had been a family-oriented event. Its purpose was to raise funds for AIDS organizations. To this, the owner reported that one of the resort's security guards had found two men on the top of the hill having sex. "You can't come here anymore," he flatly told her. "I was not thrilled that this [had] happened," Knerr recalls. "But then I couldn't fight city hall—you know what I mean. Can't fight 'em, they didn't want us. I was exhausted. Where are we going to go next?" Facing protracted negotiations for a new site, Knerr says, "I just said no." Knerr had raised more than $100,000 for AIDS char-ities. It was time to turn the event over; she just had to give it up. "It's sad, though. . . . I was so upset." She decided to step away from the project and allow others to carry the torch.

In 1992, Dan Miller, Patrick Wallen, and Barry Loveland, local business-men and gay activists, took the festival over from Nikki. The major change that these three leaders made was renaming the event the Gay and Lesbian Pride Festival of Central PA. The trio firmly believed it was time to take a dramatic public stand and place "Gay and Lesbian" in the title of the celebration. They continued to hold the celebration in late July rather than the traditional anni-versary of the Stonewall riots in June. The Unity Festival had always been held in late July, so the organizers decided to keep the date with which attendees were familiar. This date also did not conflict with all the other Pride events in New York, Philadelphia, and Baltimore in June. Lighter competition from other Pride celebrations made it easier to attract national LGBT entertainers. The new organizers selected Reservoir Park in Harrisburg—a beautiful multi-tiered park with a band shell, park seats, and grass seating, overlooking the State Capitol Complex—as the site for the celebration.

With this move, the event received its first media coverage by the *Harrisburg Patriot-News* on July 19: "In what organizers are calling a giant step forward for gays and lesbians in the mid-state, a Pride Festival is being planned in Harris-burg next week," the newspaper reported. The article went on to quote Patrick

Wallen: "It is a major step to have a gay pride event in your community; we needed to do this in Harrisburg." The article also quoted Dan Miller, who said, "Gays and lesbians in the midstate need a day in which to take pride in their lifestyles and affirm themselves. This is very painful for people who aren't out. They want to come but they will be afraid to. We're just regular people and we want people to see that."[17] For the first time since the creation of the festivals in central Pennsylvania, the community was finally coming out.

Miller, Wallen, and Loveland dropped the admission fee for the festival and sought out local sponsors and free-will donations by attendees to fund it. There were a variety of entertainment and activities, including music from several groups, such as the Harrisburg Men's Chorus, solo acts, bands, and a dance group from Seattle.[18] People danced, shared picnics, socialized, and found joy in meeting others from various outlying communities such as Lancaster, York, and Williamsport. During the event a special award was presented to state representative Peter "Pete" C. Wambach (D-Harrisburg) for his support of the gay and lesbian community during his tenure in the General Assembly of Pennsylvania. The crowd that year was estimated at more than one thousand people. Central Pennsylvania officially now had its own gay and lesbian Pride event.

Building on the success of the first year, the fearless triumvirate decided to give the 1993 Gay and Lesbian Pride Festival a theme. Seeking to include members of the nongay community as a means of educating and fostering tolerance toward gays and lesbians, they chose the theme of Together Celebrating Pride. While other large metropolises were utilizing their Gay Pride celebrations as vehicles for gay activists and protests, the central Pennsylvania organizers were using the celebration of Gay Pride as a strategy for equal rights, employing a "sameness" argument. "It is our opportunity to invite non-gays to see who and what we are—ordinary citizens," Dan Miller opined.[19] Attendance soared that year to more than three thousand people. The event was elevated by the entertainment; Betsy Salkind, an actor, comedian, and filmmaker, served as emcee. Performers that year were BETTY, an all-woman rock and roll/cabaret trio; Fred Small, a folk singer; Nancy Day, a pianist, singer, and composer; Bobbi Carmitchell, a folk singer; Debbie Jacobs, a singer who had several disco hits in the late 1970s; and the Harrisburg Men's Chorus.

In 1993, with the success of the Gay and Lesbian Pride Festival, Miller, Wallen, and Loveland, along with others, formed the Community Action Council to serve as a steering committee for the event. With the celebration's overwhelming success, the festival was then turned over in 1994 to the Pride

Fig. 70 Betsy Salkind, comedian, serving as emcee at the Gay and Lesbian Pride Festival at Reservoir Park, Harrisburg. Photo: Pep Rox. Courtesy of the LGBT Center of Central PA History Project, Archives and Special Collections, Dickinson College, Carlisle, Pennsylvania.

Fig. 71 Harrisburg Men's Chorus, performing at the Gay and Lesbian Pride Festival at Reservoir Park, Harrisburg. Photo: Pep Rox. Courtesy of the LGBT Center of Central PA History Project, Archives and Special Collections, Dickinson College, Carlisle, Pennsylvania.

Fig. 72 Dignity/Central PA booth at the Gay and Lesbian Pride Festival at Reservoir Park, Harrisburg. Courtesy of the LGBT Center of Central PA History Project, Archives and Special Collections, Dickinson College, Carlisle, Pennsylvania.

Fig. 73 Singer Debbie Jacobs performing at the Gay and Lesbian Pride Festival at Reservoir Park, Harrisburg. Photo: Pep Rox. Courtesy of the LGBT Center of Central PA History Project, Archives and Special Collections, Dickinson College, Carlisle, Pennsylvania.

Fig. 74 Comedian and emcee Betsy Salkind, speaking with David Payne at the Gay and Lesbian Pride Festival at Reservoir Park, Harrisburg. Photo: Pep Rox. Courtesy of the LGBT Center of Central PA History Project, Archives and Special Collections, Dickinson College, Carlisle, Pennsylvania.

Fig. 75 Part of the crowd at the Gay and Lesbian Pride Festival at Reservoir Park, Harrisburg. Photo: Pep Rox. Courtesy of the LGBT Center of Central PA History Project, Archives and Special Collections, Dickinson College, Carlisle, Pennsylvania.

Coalition of Central PA, an organization specifically formed to run the festival full-time. The Pride Coalition decided to drop Gay and Lesbian from the title, believing that the word "Pride" was now an inclusive and self-descriptive word defining the gay and lesbian community. From then on, the event was known as the Pride Festival of Central PA. The year 1995 would be the last year the Pride Festival would be held at Reservoir Park. The celebration moved under the auspices of the Gay and Lesbian Switchboard of Harrisburg for several years before transitioning to a separate organization, the Foundation for Enhancing Communities, where it remains today.

The 1994 Pride Festival continued from the previous year, with Nancy Day and Bobbi Carmitchell returning as entertainment headliners. Over three thousand people attended the festival at the park, but the next year, the festival turned more political with the arrival of a featured guest, lesbian activist Candace Gingrich, sister of the speaker of the US House of Representatives, Newton "Newt" L. Gingrich. Candace Gingrich spoke at the festival to advocate for equal rights for gays and lesbians and for anti-hate legislation. It was a local coming out for Gingrich, a native of central Pennsylvania. She remarked, "A lot of people in the area had some sort of idea that Newt's sister was a lesbian for a while, but now they know for sure. He may be proud of me as a person, and he's told me that. But his voting and his policies aren't supportive of me at all."[20] Gingrich's appearance at the festival boosted attendance in excess of five thousand people.

Now under the management of the Gay and Lesbian Switchboard of Harrisburg, the Pride Festival moved to the campus of Harrisburg Area Community College in 1996. The Switchboard was able to convince Harrisburg mayor Stephen R. Reed to issue a proclamation designating that "the week of July 22–27, 1996, be declared Pride Festival Week."[21] There was no resulting negative commentary over this proclamation, compared to twenty years earlier, when Governor Shapp first issued his. The festival continued its focus on entertainment, bringing back Bobbi Carmitchell as the headliner, along with singer Natalie Darkes. For the first time the festival instituted the Pride of Susquehanna Awards, which recognized individuals who had brought pride, prominence, and positive noteworthiness to central Pennsylvania. The recipients that year were Candace Gingrich, spokesperson for the Human Rights Campaign in Washington, DC, and Joy Ufema, founder and director of York House Hospice, the region's first resident care facility for end-stage AIDS patients. In framing the purpose of the festival, Dr. Eric W. Selvey, one of the event's organizers, announced, "It's a celebration of who we are and what we are. It's also an opportunity for people to network and to get involved in the community and see what people are doing."[22] Still in the midst of finding their own voice in the larger community, central Pennsylvania's Pride Festivals were focused on pride and celebration. The festival was *not* a vehicle to promote same-sex marriage, gays in the military, or gay and lesbian adoption, as was the focus in the larger urban area Pride events.

In 1997, the Pride Festival experienced its first protester, who carried a sign that read "Repent or Perish" and, on the other side, "God is angry with the wicked every day." Undeterred by this antigay protester, an estimated four thousand people attended the event. But the feelings expressed by the protester were not lost the on crowd. Attending that year was Rita Addessa, head of the Philadelphia Lesbian and Gay Task Force, who participated to raise awareness and gather signatures in support of the organization's legislative initiatives, especially its efforts to introduce legislation prohibiting job discrimination on the basis of sexual orientation in the Keystone State. "We are second-class citizens in this state," Addessa said. "Many of the laws, or lack of rights, are grounded in homophobic presumptions. The festival and other such events are vital to the gay cause."[23] Also participating that year was Marlin Snyder, codirector of the Susquehanna Valley chapter of the national Names Project.[24] Snyder believed that the event gave participants an opportunity to see that they are not alone: "It gives us pride and self-esteem and reminds us that we're all part of the same race—the human race."[25] The Pride Festival continued with a program of entertainment, and vendors offered a variety of food, crafts, and services. Amid the protests was the recognition that the gay and lesbian community could no longer stand inactive or silent in the fight for equal rights.

In 1998, the *Harrisburg Patriot-News* reported, "Warm feelings and a carnival-like atmosphere engulfed the campus of Harrisburg Area Community College as people enjoyed the Pride Festival of central Pennsylvania." Along with a dunking booth added that year, the event continued with its usual lineup of entertainment, food, refreshments, and a host of vendors. There were information tables sponsored by organizations such as the Unity Church, the Rainbow Place of South Jersey, and the Philadelphia Lesbian and Gay Task Force. Rita Addessa was back again, collecting more signatures for the proposed state legislation to prohibit job discrimination based on sexual orientation. Addessa said that her and the task force's objective was "to organize within the state, so [we] could continue empowering people and spread knowledge about the rights of minorities. The Pride Festival was a way for the gay and lesbian community to establish some visibility."[26]

Amid this celebration, protesters appeared. Carrying signs that read "Jesus Christ can deliver you from homosexuality" and "What will the end be for denying God?," protesters taunted attendees as they arrived at the festival. At one point, some protesters left their posts and began to follow cars down the road to where the volunteers were collecting admissions fees. Eventually, the protesters retreated. After facing down this opposition, one attendee remarked, "This is the reason for the festival. It is an opportunity to teach self-worth." Rita Addessa summarized, "The Pride Festival is a good tool for conscious-ness-raising and self-affirmation. We come together out of pride."[27] As the Pride Festivals were growing, so were the local controversies surrounding them.

Because of these protests, several of the community college board members began to feel uncomfortable with the festival being held on the campus. Late in 1998, Tina Manoogian-King, director of the Parks and Recreation Department for the City of Harrisburg, approached Eric Selvey, committee chair of the festival, about moving the event back to the city. It was perfect timing. In 1999 the Pride Festival finally relocated to its final home at Riverfront Park, along Front Street and south of Market Street in a heavily traveled area of the city.

The event that year—three times as large as the previous year—was heartily welcomed by Harrisburg mayor Stephen R. Reed, who in May declared July 31 to be Pride Festival Day in Harrisburg. It was also supported by state representative Ronald I. Buxton (D-Steelton). Despite the openness of the event, many who attended suggested that central Pennsylvania was still behind the times when it came to tolerating and accepting gays and lesbians. "It's still a little backwards," said Linda, a transplant from western New York. "It's like New York was 15 years ago," she said of the area's tolerance level.[28]

The move to Riverfront Park brought swift opposition from local residents. In various editorials that appeared following the festival, outrage was vitriolic. "Shame, shame, shame on the officials of Harrisburg for not only permitting but endorsing and celebrating the Gay Pride festival held at Riverfront Park on July 31. They scornfully told me that they were indeed 'very proud' of what they were doing, and constantly quoted scriptures that reinforced the fact that 'God loves everybody.' Let me remind them of this: God hates pride. Pride is what brought Satan down to earth. How far do Harrisburg officials, including Rep. Ron Buxton, intend to let this 'gay pride' thing go?"[29] In another editorial, a citizen supportive of the festival blasted a local radio station for its position: "Radio 580AM, not known for the rationality of its program hosts, spent the better part of two mornings ranting against the Pride Festival. 'Right in your face!' was the frequently uttered incendiary refrain. Thirty years ago, they would have been saying the same thing about NAACP rallies. It has to stop."[30]

As the twentieth century came to a close, the lesbian and gay community in central Pennsylvania was still struggling with making its voice heard through Pride celebrations. The opposition was in sharp contrast to large urban areas that were not only celebrating their LGBT pride but were now being supported by local and national politicians endorsing gay and lesbian activists' positions. Lesbian and gay families, open military service, the Defense of Marriage Act, and antidiscrimination initiatives were all center stage at Pride celebrations in large metropolitan areas. In central Pennsylvania, however, the right to exist and "be who you are" was still an uphill battle, and so their celebrations were focused more on unity, self-affirmation, and pride. The 1990s evolved to be an era of greater gay and lesbian awareness nationwide. But this awareness, openness, and acceptance had not totally come to central Pennsylvania. Here the LGBT community would still face challenges as it moved into the twenty-first century. The Pride Festival needed to confront these challenges to effectively adapt and evolve.

In 2001, the event adopted a theme of "Embrace Diversity." Organizer Mike Grabauskas said it was a celebration of unity and a call for a new definition of equality. Participants traveled from as far as Ohio, New York, and Delaware, with attendance reaching more than 2,500 people. Protesters again showed up at the festival, but they were not allowed into the park. Stephen Garisto, a minister from northern York County, told the *Harrisburg Patriot-News* that he was disgusted the protesters were not allowed into the park. In response, Grabauskas argued that the "anti-homosexual protesters are welcome to their opinion, but festival participants were not there for confrontations."[31]

Politics entered into the event in 2002, when Democratic gubernatorial candidate Ed Rendell addressed the crowd.[32] By 2003, there were two groundbreaking events for LGBT rights that the central Pennsylvania Pride Festival wanted to celebrate. First was a recent Supreme Court ruling, *Lawrence v. Texas*, which overturned the nation's remaining antisodomy laws. The second was that two Canadian provinces, Ontario and British Columbia, had legalized gay marriages. In addition, Massachusetts was considering a high-court ruling that could make it the first state to legalize gay marriage. In celebration of these events, the Pride Festival decided to hold a commitment ceremony, where fifteen gay couples publicly declared their love in a group wedding on the banks of the majestic, mile-wide Susquehanna River.[33]

Commitment ceremonies continued throughout the following years, as did the beginnings of the PrideFest parade. Crowds by 2007 were numbering more than four thousand people. Dan Stroup, parade chair, said, "Everyone said we were too small of a community to have a parade. We showed them wrong." The parade, which started as a one-person operation, had blossomed into a full-blown organization. Stroup added a much-needed staff and a corporate sponsor, Sovereign Bank (now Santander Bank). The staff doubled parade fundraising over the previous year and brought in more than twenty-six organizations to march.[34]

Fig. 76 Pin by Equality Pennsylvania, advocating marriage equality in Pennsylvania. Photo: Sue Blosser. Courtesy of the LGBT Center of Central PA History Project, Archives and Special Collections, Dickinson College, Carlisle, Pennsylvania.

By 2010, the event spanned an entire weekend. The PrideFest Unity parade kicked off the event and preceded the usual festivities. In addition, the Pride Festival was tackling some of the major LBGT equality issues, such as the military-service policy for gays and lesbians. The day concluded with an interfaith service at the Metropolitan Community Church of the Spirit on Sunday. "The gay community here gets bigger every year as new people move in and gay-oriented people come out of the closet," remarked Governor Rendell. "The gay community here has always been strong." He added, "The protesters will be [at the parade] telling us we're all horrible perverts and we're all going to burn in hell. Of course, I've already been told that many times, so maybe I'll triple burn."[35] One of the biggest signs that the PrideFest had grown was in the number of corporate sponsors the event had attracted. The Hershey Company, Home Depot, Hilton Harrisburg, and Four Points Sheraton were among the regional sponsors, along with the lead sponsor, Highmark Blue Shield, all supporting the LGBT community in central Pennsylvania.

In 2013, the festival celebrated the Supreme Court's decision striking down the Defense of Marriage Act, clearing the way for federal recognition of same-sex marriage. Brad Martin, president of the board of directors of the festival, commented, "We have a lot to fight. All we want is equality. We want to be equal to everybody else." Martin estimated that 4,500 people had come through the festival's gates that year. He attributed the good turnout to mild weather and a collectively charged passion people had felt with the current events involving LGBT issues.[36]

Central Pennsylvania's Pride Festival has become an all-encompassing, inclusive, unifying, and affirming event. It was never a highly political or protest-driven event. Instead, it was infused with a commitment to coming out and celebrating the LGBT community. A sense of pride and empowerment flowed through the crowd each year. No longer gathering in secret, shy of media coverage, the LGBT community proudly proclaimed, "We are just like you."

Celebrations Begin in Lancaster

In February 2007, the Rainbow Rose Community, a newly formed nonprofit service group, announced plans to hold the first Lancaster Pride Arts and Entertainment Festival in June. After researching what other cities had achieved to develop a Pride Festival, Barry Russell, founder of the Rainbow Rose Community, recruited a steering committee and started the process of getting a city permit for the event. According to Russell, the organization had an unofficial permit to close Queen Street at Binns Park in Lancaster to hold the festival.[37]

The planning committee was seeking artists, craftspeople, and vendors as well as entertainers to fill both stages at Lancaster Square and at Binns Park. "We like the entertainment to include everything from poetry to musical and dance groups—a good representation of the community," said Russell. Lancaster's mayor was supportive and had no problem with the festival. "If they want to celebrate themselves, it's fine with me," he said. "The city is a good place to do it. They have a right to rent public facilities."[38]

In May, however, the festival was forced to change venues when the City of Lancaster denied the organizers' application for Binns Park. The city claimed it had not received a complete application and necessary fees in time for the application deadline. Russell and his committee immediately started negotiating with Millersville University of Pennsylvania to use its Student Memorial Center and the adjacent quad area.[39]

Within less than a month, these plans fell apart. The university released the following statement: "A formal agreement to host the festival was never signed. In addition, there is not sufficient time to organize all the necessary components (safety and security, technical support, generators, etc.) to have a successful festival. Unfortunately, given the potential enormity of such an event, it is unlikely that an event of this size could be accommodated on campus, even with adequate notification." Barry Russell responded, "This is what happened here. We're brand new. We all worked our hardest, but the

Fig. 77 Booths at the Lancaster Pride Arts and Entertainment Festival. Courtesy of the LGBT Center of Central PA History Project, Archives and Special Collections, Dickinson College, Carlisle, Pennsylvania.

Fig. 78 Entertainment tent at the Lancaster Pride Arts and Entertainment Festival. Courtesy of the LGBT Center of Central PA History Project, Archives and Special Collections, Dickinson College, Carlisle, Pennsylvania.

parade won't happen this year. I apologize for any extra work we've caused the university and the thousands of people who expected to attend the parade."[40] Russell promised they were going to learn from their mistakes, regroup, and have a successful event the following year.

Lancaster Pride became a reality in 2008, when more than 2,500 people gathered in Buchanan Park to celebrate. According to the *Intelligencer Journal*, "Under picture-perfect, sunny skies, the festival had all the elements of a midsummer's carnival in Lancaster County: cotton candy, funnel cakes, stained glass, artsy t-shirts, and handmade jewelry vendors. Along with drag shows, there was face painting for children and G-rated musical entertainment."[41]

Protesters appeared, too, numbering approximately a half dozen, representing Repent America and Life and Liberty Ministries. They held up placards quoting biblical verses and messages about abomination, damnation, and salvation. Michael Marcavage, director of Repent America, said his group had come to warn festivalgoers of the judgment that is to come.[42] The protesters, however, never went inside the festival, refusing to pay the five-dollar admission fee. Lancaster Pride continued on successfully at Buchanan Park through 2015. In 2016, the festival moved to Binns Park, on North Queen Street, the site where, ironically, the original event had been planned all along.

Fig. 79 Program brochure for the Lancaster Pride Festival in 2011. Courtesy of the LGBT Center of Central PA History Project, Archives and Special Collections, Dickinson College, Carlisle, Pennsylvania.

Celebrating in York

In 2015, when same-sex marriage became legal in all fifty states, a group of LGBT activists in York decided to celebrate. To mark the historic milestone, the first York Equality Fest was held, with more than one thousand people attending to celebrate. By 2017, the York Equality Fest had grown both in size and purpose. Held in Penn Park in downtown York, Equality Fest had become a daylong, family-friendly community, arts, and cultural celebration.

The festival was free of charge and open to the public. The event featured multiple stages with speakers, music, dance, theater, poetry, and spoken word and performance art as well as live visual art. There were strolling performers and a fully interactive children's area with games, workshops, and activities. Sixty retail, informational, food, and organizational vendors lined the park with their tables and booths.

The York Equality Fest's celebration and mission was in vivid contrast with other Pride events. The festival honored multiple marginalized communities and showcased the contributions of LGBT individuals, women, immigrants, students, young people, seniors, and the differently abled, highlighting York's community efforts to strive for opportunity, safety, and hope for all of its residents.[43]

According to Carla Christopher, president and founder of York Equality Fest, the festival evolved into more than a one-time event and had become a catalyst that anchored an entire year of community engagement. "Part of raising awareness is creating space for conversation." Christopher states, "We are trying to make it okay to ask the questions to get those answers. Free speech applies to everyone, not just the people who say what you want to hear. Everyone who comes to Equality Fest is asked to be respectful of others. Equality Fest is all about encouraging people to engage and interact on that day. Everyone is welcomed. You can come and whatever your flag is, let it fly."[44]

The LGBT community, since the 1969 Stonewall riots, celebrates its pride annually across the nation and the world. Pride parades and celebrations in large cities have changed over the years, from revelers to protesters to politicians in support of LGBT equality and equal rights. In all cities it is a celebration of coming out and acceptance. Central Pennsylvania found its own voice in its Pride celebrations—different and distinct from those seen in large metropolitan areas, but just as powerful.

CHAPTER 8

Fruition

For many Americans, the new millennium ushered in a world of uncertainty, fear, and conflict. The events of September 11, 2001, seemed to define a new epoch. The biggest terrorist attack on the United States was followed by two lengthy and intractable wars in Afghanistan and Iraq. In 2008, the economy experienced its most severe meltdown since the Great Depression, and, despite the eventual recovery, many Americans remained uneasy. Hotly contested and controversial presidential elections in 2000 and 2016 tested democratic institutions and yielded deep and contentious divides among the nation's people and its leaders. For the LGBTQ community, however, the new era brought some dramatic breakthroughs. The restrictive "Don't Ask, Don't Tell" policy, which had been in effect since 1994, was scrapped in 2010, allowing LGBTQ people to serve openly in the military.[1]

In June 2013, the 1996 Defense of Marriage Act was overturned by the Supreme Court in *United States v. Windsor*. The court ruled that the act's denial of federal recognition of same-sex marriage violated the due process clause of the Fifth Amendment. This case had a profound effect on Pennsylvania, when US District Court judge John E. Jones ruled in 2014 that the state's 1996 ban on same-sex marriage was unconstitutional. Pennsylvania became the nineteenth state to legalize same-sex marriage and the last state in the Northeast to do so.[2] In June 2015, the Supreme Court ruled in *Obergefell v. Hodges* that same-sex couples had a right to marry, based on the due process clause in the Fifth Amendment and the equal protection clause of the Fourteenth Amendment. Marriage equality was now the law of the land.

By 2018, more than seven hundred LGBTQ political candidates had been elected to office in forty-six states. With 2 governors, 10 members of Congress, 34 mayors, and 106 judges, LGBTQ citizens are taking an active role in state and local government. In Pennsylvania there are currently 36 LGBTQ citizens holding elected positions, including 4 mayors and 2 state legislators. In central Pennsylvania—Harrisburg, West Reading, Susquehanna Township, and Millersburg Borough—7 LGBTQ people are serving in positions as city treasurer, tax collector, and city council members.[3]

While there have been major gains for the LGBTQ community nationally, in Pennsylvania, as of 2018, only 36 percent of cities and towns had passed antidiscrimination legislation, with the vast majority of the state's LGBTQ residents in towns and cities living without prohibitions against discrimination. Since the passage of antidiscrimination ordinances in Harrisburg, York, and Lancaster, no other city or town in central Pennsylvania had passed an antidiscrimination ordinance. It would be another six years before State College would pass such an ordinance in 2007, followed by Reading in 2009, Susquehanna Township in 2011, Carlisle in 2016, and Camp Hill in 2017. The rest of the commonwealth remains unprotected, leaving discrimination and harassment based on sexual orientation and gender identity a constant threat. The threat of discrimination still lingers in central Pennsylvania, whether on campuses, in workplaces, or in the communities where LGBTQ people reside.[4] Campus protections, while more prevalent in the early 2000s than in earlier decades, did not prevent discrimination from occurring, as was evident in a case that made the national news in 2005 at Penn State University.

Jennifer Harris

In December 2005, Penn State student athlete Jennifer Harris filed a lawsuit against Penn State University; her basketball coach, Maureen "Rene" Portland; and Penn State's athletic director, Timothy Curley, claiming race and sex discrimination.[5] Penn State's policy, which prohibits discrimination and harassment on the basis of race, sexual orientation, and other personal characteristics, had existed for more than a decade.[6] The events surrounding the lawsuit brought to light cracks in the system and raised tensions both at the university and in the surrounding community.

Portland, the longtime women's basketball coach at the university, had amassed a winning record of more than six hundred wins and taken her team to twenty-one National Collegiate Athletic Association (NCAA) tournaments.[7] But she also expressed open hostility toward lesbians. In a 1986 interview with the *Chicago Sun-Times*, Portland said one of the first things she brought up during any recruiting visit with a prospective player and her parents was lesbian activity. "I will not have it in my program. I bring it up and the kids are so relieved and the parents are so relieved. But they would probably go without asking the question otherwise, which is really dumb."[8] Though Penn State adopted a nondiscrimination policy in 1991, this culture of bigotry lived on under Portland's tenure and was encountered by Jennifer Harris.

Harris played in every game during her first two years on Penn State's women's basketball team. In her sophomore year she started twenty-two out of thirty-four games. She scored a total of 313 points, averaging 10 points a game, with 42 assists, 45 free throws, and 76 rebounds.[9] Then, at the end of her second year, in March 2005, Portland abruptly kicked Harris off the team. The coach claimed that Harris was dismissed for her poor athletic performance, lack of commitment, and bad attitude.[10]

Fig. 80 Jennifer Harris, playing in a women's basketball game for the Penn State Lady Lions against Northwestern, February 20, 2005. "PSU Women B-Ball vs N-Western 02.20.05: Harris, Jennifer," University Photographic Records, 1943–2007 (9825), Pennsylvania State University. Used with permission from the Eberly Family Special Collections Library, Penn State University Libraries, University Park, Pennsylvania.

After her dismissal from the team, Harris fell into a deep depression. She kept asking herself, "Will I ever love basketball or anything else in the same way again? It broke my spirit."[11] Instead of succumbing to dejection, she bounced back and sought help from the National Center for Lesbian Rights (NCLR) later that year. On her behalf, the organization filed a federal lawsuit, claiming racial and sexual discrimination. In her suit, Harris alleged that she was repeatedly asked by Portland if she was a lesbian. Portland also accused Harris of dating another teammate during Harris's first season. Convinced that the teammate was a lesbian, Portland dismissed the player. The following season, Harris says that Portland again accused her of having a lesbian relationship with another player and repeatedly tried to catch the two of them together. Harris says Portland asked the team members to spy on her. According to Harris, Portland told the team that she would "do whatever it took to prove that Jennifer was gay," an allegation that Portland denied.[12]

Portland instructed her team on how to wear their hair and use makeup. Harris was told to "dress in a more feminine style and to stop wearing her hair in corn rows." When Harris refused to do so, Portland would say things like

"That's why they don't let coaches carry guns" and "Break a leg so you can't play and put me out of my misery." It was apparent to Harris by Portland's instructions—"to be more feminine and stop wearing baggy clothes and cornrows"—that she did not comport with Portland's feminine, heterosexual ideal of her players. Portland's behavior could be interpreted as both racist and discriminatory.[13]

Harris's complaint alleged that Portland was racist in how she dealt with players she recruited, terminated, and kept on the team. The disparities were pronounced: "Portland recruited a majority of White players—60% of the players recruited from 1997 to 2005 were White—yet over that same time period, African American players constituted the majority (60%) of the players who were terminated or quit. Portland terminated all the African American players who were eligible to return for the 2005–2006 season—Harris, Amber Bland, and Lisa Etienne—and retained all three of the White players who were eligible to return."[14]

The NCLR asserted that Portland had harassed players, including Harris, throughout her coaching career at Penn State. "What Rene Portland is doing is not only against university policy, but it is also illegal," said Karen Doering, Harris's attorney. "Penn State has a policy on harassment and discrimination, Policy AD42, issued in 1991." The policy included race and sexual orientation.[15]

Penn State conducted a six-month internal investigation as a result of Harris's lawsuit. Its findings vindicated Harris's allegations. Penn State found that Rene Portland had in fact discriminated against Jennifer Harris on the basis of sexual orientation, violating the university's antidiscrimination policy. Portland was fined $10,000. She was warned that if she violated Penn State's antidiscrimination policy again, she would be dismissed. The investigation also found, with respect to race and sexual orientation, Portland had created a "hostile, intimidating, and offensive environment."[16] In addition to the fine, Portland was ordered to attend diversity training, and a reprimand was issued and placed in Portland's official personnel file. At a press conference following the announcement of Penn State's decision, Portland expressed doubts about the investigation and its results but vowed to return to the basketball court the following season to lead the Lady Lions.[17]

Reactions among students and faculty were mixed. Some called for Portland's resignation, while others claimed Portland acted within her First Amendment rights.[18] An undisclosed settlement was reached in February 2007. In March, however, Portland suddenly resigned as Penn State's head basketball coach without offering an explanation. In a press release Portland said that she was "appreciative of the opportunity to coach at Penn State" and "proud of what we have been able to accomplish." Athletic director Timothy Curley stated that it was "Rene's decision," adding, "I did not try to change her mind." According to the *Daily Collegian*, "because the terms of the settlement are confidential, Curley could not comment on whether or not Portland's resignation was a stipulation of the lawsuit's agreement." Karen Doering remarked, "As far as I know this has nothing to do with the lawsuit. Portland's status as an employee at Penn State is between her and the university."[19]

Local and national gay rights activists applauded Portland's resignation. The gay rights student group SpeakOut issued the following statement: "For nearly three decades, Coach Portland has had a documented history of discrimination and prejudice toward lesbian, gay, bisexual, and transgender athletes. Her resignation is just one of many steps that need to occur at Penn State to improve campus climate issues both within and outside the athletic department."[20] After the settlement, Jennifer Harris continued her college basketball career at James Madison University. Harris does not consider herself a hero or an activist: "I hear people say I did a great thing, that I am a hero. I don't feel that. It was a horrible situation that I don't want anyone to go through. It was humiliating. It was painful. I want as many people to avoid that as possible."[21]

Penn State has come a long way since its efforts in 1971 to prevent the Homophiles of Penn State (HOPS), the gay student organization, from obtaining its charter to operate as a student organization on campus, and even since it faced the embarrassment of Rene Portland's homophobic views and actions in 2005. The journey toward LGBTQ equality has been slow, but today a Lesbian, Gay, Bisexual, Transgender, Queer and Ally (LGBTQA) Student Resource Center on campus sponsors a wide range of programs for Penn State's students and faculty. It is operated by a professional full-time staff and several students. Penn State also has a Commission of LGBTQ Equality and an advisory group that makes policy recommendations to improve campus life for LGBTQ students and faculty. In 2017 Penn State received a "five out of five stars" ranking from Campus Pride, a national nonprofit organization of LGBTQ groups and leaders, and is on the list of the top twenty-five LGBTQ-friendly colleges and universities in the country.[22]

The Transgender Community Comes Out

One group that has sustained much discrimination, even from within the LGBTQ community at large, and continues to face hardship is the transgender community. Before the early 1990s, transgender persons were often referred to as cross-dressers, transvestites, or transsexuals, terms that conflated gender and sex. Support groups were rare and hidden, as was the community itself. Deciding to transition to their true gender identity often resulted in the loss of family, job, friends, and possibly even home. They endured harassment and discrimination. It was not until 1997 that the transgender and bisexual movements had gained significant attention and demanded inclusion in the gay and lesbian movement. The National Gay and Lesbian Task Force revised its mission statement to include the transgender community. The 2000 March on Washington was titled the Millennium March on Washington for Lesbian, Gay, Bisexual, and Transgender Equality. The acronym LGBT officially came into existence, and transgender people became recognized as part of the lesbian, gay, and bisexual community.[23]

In 1987, the International Foundation for Gender Education (IFGE) was founded in Waltham, Massachusetts, and began publishing a monthly magazine, *Tapestry*, which contained listings of support groups available in various cities throughout the country. *Tapestry*, although not pornographic, was sold only in gay bookstores, the only place where transgender people could find any information in the 1980s.[24] In Pennsylvania, the Renaissance Education Association was founded as a statewide organization. Renaissance was a nonpolitical, educational, social-support organization founded and designed to educate and support persons regarding transgender issues, sexual orientation, sexual identity, or gender identity. The group did this through a variety of educational programs, support groups, and resources for transgender community care providers, as well as personal and recreational resources for anyone who identified as transgender and persons who were close to them.[25] By the late 1980s, they had chapters not only in Philadelphia but also in the Lehigh Valley in Trexlertown, southeastern Pennsylvania in Mountville, and the Lower Susquehanna Valley in Harrisburg.

With the dawn of the new century, the transgender community had begun to come out from the shadows and gain in visibility and acceptance. They began to form support groups and political organizations. In 2001 the Transgender Foundation of America was formed; in 2003, the Transgender Veterans Association was created, and central Pennsylvania native Mara Keisling founded the National Center for Transgender Equality. These organizations fought for the rights of trans people and countered the discriminatory backlash that arose as trans visibility increased.

In 2003 Gov. Ed Rendell of Pennsylvania signed an executive order extending nondiscrimination rights and protections to transgender people working in state government.[26] On a national scale, transgender service members were finally permitted to serve openly in the military starting in 2016, a policy that the Trump administration has since reversed.[27] In Pennsylvania in July 2018 the Third District Court of Appeals rejected the antitransgender arguments in *Doe v. Boyertown*, allowing transgender students to use the bathrooms and locker rooms according to their gender identification. In May 2019 the Supreme Court declined to review the case.[28]

In central Pennsylvania, a dynamic group of people formed TransCentralPA in 2006. Their story reflects how they helped countless other transgender people locally and nationally. In 2009, the group launched the Keystone Conference, which offered a series of workshops and seminars dealing with issues facing the trans community and would soon draw more than eight hundred people annually.

The TransCentralPA Story

In 2003, Jeanine Ruhsam was seeking resources for transgender people. Born in 1954, she began identifying as a girl from a young age. But conforming was necessary for survival, so she grew to adulthood as a man—attending college, becoming a jockey and horse trainer, and eventually designing and building homes. She was living in Washington, DC, and attending meetings of the Transgender Education Association (TGEA) when fellow group members suggested that she visit a meeting of Renaissance in Harrisburg. She started attending meetings regularly and soon after began the process of transitioning. By 2006 she was elected to lead the group.[29] Before long, Ruhsam wanted to make some changes, and with a hands-up vote the group decided almost unanimously (only two in attendance dissented) to leave the Renaissance Organization and rebrand to become their own organization. Founded in Philadelphia in the 1980s, Renaissance had expanded to a number of chapters by the early 2000s. Renaissance Lower Susquehanna Valley had the largest membership. Ruhsam remembers, "[We] were paying dues regularly to Renaissance in Philly for the privilege of running our group down in Harrisburg, and we had no support from them. They just wanted our money. And then they decided we couldn't do any sort of outreach unless they trained us. And at this time, we were doing good stuff. So the group decided, 'You know what? Let's go out on our own.' So we did. And I coined the name [TransCentralPA]."

Fig. 81 Jeanine Ruhsam, founder of TransCentralPA, speaking at a Fall Achievement Benefit fundraiser for the LGBT Center of Central PA. Photo: Dennis Martin, Posh Studio.

In the beginning, the group was focused mainly on support. The group's monthly meetings were held at the Metropolitan Community Church of the Spirit in Harrisburg. Ruhsam explains, "We recognized early on the real foundation of the monthly meeting was all about support for trans and gender non-conforming people in central Pennsylvania. And of course [at] our meetings, from the earliest times, we had people from Scranton, and from north of State College, and all over the state. [They] would drive down once a month to come to our meetings, because rural Pennsylvania's just not a place you get that kind of support. We would have full-time, fully transitioned people coming down just to be with their own kind, and we'd have people that would identify as cross-dressers but come down just to be able to have a chance to express the gender that gave them comfort."

Ruhsam and fellow member Kristy Snow came up with the idea to begin socializing outside of the closeted church meeting room. The decision was made to go out for dinner, before the meetings, for a "chance to be out in the public." As Ruhsam describes it, the public would see "trans people that aren't closeted people that feel guilty about doing what they're doing. Realizing that most of the public at the time figured that . . . all [trans people] were some kind of drag queens, we just had this really poor public brand. And so I said, 'What not?'"

That began a series of public forays for TransCentralPA. Before long there were fifteen to twenty trans women and men attending these dinners. They developed standards and guidelines for the dinners. As part of TransCentralPA's strategic rebranding process, dress codes and rules of behavior were established in order to go out in public. By 2008, members of the organization were marching in the Pride parade in Harrisburg and hosting informational booths at the Pride festivals in Harrisburg and Lancaster. Increased public exposure led TransCentralPA to their next phase of growth, advocacy, and education.

The support group meetings were essential in helping trans people deal with issues of coming out, sharing identity in the workplace, maintaining relationships, and dealing with family. According to Ruhsam, "These were the [problems] of being trans and coming out. What do you do about it? These are the necessities of having a support group meetings, to hold each other's heads above water and support those that needed support and try to keep people from literally jumping off the bridge because all their options had run out and their lives had been destroyed." Because these issues were so paramount, in 2009, Ruhsam and Snow decided that the best way to further address these needs would be to hold a conference that would reach the larger trans community. The idea of the Keystone Conference was born.

In the first year, it was up to Ruhsam and Snow to fund the inaugural conference. They both signed personal guarantees and used their own credit cards to finance the conference. As Ruhsam remembers, "The easy part is having an idea and putting together a few speakers and a few workshops. . . . Then you have to find the location for it." In this case, the Sheraton Hotel in Harrisburg was chosen. "In case we couldn't raise enough money, we were still liable for renting this space and paying for meals. . . . We asked each of the members of TransCentralPA to volunteer to help run [the conference] and to do so with enthusiasm and happiness. And they did." It was a big success.

The inaugural conference had workshops for couples, parents, and children of trans people. "No other trans conference in America at that point had had workshops that were for spouses and couples. Because, historically, if . . . the husband came out as trans, that resulted in divorce." Ruhsam adds, "We knew this from all the various support group meetings. One of the big questions will be, 'Oh my God, I can't come out to my wife because it will be the end, we'll get divorced. And then what happens to the kids?'" Trans men were equally affected. "They had typically been in a relationship with a woman, and they would both identify as lesbians. . . . The trans men would identify as [trans] and start moving towards transition, and that would be the end of the relationship." The conference brought in trained counselors to the workshop discussions.

Over time, in addition to family and youth workshops, the conference offered workshops in continuing education with professional counselors, marriage therapists, and social workers. Seminars and workshops were offered on a wide variety of topics including medical surgery, coming out, beauty and image, religion, avoiding confrontation, trans rights, and explaining transgender and transitioning to children.

TransCentralPA members Gretchen Little and Joanne Carroll were also involved that first year, and they have seen the conference grow over the years. As Little remembers,

> I really got to appreciate the work [TransCentralPA was] doing, and so I ended up actually being an officer for a couple of years. I was involved as an officer when we made the initial decision to start doing the Keystone Conference, which has just blossomed into one of the major gender conferences worldwide now. We were on a shoestring budget the first year, and we figured that we were either going to bankrupt ourselves putting on Keystone or it was going to work, and it did. . . . The first year we had, like, 125 or 150 attendees. Now we're up in the 600–700 range.

She adds that many medical professionals—surgeons, doctors, therapists—and others have helped underwrite the conference. Little also spearheaded the effort to obtain 501(c)(3) tax-exempt status for TransCentralPA, which has continued to pay dividends for the organization. "We are now able to accept donations on a tax-free basis, and, with organizing something like the Keystone Conference, [it has become] very helpful."[30]

Joanne Carroll, who took over as president of TransCentralPA in 2015, says, "We now have a website that supports the conference. We have had over sixty thousand hits from 140 different countries, including places like Iraq and some of the places you wouldn't suspect. Communist China is the fourth heaviest hit we've had. So, I would tell you we're international in scope. In 2016, we had all fifty states represented, people from Canada, and twelve foreign countries. In prior years we had as many as 130 apply for workshops and only approved 70 because of [space limitations]."[31]

With attendance at the five-day conference now approaching eight hundred by the 2019 conference, the evening dinners in Harrisburg also began to grow. According to Ruhsam, "We've gotten to the point that it's not unusual . . . to see two hundred some trans people in downtown Harrisburg. To increase the visibility of trans people. So obviously, the more the public sees them, the more used they get to trans people, the more they go, 'So what?'" At one of the dinners in 2009, Gov. Ed Rendell was in the same restaurant. He chatted for a few moments with the conference attendees. "We [took] a bunch of pictures with him, and that was kind of fun. But that was part of the outreach [TransCentralPA was doing]."[32]

Over time, TransCentralPA also became involved in the legislative arena. In 2010, Ted Martin, president of Equality Pennsylvania, asked Jeanine to help with a recent case involving one of the Dauphin County judges and the Pennsylvania Department of Transportation. The judge had refused to allow a male-to-female transgender person to change her name on her driver's license and thereby obtain a state-issued photo ID. The judge forbade the change unless the person could provide proof that they had gone through gender-confirmation surgery, or "sex-reassignment surgery" (SRS), as it was known then.

Fig. 82 "Meet Me at Keystone" pin, from the Keystone Conference of TransCentralPA. Photo: Sue Blosser. Courtesy of the LGBT Center of Central PA History Project, Archives and Special Collections, Dickinson College, Carlisle, Pennsylvania.

"That was really huge," Ruhsam recalls. "A lot of people couldn't afford to have surgery, or didn't want to for health reasons, or didn't want to [simply] because they didn't want to. And so, of course, what that meant was if you're a full-time, fully transitioned trans person, man or woman, that you'd have an ID stating the opposite. And this is something that came up over all the years, [in] every single one of our support group meetings. Invariably, somebody would be telling a story of how they got outed at work and lost their job, or, at a minimum, suffered abuse from their fellow employees for being outed as not what they appeared to be." TransCentralPA and Equality Pennsylvania helped to appeal the Dauphin County case and won. The court overturned the judge's decision and ruled that anyone would be allowed to pick the name of their choosing, unless they were trying to avoid criminal behavior or paying their debts.[33]

TransCentralPA and Equality Pennsylvania continued their partnership in lobbying the state legislature in the ongoing effort to pass House and Senate Bill 300. The legislation is a fully inclusive nondiscrimination bill, including gender identity, for the entire commonwealth. The legislature has yet to pass the bill as of 2019, leaving 64 percent of the commonwealth's LGBT citizens unprotected. The 36 percent of the population that is protected live in cities and towns (mainly Philadelphia and Pittsburgh and their surrounding suburbs, along with Harrisburg, York, Lancaster, Scranton, Allentown, and others) that have passed ordinances on their own to protect the LGBT population.[34]

Under the leadership of Joanne Carroll, who took over after Jeanine Ruhsam left to obtain her PhD and pursue a career in academia, TransCentralPA has continued to enhance its educational and advocacy programs. TransCentralPA participates with the Widener Law Diversity Forum in Harrisburg, discussing barriers faced by trans people in employment and how employers can eliminate biases. They are also working with the Pennsylvania Department of Corrections to help set up a support system for 150 trans-identified inmates. In addition, they provide educational support programs and groups for the Geisinger Health System in Danville, as well as the Pennsylvania Department of Health.[35] "The group has really stepped up and become an important, vital part of the greater efforts, and I think that's great," Gretchen Little commented. "I think that the community sees us more clearly and respects and seeks out our viewpoints. The fact that we have grown the Keystone Conference from sort of a regional niche two-day conference to one of the . . . major heavy-hitter conferences in the world in five or six years is a big deal."[36]

There is still work to be done, Little emphasizes. The first issue to tackle would be to pass a statewide law banning discrimination, including gender identity. "I hear a lot of legislators often say, 'Well, we don't want another protected class.' Yeah, but if you're not so much creating a protected class as you are preventing wholesale discrimination . . . that's by far the largest and most important objective that I see right now."[37]

The second priority for Little is having certain treatments covered under standard medical insurance. "Presentation issues are huge," she says.

> I'm still, quite honestly, wrapping my head around the treatments that are available to trans youth now. You know, I would be a very differently presenting person had I been able to be involved in some of those treatments when I was in my teens. . . . From that perspective, making sure that treatments are covered under standard health insurance policies is a really important thing. If this level

of medical intervention is going to be a part of the treatment protocol, then it's indefensible to only allow it for people who can afford it. It's like, sorry, *you* get to be yourself, [but] not you.[38]

The work that Renaissance and TransCentralPA and its Keystone Conferences have done has been remarkable. In reflecting back on her journey, Ruhsam commented,

> I've managed to get through this thing alive. And I've gotten strong because of it. . . . I showed up at those support group meetings and went, "Oh my God, these poor people, they're suffering horribly. And we've got to help them. We have to stabilize them. It's going to take a long time to change the public because that's what really needs to happen, but in the meantime, what do we do about both of those things?" . . . So that was why I got involved. . . .
>
> And how did I benefit from that? What did I seek out of it? You know, just that incredible sense of satisfaction that you are doing some good, even if it isn't that obvious. [After] some of the meetings, it was obvious because people would come up to you and say, "Boy, that last meeting really helped. I got through a whole month, and I'm here again. And I feel good about being here." . . . It's like Kristy and I said after the first Keystone Conference concluded [and after each one]: "Well, that was a lot of work. We took a lot of risk on. But the big question is, Did we do good? If it does good, we'll do one next year." . . . And then we started hearing from people, "It changed my life." Then Kristy and I would look at each other and say, "[We've] got to keep doing these Keystone Conferences." You know? We've got to keep doing this.[39]

Sadly, Jeanine Ruhsam passed away on March 13, 2019. An avid skier, she was downhill skiing in Vermont when she suddenly collapsed. Her aorta had burst. Ruhsam left a legacy of strength, courage, and perseverance. Her death was mourned by hundreds, and at the 2019 Keystone Conference she was honored and remembered.

The work of TransCentralPA continues. With more than two hundred members and six thousand on its mailing list, the monthly support meetings now tend to number between forty to sixty trans people. Their mission is focused, says Joanne Carroll. "We are committed to providing care and support for transgender-identified persons, their families, their friends, and allies. We provide advocacy on behalf of the community and conduct educational programming for businesses, schools, and government."[40]

TransCentralPA and its Keystone Conferences have not only transformed countless lives but also reshaped public opinion about trans people in central Pennsylvania. The organization has brought about the emergence of a dynamic, energized, and multigenerational transgender community. It succeeded in bringing together as many as eight hundred transgender people and supporters from all over the world to attend TransCentralPA's annual Keystone Conference in 2019. This increasing visibility has been further magnified by having two of its former members on the national stage. Mara Keisling founded and became the first executive director of the National Center for Transgender Equality, and Dr. Rachel Levine, also a former member, was appointed as physician general of Pennsylvania. Levine was asked by Gov. Tom Wolf to serve as physician general the day before his inauguration. She had to be confirmed by an overwhelmingly conservative state senate. As Levine remembers, "I had the pleasure of going to meet all of the state senators, which was a learning experience for me. . . . I think it was a learning experience to them, to have an openly transgender woman come to their chambers and talk about public health. One of the things I'm most proud of is that I was unanimously confirmed by the Pennsylvania state senate." At first, all the press coverage was about having a transgender physician general. "That's no longer included in every article. I'm just Dr. Rachel Levine, physician general of Pennsylvania, who is advocating about health, prevention of overdoses, or other things."[41] Both of these accomplished leaders have not only become spokespeople for transgender civil rights but also served as visible role models for transgender youth.

Even with all the progress and visibility the trans community has experienced, major challenges remain. Trans people face high levels of physical and

Fig. 83 Louie Marven and Dr. Rachel Levine, attending a reception for an LGBT history exhibit in the State Museum of Pennsylvania. Photo: Andrea Glass. Courtesy of the LGBT Center of Central PA History Project, Archives and Special Collections, Dickinson College, Carlisle, Pennsylvania.

sexual violence. More than one in four trans people have faced a bias-driven assault, and the rate is higher for trans women and trans people of color. In 2015 the National Center for Transgender Equality conducted a survey of more than twenty-eight thousand people in the transgender and nonbinary community. The survey found that 26 percent had lost jobs due to bias, 50 percent had been harassed on the job, and 20 percent had been evicted or denied housing. As the National Center for Transgender Equality states, "The passage of clear non-discrimination laws for gender identity would help protect trans people—but it would not always guarantee fair treatment or end prejudice."[42] The battle continues, and organizations like TransCentralPA and the National Center for Transgender Equality are taking up this fight.

A LGBT Community Center

By the late 1990s, central Pennsylvania had various social and political organizations that had been formed to serve the needs of the LGBT community: the Gay and Lesbian Switchboard of Harrisburg, Common Roads, Harrisburg Gay Men's Chorus, Central Pennsylvania Womyn's Chorus, AIDS Community Alliance, Pink Triangle Coalition, York Area Lambda, and Pennsylvania Justice Campaign (which published an annual voters' guide for candidates supportive of LGBT rights), along with many others. Tish Frederick, an attorney in Harrisburg and a LGBT supporter, knew that many of these organizations were financially

Hershey Lodge and Convention Center
Saturday, November 14, 1998

Fig. 84 Event program from the third annual Fall Achievement Benefit fundraiser, held November 14, 1998, to benefit the LGBT Center of Central PA. Courtesy of the LGBT Center of Central PA History Project, Archives and Special Collections, Dickinson College, Carlisle, Pennsylvania.

strapped. To help remedy this, she, along with a group of volunteers, decided to plan a benefit to support these organizations. The event was a black-tie gala called the Fall Achievement Benefit (FAB), which honored select LGBT persons each year for their contributions to the community. The gala soon became one of the more popular and well-attended events for the LGBT community in central Pennsylvania. The proceeds from the event funded one or more of the established LGBT organizations.

Frederick approached Ben Dunlap, an attorney practicing in Harrisburg, to help her with the FAB galas, with the expectation that he eventually would take over the planning of the event. Dunlap became actively involved and after his fourth year, in 2000, was contacted by Candy Free, a member of the Foundation for Enhancing Communities (TFEC) in Harrisburg (formerly the Greater Harrisburg Foundation), a community-service organization. Free said to Dunlap, "Hey, I heard about this fund-raising you're doing, and we have the opportunity to raise $200,000 for the LGBT community in town through this group called the National Lesbian and Gay Community Funding Partnership [NLGCFP] out of New York."[43] NLGCFP was going to fund only two communities in the country that year. Dunlap was intrigued. "It had to be done through community fund-raising," he recalls. "If we raised $100,000, we got another $100,000 from the National Lesbian and Gay Community Funding Partnership. We had this vehicle to do it, the FAB galas, which was why Candy came to me. So we initiated the process."

Dunlap immediately took on the challenge and asked Marlene Kanuck, Greg King, and Ted Martin, all central Pennsylvania residents and LGBT supporters, to be members of the steering committee to drive the initiative. One of the requirements from the NLGCFP was that participating organizations perform a needs-assessment survey. The steering committee hired TFEC to tackle this task, and it formed the Institute for Cultural Partnerships Fund (ICP) to execute the assessment.

ICP did more than six hundred surveys and focus groups in the eight counties that made up the intended service area: Dauphin, York, Perry, Lebanon, Cumberland, Lancaster, Adams, and Franklin. Dunlap remembers, "Gay and lesbian people made up about 90 percent of those surveyed, straight allies the remainder. We tried to have a mix of people. We got people involved who got into the minority communities; we sought out elders and young people as well."

In 2001, when the final report from the needs assessment was delivered, the overriding theme from all the surveys and groups was the need for a community center. "They all felt that we needed some way to bring together the community," Dunlap recalls. Once the committee saw this overwhelming consensus of opinion, they knew in which direction to head—the establishment of a community center for central Pennsylvania. In conjunction with TFEC, they established a separate fund within the foundation for any monies raised toward the new community center.

Dunlap had prior experience with trying to open a LGBT community center when he lived in Allentown, in Lehigh County. "I was part of an effort there to start a community center. It was done with great intentions, but it was done on a shoestring. We had a space; it was all volunteers, and it fell apart. There were bad feelings all around. There are two things that I learned from that. You can't do just an all-volunteer operation, and you have to have a plan. You can't just come in and wing it. So this was going to be different. We would have a plan and a paid staff."

To help with the planning process, the steering committee convened additional small groups to discuss their activities and seek their input. They solicited people from of all ages and genders. They also tried actively to recruit members from the African American LGBT community, but it was a struggle to engage them. Marlene Kanuck remembers, "There's a stigma in the minority community, particularly in the African American community, to be gay. I believe [that] . . . it's very influenced by their religious beliefs. And I think it's just hard for people. Particularly in an area that's small-townish, to be out in the African American community. . . . It's still a struggle sometimes to get minority people to come out for various activities."

Fig. 85 *Left to right*: David Leas with his husband, Ben Dunlap, and Dr. Eric Selvey, at a Fall Achievement Benefit fundraiser. Courtesy of the LGBT Center of Central PA History Project, Archives and Special Collections, Dickinson College, Carlisle, PA.

To help solve the problem, the committee turned to two prominent African Americans: Dr. Eric Selvey, an optometrist, and Rosemary Brown, a graduate of Howard University and a member of the Greater Harrisburg Foundation. They were able to involve many of their friends in the discussion groups. "We did get enough to have a minority focus group," Ben Dunlap recollects. "We wanted to have a center that would be inclusive, and it would meet the various needs of the LGBT community. We worked very hard to build a rapport and not have them say, 'It's just a bunch of white people and they're not going to listen to us.'"

By 2002, the steering committee had a viable framework in place for programs for the future community center, but now it was time to enlist a board of directors, establish a set of bylaws, and start the fundraising process.

Under the auspices of TFEC, the steering committee members soon started referring to themselves as "the coalition," although it was still not yet a legal 501(c)(3) entity. The next five years were spent raising needed funds. By 2008, the $100,000 goal had been met and the matching grant from the NLGCFP had been received. They had finally formed a board of directors, with Ted Martin, president; David Zwifka, vice president; Elizabeth Mullaugh, secretary; and William J. Wollyung III, treasurer. During that time, the coalition had distributed some of the contributed funds to various LGBT organizations such as the Gay and Lesbian Switchboard of Harrisburg, Harrisburg Gay Men's Chorus, Central Pennsylvania Womyn's Chorus, and Equality Pennsylvania, while continuing to conserve monies for the future community center.

In 2008, the coalition hired its first part-time employee, Louie Marven, a recent graduate of Messiah College (located in Mechanicsburg, Cumberland County), as office manager to begin developing programming. Louie had office space at TFEC, where the coalition would conduct its monthly board meetings. It was at this time that several members of the board of Common Roads approached the coalition and floated the possibility of a merger of the two organizations. Common Roads had been working with LGBT youth in central Pennsylvania since 1993. But Common Roads had started to run into problems of staffing and funding. Board members believed that it was going to be difficult for the organization to continue as a separate, independent entity.

Elizabeth Mullaugh remembers, "One [organization was] not quite an organization yet, and one [was] an established organization that had a track record, doing community work for a long time. I was really excited about that opportunity because we needed our own legal entity to really go out and do something. . . . To tie the development of the center to an organization [Common Roads] that did have a long track record, a good reputation in the community, and had been doing good work just made a tremendous amount of sense to me." Merger talks began, and it was soon decided that the center would become the umbrella organization, with Common Roads functioning as an arm within it. Common Roads would retain its name and all of its programs. The coalition soon became a legal corporate entity, renamed the LGBT Center of Central PA, and Common Roads was a subsidiary of the center.

Marven's part-time role turned into a full-time position. Common Roads' youth coordinator had left, so Marven became youth director and administrator for Common Roads and the LGBT Center. There was initial concern that that the center would swallow up Common Roads, but that soon proved not to be the case. Under Marven's guidance, Common Roads continued to grow in attendance as well as in adult programming. Both groups were meeting at St. Stephen's Episcopal Cathedral in Harrisburg, and it was evident that they were outgrowing the space.

During the following several years, other programs were added. There was a book club that met at the Midtown Scholar Bookstore in Harrisburg, as well as a group for elders and an outdoors group organized for camping and field trips. In 2008, the center helped found and sponsor the first Gay Pride event in Lancaster. Under Marven's leadership and based on previous work by Michelle Simmons, the former director of Common Roads who helped developed the Gay-Straight Alliance (GSA) student clubs in various schools throughout the region, Common Roads dramatically expanded. "I think Michelle's big legacy in Common Roads [was] getting out into schools and developing youth conferences and really developing training to do it internally," Marven recounts. "I think that she really raised the bar, and when I started, there were already folks who knew that we did this training. So I learned how to do that. They were coming to us looking for that education. When people think about Common Roads, they think about weekly meetings, which, of course, is a core program, but there's also technical assistance to GSAs, training to schools, and enabling youth conferences that Michelle started."

By 2011, it had become obvious to the board that the center had outgrown the space in St. Stephen's and needed its own space. There were many discussions on where to locate the center, since it was serving an eight-county region. Board members had learned through the needs assessment that they were dealing with an extremely diverse socioeconomic and geographic community. LGBT people were living not only in the cities of York, Lancaster, and Harrisburg but in rural, remote regions throughout central Pennsylvania—in communities such as unincorporated municipalities, small boroughs, towns, crossroads villages—that were severely conservative.

"It is somewhat of a paradox—to have a community center and to serve a region," Marven contends. "I mean, those are two different things, in some ways. . . . The center isn't operating in a vacuum. It's part of this bigger central Pennsylvania community, and public transportation isn't great. It's not like people are driven to this urban center of Harrisburg, where you get services, and there's more of this colloquial idea of having something in my neighborhood."

While some ardently believed the center should be located in Harrisburg, others worried that having the center there would be detrimental. The board looked at spaces outside of Harrisburg but found they were not centrally located and that people would have a difficult time getting there to access their programs. Once again, they turned back to Harrisburg. They would locate the center in Harrisburg while maintaining programs in York, Lancaster, and Carlisle. They looked at an abandoned church in midtown, a vacant technology center, and various other places, but all were too expensive. Finally, a storefront location was found in midtown Harrisburg at 1306 North Third Street.

Work began in earnest on the new location. Jeanine Ruhsam, who owned an architectural design-and-build business and was the founder of TransCentralPA, spearheaded renovation of the space. Ruhsam and her contacts were able to arrange contracts with electricians and vendors such as Home Depot and others to build out the center. Community members laid the floor and painted the walls. The board instituted a development plan to raise additional funds for the center. In addition to money received from the initial grant from NLGCFP and the annual FAB benefit, they commenced soliciting grants and sponsorships. The Hershey Company and Hershey Entertainment and Resorts Company became steadfast partners.

In the summer of 2012, the LGBT Center of Central PA was ready to open. In July it welcomed visitors with an art exhibit as part of the 3rd in the 'Burg, art gallery open houses held on the third Friday of every month. Thanks to good planning, the center had enough space to enable LGBT artists to display their work and be part of the event. "We found someone to curate the gallery, and so that was an immediate way to invite the public into the space. I thought that was a great way of having the center take off and have some public profile," Mullaugh remembers. Marven adds, "It was about being assertive, that we're part of this community. I think people got that."

Once the center opened, programs skyrocketed. For years, the center had struggled to establish a women's group, but to no avail. But with the new center, Mullaugh recalls, "we had to do it. There were attempts at that, and it never really just took off for whatever reason. Once we [opened the new center's] doors, the first women's group—I think there were 120 women in this room. It was crazy. . . . Where did all of these women all come from?" She adds, "[It was] an incredibly diverse array of women from all over the region. Finally, some racial diversity. . . . It was amazing." From that first group, Shaashawn Dial-Snowden, a young African American woman who was in attendance, eventually became president of the LGBT Center of Central PA's board of directors, serving through 2017.

The women's group ended in 2019, as did the LGBT group for adults, but an innovative program for seniors, "Aging with Pride," was established. In addition to Common Roads, the LGBT book group still meets. The center also developed the LGBT History Project, which collects oral histories and memorabilia of LGBT citizens in central Pennsylvania and archives them in the Dickinson College Archives and Special Collections in Carlisle. The center works in conjunction with TransCentralPA to meet the needs of the transgender community. Many in the Common Roads meetings are transgender and gender nonconforming. Another support group was formed for Queer and Trans People of Color (QTPOC) as part of the center's ongoing mission to meet the needs of the community.

Common Roads began to hold GSA leadership summits in 2009 at Harrisburg Area Community College, with more than one hundred attending. Representatives from GSA organizations would gather for one day to hear from a keynote speaker, attend workshops on relevant topics, and meet other community members. After the center opened, these summits grew to two-day events, one for high schools and one for colleges, on the campus of Dickinson College. Attendance now reaches more than four hundred students over three days. According to Louie Marven, "The event was really developed to bring those groups together, and the 'being together' part is really important. We spent a lot of time making sure we had great workshops, but it's almost secondary to being in the same room as other queer young people, which, in central Pennsylvania, where else would you possibly get that?"

The LGBT Center of Central PA has made important contributions to the community. Elizabeth Mullaugh says, "The challenge and opportunity of having a community center is to know you need to reflect the changes that are happening. Be nimble enough to keep growing." Marlene Kanuck adds, "We wanted programming for all these different groups—elders and all of that—because we wanted to have an alternative to the bars. This was going to be the place you could come and meet and you wouldn't feel like you had to go to the bar if you didn't want to. Sometimes people that didn't want to go to the bars felt that they didn't have any other place to go. . . . We were hoping that this would create that place to go."

Besides giving the LGBT community a place to go, the center has also become a representative of the LGBT community itself. "I think the idea of cultural competency training has been one of the great legacies that the center has laid down," says Mullaugh. "Going out into communities to non-LGBT spaces and just talking to folks . . . pure education about who this community is and how every other community could be more inclusive. That's been tremendously helpful. It was always a great demand from organizations to come give those talks."

Not only has the LGBT Center helped bring the LGBT community together; it has also become a voice. It has helped inform and educate the citizens of central Pennsylvania about LGBT rights and equality. It has had a profound impact on LGBT youth and adults and those in need. As Jeanine Ruhsam comments,

> The biggest difference I noticed as soon as I got involved in the Harrisburg area was how much closer the LGBT community is in Harrisburg than it was back in DC. You know, it's just like once people got over their initial issues, they just went, "Oh, okay. You know, we think we get you people, and that's okay. We like you. We're all together in this." You don't see that in other areas. I mean, I didn't even see lesbian and gay people in DC getting along the way they do in central Pennsylvania. It was great to see the [LGBT Center] grow the way it did and become what it has. . . . Just really good people, very few biases that last, and overall, a good community.[44]

The LGBT Center is truly a symbol of the how far the LGBT community has evolved over time and come to fruition in central Pennsylvania.

Profiles

MJ DOUGHERTY

MJ Dougherty grew up in Williamsport, Lycoming County, in a large Irish Catholic family. As one of six children, MJ describes her parents as "Kennedy Democrats," who simultaneously held liberal views but strong conservative values. In this environment, MJ went through the traditional Catholic rituals of baptism, confirmation, and communion, trying to live the life that was expected of her. In 1980, she married and moved to Harrisburg, where her new husband had recently accepted a job. On the day of her wedding, MJ remembers standing at the back of the Catholic Church, her arm tightly intertwined with her father's, thinking, "What are you doing?" As MJ recounts, "I knew since I was probably about ten years old that I was gay, but I grew up in a large Irish Catholic family. I wanted to make my family happy, and I wanted to do what I thought was the right thing—the traditional thing— and so I did it."[45] MJ knew on her wedding day that the marriage wasn't going to work, but she stayed married for eighteen years, in full cognizance that she was gay the entire time. She finally met a woman, filed for divorce, and moved out.

Before and after her marriage, MJ was intently focused on her career. Prior to moving to Harrisburg, she started as a file clerk for the largest insurance firm in the country, Liberty Mutual Insurance, advancing upward to two different executive positions. When she relocated to Harrisburg, she found employment with the Ohio Casualty Insurance Company and was employed with the company for more than seven years. When she applied for a promotion at a higher level, she was told by her supervisor that the company would not "promote women into those positions." Emotionally devastated by this, MJ sought help by seeking out Gene Veno, then from northwestern Pennsylvania, who later became Harrisburg School District's chief recovery officer. Veno was holding résumé-building classes in Harrisburg. He, according to MJ, was supportive in every way, assuring her that "other people don't define you; you define yourself." With his help and guidance, MJ was able to obtain a position at Marsh and McLennan, a large global insurance brokerage firm. She moved up quickly to become the services manager at the office in Harrisburg, managing a large portfolio of clients, including Bucknell University. MJ's job entailed traveling not only to Philadelphia but to other parts of the country as well, including New York City.

On the evening of September 10, 2001, MJ found herself in New York City having dinner with others from Pennsylvania, Massachusetts, Virginia, Connecticut, New York, and New Jersey for the mid-Atlantic regional meeting of Marsh and McLennan. The meeting was to begin the following morning, September 11, at 9:45 on the ninety-ninth floor of the north tower of the World Trade Center (WTC 1). The meeting had been pushed back from its earlier start time of 8:00 a.m., since it was Election Day in New York and the first day of school in New York and New Jersey. On the morning of September 11, MJ arose around 6:00 a.m. in her hotel room at the Marriott World Trade Center (WTC 3) to begin her day. Her partner, Christy, telephoned MJ around 8:30 a.m. to say good morning and to discuss the progress she was making on the reseeding of their lawn back in Harrisburg. Christy ended the call asking why they had postponed the meeting and adding, "Well, just whatever you do, be careful, and I'll see you tonight." MJ hung up and began to gather her things for the meeting, when suddenly there were two violent explosions. "I felt the building I was in literally rock off of its foundation. It just went sideways." MJ dashed to the window and looked down, where she saw people running away from the tower and enormous chunks of debris crashing down on the streets. At that moment the fire alarm went off in the hotel. People were flooding out of their rooms, into the halls, and out to the stairs. No one knew what was happening. The time was 8:50 a.m., just after the first airplane had hit the north tower.

MJ grabbed her briefcase and rolling suitcase and fled down the nineteen flights of stairs onto the street. When she got to the lobby, there was smoke and burning debris. She made her way out onto Liberty Street, in between the hotel and the south tower (WTC 2). A police officer was standing in the center of the sidewalk looking up, yelling, "Run, run!" At this point, MJ looked up at the north tower. "I had no idea of what had happened. I knew that it was a fire, and I thought in my mind that it must have been a boiler that exploded. I crossed the street, and I started to walk away from the building, and I just remembered looking back and then realizing that whatever happened, it was on my floors. My company had [floors] 93 to 100 in Tower 1 and the first plane went right in at 95. So it went right into my floors."

MJ fled the chaotic scene. There were thousands of people on the street by this point, in various states of confusion. MJ turned and looked up again and, to her horror, started to see people jump out of the windows of the tower. "I watched a couple, a man and a woman, come to the window holding hands and jump together. That was the last time I turned around." MJ kept plodding through the debris and white dust, eventually stumbling on clutter that had fallen from the plane that had sliced through the tower. Approaching the West Side Highway, she came across a terrifying discovery: part of a human torso. That is when she said to herself, "Okay, enough, I've had enough. I can't see any more. I don't want to see any more. I just want to figure out how to get home." In this state of shock, with thousands of people on the streets, MJ started asking anybody who would listen, "How can I get to Pennsylvania?" MJ kept walking, eventually ending up at Battery Park, when she heard the second plane fly over and watched it slice its way into the south tower.

In desperation, MJ finally found a pay telephone, where she was able to reach her office in Harrisburg. She was finally connected to the office manager, Jim, who told her to go to the corporate headquarters in midtown Manhattan. But in the middle of their conversation, the first tower collapsed, and then the phone went dead. In a panic, everyone started to run, including MJ. The only safe haven was the ferry to Staten Island. MJ and hundreds of others pushed and shoved their way onto the boat, and eventually she was on her way to temporary safety. Landing on the island, MJ found her way to the bus station, which took her to the Staten Island Mall. She found her way to the

Staten Island Hotel, which was crowded with throngs of panicked people. MJ made her way to the front desk and asked for a room. She was despondent. There were no rooms available, with more than one hundred people on the waiting list. MJ collapsed in a chair in the lobby, exhausted, when a woman, Rosemary Flick, sensed MJ's dilemma and approached her. She said that she had a room with two double beds and that she would be happy to share it with MJ. They spent the night there "and watched, from where we were, the towers smolder and burn all night. . . . It was literally forty-eight hours with absolutely no sleep."

By the next morning, MJ was able to get through to her partner and her mother, both of whom had been desperate for word, not actually knowing if MJ had survived the attack. They devised a plan. MJ would stay in Staten Island until the next morning, when Rosemary could take MJ to New Jersey, and from there she would be able to eventually rendezvous with her family in Pennsylvania. Upon her return, MJ learned that everyone with whom she dined on the evening of September 10 in New York City had been killed by the first plane that hit the north tower. Marsh and McLennan, MJ's parent company, suffered the tragic loss of 295 of its employees on September 11.

MJ had just been through the most harrowing experience of her life, but upon her return home the pain and suffering escalated. MJ was not out in her office about her sexuality, not to anyone, especially her supervisor. She always considered it a private matter, and, given the conservative views espoused by most of her associates, MJ was fearful of their potential negative reactions. On the day of the attack, MJ's boss was in a rage for not having heard from her. When MJ's partner, Christy, heard the news on the radio about the towers, she called the office and reached MJ's supervisor. She asked him if he had any word from MJ. She explained that she was trying to determine where MJ was and if she was all right. He asked who she was, and she told him, "I'm Christy, MJ's partner." He told her that the office hadn't heard from her, and that any information they might have would be given only to family members. He then abruptly hung up. That was the turning point. MJ had been outed, not by any malicious act, but out of love and compassion by her partner. Until that point, MJ had been promoted by the company, eventually becoming vice president. Now, upon her return, unhurt physically but mentally exhausted and emotionally traumatized, MJ was facing a new horror.

Marsh and McLennan was keenly aware of the psychological impact the attack would have not only on the survivors but on the company as a whole. Management offered to make available psychologists and psychiatrists to every office throughout the country to counsel and help heal. In the Harrisburg office, MJ was the only survivor of the attack. Her boss refused the offer for help from the parent company. The company's mantra emphasized "business as usual" and "let's take care of our customers." Everyone was paralyzed by the attack, and everyone who worked for Marsh and McLennan across the country knew that MJ was one of the few survivors from their company of the September 11 tragedy.

MJ sought psychological help, engaging a therapist to work through her problems. She was diagnosed with post-traumatic stress disorder (PTSD). The therapist helped MJ adopt a normal routine, to "put one foot in front of the other," and at work to perform "business as usual." MJ struggled that first year. It was difficult for her to function and to focus. She kept reliving the harrowing experience every day, eventually learning how to cope and adjust. Her relationship with her boss fell apart, and the evidence of that was apparent during her annual performance review in 2002. When he met with MJ, he advised her she was completely ineffective in her job, dragging down colleagues, and therefore no longer in good standing with the company. Because of this, she was not given a raise and not entitled to her bonus. In response, MJ pointed out that the measurements for success were numbers driven and she had met and surpassed each of these metrics—revenue, sales, and new accounts, among others. She argued that his review was not objective, but subjective and biased.

MJ appealed the review through the corporation's chain of command, asking to be put back in good standing. She refuted her boss's criticism by defending her results through a strict analysis based on the generally accepted key ratios and metrics she satisfied or exceeded. Her results proved she was doing her job and therefore made it impossible for her supervisor to claim she was failing to lead or was unsuccessful. The company, however, rejected her appeal.

In her frustration, MJ hired an attorney and filed a lawsuit against her company with the Pennsylvania Human Relations Commission, asking only for reinstatement in good standing, her bonus, and her salary increase. MJ's lawyer believed they had a strong case. At the hearing, only the parties involved were allowed to speak. The human resources department personnel at Marsh and McLennan never interviewed MJ; they only read her complaint. The Human Relations Commission thought MJ needed to prove that she was treated differently from others similarly situated in the office or in offices throughout the region. The only problem was that MJ's job was unique in the region, and no one else held a similar position. Because of that, the commission felt that she did not adequately prove her case. She told her lawyer she realized the underlying reason was because she was gay, and that was why her supervisor had taken this sudden turn. Her lawyer responded that being gay was not a protected class in Pennsylvania; therefore, it would be worthless to pursue that argument. But, during the course of the meeting, her diagnosis of PTSD was brought up. Her supervisor claimed that he had no knowledge of MJ's condition or struggle. The director of the region, however, was at the meeting, hearing in detail MJ's case and the effects of PTSD disorder. Because PTSD falls into the category of a disability, MJ was protected by the Americans with Disability Act (ADA). Unable to argue her discrimination was rooted in her sexuality, MJ and her lawyers instead argued discrimination under the ADA.

The regional director for Marsh and McLennan responded positively. He reversed her supervisor's rating, placed MJ back into good standing, restored her bonus, and gave her a raise. He placed MJ in the Philadelphia office, so as to separate her from her old supervisor. Her career began to thrive again. In reflection, MJ states, "When you are under the effects of PTSD, there is just something about your brain that doesn't quite engage. You are not in a place where you can adequately defend yourself. You have to be able to articulate how it is that you are feeling and why it is that you feel wronged. Then [there was] the whole issue of that fact that I thought he was being prejudiced because I was a lesbian, and it was as simple as that. I knew it. He knew it too. But . . . not being a protected class in Pennsylvania, there is absolutely nothing you can do." Unable to bring it up in the hearing, MJ and her lawyer did the only thing they could do—make the case about PTSD and use the protection offered by the ADA. As MJ concludes, "That is how it was approached, but it was never approached that, yes, she is gay, and that is why he did what he did."

MJ Dougherty came out late in life. She built a solid, successful career and had a wonderful, loving relationship with her partner. MJ was a survivor of the horrific September 11 attacks on the United States and suffered the traumatizing aftermath. When she was unintentionally outed, her supervisor turned on her, seeking to derail her career. MJ fought back, seeking the only protection she had available to her, the ADA. Her sexual orientation was not protected, allowing her to fall prey to a subjective review that could have destroyed her career. MJ had to experience the hell of September 11 and then use her PTSD diagnosis resulting from that horrific experience to battle discrimination.

Mara Keisling was born in Scranton, Lackawanna County, the third oldest of seven children. Her parents moved to Harrisburg when she was three, and her twenty-seven-year-old father, William "Bill" J. Keisling, was appointed assistant to newly elected governor William Warren Scranton. Mara was aware of her gender identity as early as the age of four, when she started wearing her sister's Brownie uniform. "I thought that that would help [my parents] understand that I was really a girl. . . . But my father very nicely said, 'No, you're a boy, you have to be a boy,' and then that was the end of it. I [knew] I couldn't talk about it again. I don't fault my dad for that at all. That was what anybody knew in 1962."[46]

A shy child growing up, Mara later enrolled at Penn State University, which she found to be overwhelming. She transferred to the University of Chicago for her next two years, but then took a year off, when she began working as a pollster in Harrisburg. This led to a job at the Survey Research Center at Penn State–Harrisburg, where she was able to complete her undergraduate degree in history. As Mara remembers, her partner at the time "wanted to go to law school, and I had been working at Penn State, noticing all of these professors who basically were on campus ten to fifteen hours a week and then did whatever consulting they wanted. . . . I thought, 'Well, that would be good to be a college professor.' So my partner and I started looking for a place where she could go to law school in a good program and I could go to grad school." They finally ended up at Harvard.

Even though she was in a relationship, Mara was continually aware of her identity. "When we were moving to Boston, it was getting harder, as I got into adulthood, to outrun the trans thing. But there was still nothing to do except to try to outrun it." Mara and her partner had a son, and she drove up to Boston to find the family a home. While she was in the city, she called the number of a support group she found through *Tapestry* magazine, published by the International Foundation for Gender Education. Mara met with the leader of the support group, and they sat for hours on a snowy day. "It was kind of terrifying, but it was my first real connection with the trans community and a transgender person." Mara would attend support group meetings occasionally during her time in Boston, but she was not yet ready to make any major changes.

After three years in Boston, her partner got a job in Washington, DC, and they moved. Mara completed her graduate thesis and became an adjunct professor at George Mason University. She also took a part-time job representing various state agencies and advertising firms that required her to go to Harrisburg several times a month to advocate on their behalf.

By 1996, Mara and her partner had ended their relationship, and at that point she made a strategic life decision. "I finally had the guts to go up to this Fantasia Fair thing [in Provincetown, Massachusetts]. What was pivotal about that was at the time, I was, among other things, teaching [political science as an adjunct professor]. . . . In Provincetown I met a [trans] 6' 2" tall college professor, and I was that. And that meant, somebody like me could be trans and could transition. And then, I knew I had to do it." During the next two years, Mara thought, "'I got to do this. I can't do this. I got to do this.' I was seeing a gender therapist, talking it through. You have to remember, in the late '90s what we told each other in support groups and on the internet was, 'When you transition you will lose your job, you will lose your family, you could lose your home, you could be bashed, you could lose your health.' And it was really dangerous."

In 1998, Mara decided to attend another conference, called Southern Comfort Transgender Conference, in Atlanta, Georgia. "I went down there, [and] I knew while I was at the conference I would have to present as a woman [and] didn't know how I was going to do that, and I didn't have a name. And on the airplane down, I actually [had] a list of ten names that I was trying to figure out which one I was [going to use]."

The conference had an immediate impact on Mara. She met some amazing trans women there—people such as Holly Boswell, an early activist and writer in the trans movement; Sabrina Marcus, an aeronautical engineer who was fired from the space shuttle program for coming out as trans; and Marissa Richmond, founder of the Tennessee Transgender Political Coalition. According to Mara, "It just radicalized me, [and] I mean that in the political sense. It made me understand that I had to not just transition, but I had to do activism. I had to be a leader in some way."

Mara spent the next two years planning how she was going to survive this and how she was going to afford the expense. She arranged a job through a good friend to continue her work at the advertising agency in Harrisburg. In 2000, Mara moved back to Harrisburg to fully transition and begin her work and involvement in the trans community. She met with her parents to tell them of her plans to transition.

Mara's mother's reaction when she told her was to use her grandmother's words: "Jesus, Mary, and Joseph!" Then her mother started to cry. She said,

"I wish you would have told me when you were little, so I could help." Then Mara told her father: "His first words were something like 'Wow, well what can I do?' or 'How can I help?' or something like that." Mara's parents were truly supportive. According to Mara, "My parents came to me and asked if they could rename me. They said as my parents they had a right and obligation to name me. And they helped me pick the name . . . they basically picked the name. I'm still the only trans person I know like that."

When Mara arrived in Harrisburg, she immediately started attending monthly support group meetings of Renaissance. It was there one night that one of the members told her that he was going to State College to hold a job-fair panel for LGBT students at Penn State, and they were having trouble finding a trans Penn State grad. He asked Mara if she would go, and she agreed. According to Mara, "What's important about that is the person who is putting on the panel was Sue Rankin [associate professor of education at Penn State]. . . . [She] had been working hard, really hard, to get the LGBT center off the ground. . . . And Deb Sieger, who was a social work professor at Kutztown [University of Pennsylvania, in Berks County]." They were involved in convening a statewide meeting for activists in 1996 at Penn State University, in which the Statewide Pennsylvania Rights Coalition [SPARC] was founded. Sue and Deb were running SPARC along with its chairman, Steve Glassman. Steve was a resident of New Oxford, Adams County, who later became the first openly gay chairman of the Pennsylvania Human Relations Commission from 2002 to 2011, under Gov. Ed Rendell. SPARC was working in conjunction with the Center for Civil Rights; both organizations would eventually evolve into another organization called Equality Pennsylvania.

It was through meeting Sue that Mara became involved with SPARC. Soon Mara was actively involved in SPARC's lobbying efforts with the state legislature to pass a hate crimes bill, becoming one of the four primary lobbyists from 1998 through 2001. She and Steve Glassman lobbied the state senate for the bill and met with the Democratic senate minority leader Robert Mellow. They were trying to get gender identity included in the hate crimes bill because it encompassed only sexual orientation. As Mara remembers,

> He said, "No, you'll lose all the Democrats." There were nineteen Democrats and thirty-one Republicans at the time, and he said, "With just sexual orientation we'll get seventeen out of the nineteen Democrats. If we put gender identity in, we lose everybody but [the sponsor]." . . . We [eventually] got it in, and we passed it in the senate with every Democrat and thirteen Republicans. Still, the point of

'Mara, look at the bright side. Five years ago I wouldn't have let you in my office.'"

Mara briefly became the managing director of SPARC, and then she founded another organization, called Gender Rights Pennsylvania. According to Mara, "This was primarily a vehicle, for me, to say that there was a trans group that was lobbying Harrisburg. It's super closely tied with SPARC, but it gave me a title. Unfortunately, when you're doing lobbying and other kinds of governmental advocacy, it really helps if you're not just some person. You need a title." She adds, "At the same time, all over the country, there were fifty or a hundred people who were really trying to get a national movement going. . . . Until 2001, there was not a single attorney in the country whose job was to do trans rights."

At the turn of the century, very few organizations were using the acronym LGBT. The National Gay and Lesbian Task Force and the National Center for Lesbian Rights were referring to the LGBT community, but many organizations were still resisting the *T*, which made lobbying and acknowledgment of the trans community difficult. Mara recalls, "There were a couple of Lobby Days in DC that you only got twenty to thirty legislators, which is amazing. Nobody ever had seen anything like it, and everyone was terrified their picture was going to be used against them."

By 2002, things began to change for Mara. "I passed the point where my activism was getting in the way of my job to the point where my job was getting in the way of my activism. And about that time, we lost our biggest client, which was the Pennsylvania Department of Health [to a rival agency]." At that point, Mara and some others founded the National Center for Transgender Equality (NCTE).

Mara moved to Washington, DC, and opened the offices of NCTE inside the National Gay and Lesbian Task Force, which gave them free office space, copiers, and telephones. Mara funded the center without pay for the first three years. Today it has a staff of twenty people and is funded through grants, individual donors, and corporate sponsorships. With roughly a $2 million budget, NCTE has been able to lobby, educate, and advocate for transgender equality for the past fifteen years.

In 2007, NCTE lobbied for the inclusion of gender identity in the federal Employment Non-Discrimination Act. When the Trump administration announced its ban on transgender military personnel, thirty-six members of the US House of Representatives, along with Mara, conducted a press conference on the steps of the US Capitol, among them Congressman Joseph "Joe" P. Kennedy III (D-MA) and House Minority Leader Nancy Pelosi (D-CA). Mara says, "They're not afraid to be with us anymore." When they hold their Lobby Days now in Washington, instead of 20 to 30 legislators, more than 260 now appear with Mara and her staff.

In looking at the trans community today, Mara observes,

> [It] is changing so much. It's almost ridiculous saying that there's a trans community. The trans community is getting younger; folks are coming out very frequently now at age three, seven, and ten. There's more and more parents involved. In different ways, this isn't just a PFLAG [group saying] "I support my kids." This is much more akin to parents of children with special health-care needs. Parents who realize their kid is at risk if they don't throw their whole lives into it. . . . Our survey of twenty-eight thousand trans people a couple years ago showed that a third of our folks are saying the trans that they are is a nonbinary trans. It's not male or female; it's not transitioning that way. It's transitioning from one of those things to a very personal, individualized gender space, which might be a fluid gender space, or it might be a rigid gender space. But on a spectrum, not either fully male or fully female.

Given the rapidity of the growth of the trans community, the need for advocacy and education for equality is even greater today. The work that Mara and NCTE are doing is essential as well as groundbreaking. As Mara reflects, "I've been so lucky. This movement has gone faster than any other social justice movement in history, and to get to be a part of it is just amazing."

Conclusion

Many LGBTQ people have chosen to move to larger metropolitan areas that provide more anonymity and a wider variety of LGBTQ life, but those who stayed among the Amish farms, majestic Appalachian Mountains, and the smaller cities of the Susquehanna Valley were able to build a LGBTQ community that had most of the elements found in larger cities. They lived in a culturally conservative environment, but they did so by choice. For many of them, this is where they were raised, put down roots, had a family, and built careers. With no laws to protect them, no distinct LGBTQ neighborhoods in which to live, and no centralized space to congregate, they collaborated to find inventive ways to form social networks and organizations, fight successfully for civil rights protections, and build a dynamic community. Each succeeding generation produced advocates and activists who took up the mantle of leadership and worked to overcome the challenges each decade presented.

The LGBTQ community in central Pennsylvania has made major progress in improving its quality of life, and, for most of these residents, it continues to improve. Like elsewhere, the importance of LGBTQ bars in central Pennsylvania continues to diminish as more straight bars, restaurants, coffeehouses, and other social gathering places make LGBTQ patrons feel welcome. More religious denominations and congregations describe themselves as welcoming LGBTQ worshippers, as is evident in the increasing number of congregations that host vendor booths at various local Pride events. More Fortune 500 corporations and even smaller companies—many of which have offices, warehouses, manufacturing plants, or other facilities in central Pennsylvania—have enacted LGBTQ nondiscrimination policies and have encouraged the formation of LGBTQ employee organizations.

Colleges, universities, and high schools throughout the region continue to evolve and offer more supportive programs for their LGBTQ students. There has been an increase in the number of school districts with gay/straight alliance (GSA) groups, reflected in the increasing numbers attending the annual GSA Leadership Summit sponsored by the LGBT Center of Central PA. Most colleges and universities in central Pennsylvania now have LGBTQ student organizations, and their administrations have staff devoted to outreach, along with services and programs, for their LGBTQ students.

Like many similar cities, Lancaster, once a fairly conservative enclave in the middle of Amish and Mennonite country, is becoming more liberal with the influx of younger people and immigrants along with burgeoning arts, retail, restaurant, and nightlife scenes. This has created not only a vibrant and active downtown but also a rebirth of neighborhoods and a more welcoming atmosphere for its LGBTQ residents.

Harrisburg also has benefited from two decades of growth in restaurants, nightclubs, art galleries, and other cultural amenities. Its LGBTQ population led a neighborhood preservation movement that began several years after Hurricane Agnes flooded the Susquehanna River in 1972. Momentum picked up after the turn of the century, when several neighborhoods in and around the city's midtown area, anchored by its LGBTQ center, developed a higher concentration of LGBTQ residents.

Despite these advances, discrimination has not been eliminated. It will likely exist for decades more here, as in many other places throughout the country. Anti-LGBTQ discrimination remains a pervasive problem in the United States, and legal remedies are limited. As of 2018, fourteen states and countless local jurisdictions have no specific laws that restrict discrimination based on sexual orientation, gender identity, or gender expression.[1] In such states there is little legal recourse when people are fired from their jobs, denied housing, or excluded from public accommodations because of anti-LGBTQ prejudice. In fourteen other states, some municipalities have passed antidiscrimination laws, but there is no statewide protection. And in other states and many municipalities, antidiscrimination laws do not apply to gender identity or gender expression or apply only to public-sector jobs.[2]

This is the double challenge that faces central Pennsylvania: the region is culturally conservative in nature, and Pennsylvania has yet to pass a statewide antidiscrimination law to protect its LGBTQ citizens. As of 2018, forty-nine municipalities in the commonwealth had passed antidiscrimination ordinances, thirty-two since 2010. Only twelve passed ordinances from 2002 to 2006. Besides Harrisburg, York, and Lancaster in central Pennsylvania, only State College, Reading, Susquehanna Township, Carlisle, and Camp Hill now have laws to protect their LGBTQ residents. In the balance of the commonwealth, LGBTQ citizens of 64 percent of the towns still remain unprotected.[3]

Equality Pennsylvania continued to lobby for the passage of comprehensive protections for LGBTQ citizens through a proposed amendment to the state Human Relations Act. At the same time, it continued to encourage and support other municipalities to enact local protections. Equality Pennsylvania has fought for LGBTQ civil rights since its founding in 1996; in 2012 it helped defeat in committee an amendment to the Pennsylvania constitution that would have banned gay marriage. In 2008, Equality Pennsylvania launched the Student Network Across Pennsylvania (SNAP), which facilitates greater communication and collaboration among Pennsylvania LGBTQ students and collegiate organizations.[4] Equality Pennsylvania is now in the midst of reorganizing, but other organizations are picking up the torch for LGBTQ rights throughout Pennsylvania.

Joining in this fight and now supplementing Equality Pennsylvania's efforts is a new statewide youth organization, the Pennsylvania Youth Congress, based in Harrisburg, with its headquarters across the street from the State Capitol. Under the leadership of founder and executive director Jason Landau Goodman, the organization's mission is to motivate LGBTQ youth to get involved in campus and community organizing and political action across the state. It helps support lobbying events and demonstrations and holds an annual statewide conference. The Pennsylvania Youth Congress focuses not only on the fight for LGBTQ civil rights but also for LGBTQ community visibility, the Safe Schools Improvement Act, the reduction of bullying and harassment, schools as affirming places for LGBTQ students, and transgender youth advocacy training for educators and students.[5] The Pennsylvania Youth Congress is preparing new leaders to continue the work of equal rights for a better quality of life for LGBTQ citizens in central Pennsylvania.

In this new century, gay millennials are stepping into positions of leadership. They have come to realize that political action works best when there are people both inside and outside of government working together—young gay men like Alex Reber, who serves on the Democratic State Committee and as the head of the LGBTQ caucus for the Pennsylvania Democratic Party. He is leading the fight for equal rights for the LGBTQ community:

> You can get married in Pennsylvania one day, and then the next day put your photo of your same-sex spouse on your desk and be fired for it. And it's perfectly legal. That to me is really disconcerting. Something some other folks and I have

talked about is trying to see if we can get an ordinance passed in Dauphin County for nondiscrimination. [We are] still pushing at the state level, but because we're so Republican controlled . . . it seems difficult to get that passed today. But it's part of the reason I'm involved in politics. I would like to elect more people who share those views, [because] no one should fear getting fired or not getting an apartment because they are LGBT. It's a shame that that still can happen. It's exciting we were able to pass an ordinance in Harrisburg and in Susquehanna Township, but not for the whole county and not all of Pennsylvania. So . . . there's a lot of work to be done.[6]

Fig. 86 Pin depicting a rainbow-colored donkey from Capital Region Stonewall Democrats. Photo: Sue Blosser. Courtesy of the LGBT Center of Central PA History Project, Archives and Special Collections, Dickinson College, Carlisle, Pennsylvania.

Reber, who is also active in Capital Region Stonewall Democrats, a local chapter of a national organization of LGBTQ Democrats, has managed campaigns to successfully elect several gay candidates to local offices in Harrisburg.[7] In January 2018, he was elected as tax collector for Millersburg Borough, to serve until December 2021.

Over the last half of the twentieth into the twenty-first century, the LGBTQ community in central Pennsylvania has evolved against strong odds. In a culturally conservative area, separated by distance, with no laws to protect and guarantee basic rights, thousands of LGBTQ people have persevered to form a community rather than flee to big cities. Central Pennsylvania now has a thriving LGBTQ community, with many social and political organizations. Discrimination and homophobia still exist, but the community is strong, and it is easier to be proud and out. The early unsung activists and pioneers who built this community have left a lasting legacy.

The voices featured in *Out in Central Pennsylvania* detail that struggle and the history of LGBT life in a nonurban area, complementing Lillian Faderman's narrative in *The Gay Revolution: The Story of the Struggle* and Eric Marcus's in *Making History: The Struggle for Gay and Lesbian Equal Rights, 1945–1990*. Much has been documented about building LGBTQ communities in major metropolitan areas. But we have seen that in central Pennsylvania an LGBTQ community was built emulating much of what exists in those larger urban centers. *Out in Central Pennsylvania* fills a void in LGBT history by recording the testimony of the resilient people who fought for their dignity. A new generation of LGBTQ citizens of central Pennsylvania are breaking barriers, working together, and applying their collective skills and resources to grow, sustain, and enhance this remarkable community. Today there are more than enough reasons to stay in central Pennsylvania, where LGBTQ people have a bright and promising future.

notes

Foreword

1. See the Bucks County tourism website describing New Hope, https://www.visitbuckscounty.com/townsmainstreets/newhopelambertville/.

2. Philip Kennicott, "At Smithsonian, Gay Rights Is Out of the Closet, Into the Attic; Activist Frank Kameny's Memorabilia Are Now Signs of Progress," *Washington Post*, September 8, 2007, C1.

Introduction

1. For an example of this view, see Scott Herring, *Another Country: Queer Anti-urbanism* (New York: New York University Press, 2010), 149.

2. Nan Alamilla Boyd and Horacio N. Roque Ramírez, *Bodies of Evidence: The Practice of Queer Oral History* (New York: Oxford University Press, 2012), 1, 47.

3. Ibid., 47.

4. Eric Marcus, *Making History: The Struggle for Gay and Lesbian Equal Rights, 1945–1990* (New York: HarperCollins, 1992), x.

5. United States Census Bureau, "Quick Facts: Lancaster City, Pennsylvania," July 1, 2018, www.census.gov/quickfacts/fact/table/lancastercitypennsylvania/PST045218; United States Census Bureau, "Quick Facts: York City, Pennsylvania," July 1, 2018, www.census.gov/quickfacts/fact/table/yorkcitypennsylvania/PST045218; United States Census Bureau, "Harrisburg City, Pennsylvania; United States," July 1, 2018, www.census.gov/quickfacts/fact/table/harrisburgcitypennsylvania,US/PST045218.

6. Marc Stein, *Rethinking the Gay and Lesbian Movement* (New York: Routledge, 2012), 5, 6.

Chapter 1

The epigraph to this chapter is from Lorraine Kujawa, "There Was a Time," in *Coffee at Hilde's: Four Provincetown Poets*, by Lorraine Kujawa, Hilde Oleson, Pat Lombardi, and Margaret Phillips (Bloomington, IN: iUniverse, 2013), 50. © Lorraine Kujawa 2013.

1. John D'Emilio, *Sexual Politics, Sexual Communities: The Making of a Homosexual Minority in the United States, 1940–1970* (Chicago: University of Chicago Press, 1983), 13.

2. Marc Stein, *Rethinking the Gay and Lesbian Movement* (New York: Routledge, 2012), 44.

3. D'Emilio, *Sexual Politics, Sexual Communities*, 40–41; Lillian Faderman, *The Gay Revolution: The Story of the Struggle* (New York: Simon and Schuster, 2015), 22.

4. Group interview by William Burton, June 16, 2016, Harrisburg, PA, transcript, LGBT Center of Central PA History Project, Archives and Special Collections, Dickinson College, Carlisle, PA (hereafter cited as History Project).

5. Nan Alamilla Boyd and Horacio N. Roque Ramírez, *Bodies of Evidence: The Practice of Queer Oral History* (New York: Oxford University Press, 2012), 7.

6. Material here and in the following paragraphs is derived from Larry Wilson, interview by Lonna Malmsheimer, November 17, 2015, Harrisburg, PA, History Project.

7. Material here and in the following paragraphs is derived from Donald Fitz, interview by Kevin W. Barns, October 25, 2014, Harrisburg, PA, History Project.

8. Material here and in the following paragraphs is derived from Lorraine Kujawa, interview by William Burton, October 28, 2015, Provincetown, MA, History Project.

9. Material here and in the following paragraph is derived from John Folby, interview by Blake Barker, March 26, 2014, Harrisburg, PA, History Project.

10. Material here and in the following paragraphs is derived from Samuel Deetz, interview by Lonna Malmsheimer, October 27, 2013, Carlisle, PA, History Project.

11. Material here and in the following paragraphs is derived from Nancy Helm, interview by William Burton, January 16, 2016, Lancaster, PA, History Project.

12. Group interview.

13. Ibid.

14. David Walker, interview by Orli Segal, March 19, 2015, Harrisburg, PA, History Project.

15. Ibid.

16. Material here and in the following paragraphs is derived from Kathy Fillman, interview by Marjorie Forster, February 10, 2015, Highspire, PA, History Project.

17. Material here and in the following paragraphs is derived from Marlene Kanuck, interview by Nancy Datres, July 1, 2013, Harrisburg, PA, History Project.

18. Material here and in the following paragraphs is derived from Richard Schlegel, oral history interview by Marc Stein, May 10–11, 1993, Philadelphia LGBT History Project, 2016, http://outhistory.org/exhibits/show/philadelphia-lgbt-interviews/interviews/richard-schlegel.

19. Folby, interview.

20. Paul Foltz, interview by Brian Pidgeon, March 20, 2015, Carlisle, PA, History Project.

21. Bob Skiba, "Gayborhood," *The Encyclopedia of Greater Philadelphia*, accessed May 16, 2019, http://philadelphiaencyclopedia.org/archive/gayborhood.

22. Material here and in the following paragraphs is derived from the group interview.

23. Len Evans, "Gay Chronicles: 1945–1970," accessed May 16, 2019, http://gayinsacramento.com/Chron-45-page.htm.

24. Group interview.

25. Ibid.

26. Wilson, interview.

27. George Centini and Gary Hufford, interview by Barry Loveland, January 30, 2017, Lancaster, PA, History Project.

28. Anthony Silvestre, interview by Barry Loveland, September 21, 2016, Pittsburgh, PA, History Project.

29. *Alternative* 2, no. 2 (1972): 2, PSUA 450, Homophiles of Penn State Records, Special Collections Library, Penn State University Libraries, State College, PA.

30. Daniel Maneval, interview by Barry Loveland, July 24, 2015, Harrisburg, PA, History Project.

31. Wilson, interview.

32. Group interview.

33. Schlegel, oral history.

34. "18 Arrested In Morals Crackdown," *Harrisburg Patriot-News*, July 3, 1965.

35. Schlegel, oral history.

36. *Harrisburg Patriot-News*, July 3, 1965.

37. "5 Men Jailed in Morals Cases; 7 Are Fined, Put on Probation," *Harrisburg Patriot-News*, September 9, 1965. "Court Here Imposes Sentences on 8," *Harrisburg Patriot-News*, September 10, 1965.

38. "Clock Bar Loses License," *Harrisburg Patriot-News*, October 27, 1965.

39. Bob Hafer, "Lipsett, Zimmerman Guests at Testimonial Dinner Here," *Harrisburg Patriot-News*, October 20, 1965.

40. Prior to 1981, attorneys general for the Commonwealth of Pennsylvania were appointed by the governor.

41. Bob Fernandez, "Hershey Chairman LeRoy S. Zimmerman Resigns from All Boards," *Philadelphia Inquirer*, November 29, 2011, www.inquirer.com/philly/business/20111129_Hershey_chairman_LeRoy_S_Zimmerman_resigns_from_all_boards.html.

42. Jim Bortzfield, interview by Barry Loveland, October 13, 2014, Harrisburg, PA, History Project.

43. Group interview.

44. "New Jersey Gay Couple Celebrates 51st Anniversary," *Washington Blade*, August 16, 2012.

45. Ibid.

46. Joe Burns, correspondence to Barry Loveland, April 30, 2017.

Chapter 2

1. Michael Bronski, *A Queer History of the United States* (Boston: Beacon Press, 2011), 177, 178. As Bronski reports, Kinsey's study found that "37 percent of all males had some form of homosexual contact between their teen years and old age" and that "4 percent of males were exclusively homosexual throughout their lives."

2. Ibid., 179, 181.

3. Ibid., 206, 180.

4. Lillian Faderman, *The Gay Revolution: The Story of the Struggle* (New York: Simon and Schuster, 2015), 187.

5. Eric Marcus, *Making History: The Struggle for Gay and Lesbian Equal Rights, 1945–1990* (New York: HarperCollins, 1992), 172.

6. Richard Hause and Steven Leshner, interview by Barry Loveland, March 8, 2017, Harrisburg, PA, LGBT Center of Central PA History Project, Archives and Special Collections, Dickinson College, Carlisle, PA (hereafter cited as History Project).

7. John D'Emilio, *Sexual Politics, Sexual Communities: The Making of a Homosexual Minority in the United States, 1940–1970* (Chicago: University of Chicago Press, 1983), 233.

8. John-Manuel Andriote, *Victory Deferred: How AIDS Changed Gay Life in America* (Bangor: Booklocker, 2011), 9.

9. Hause and Leshner, interview.

10. Richard Hill and Jerry Brennan, "History of Dignity/Central Pennsylvania," 1985, LGBT-053, Richard Hause Collection, History Project.

11. John Barns, interview by Cathy McCormick, December 16, 2015, Camp Hill, PA, History Project.

12. Ed Good and Thurman Grossnickle, interview by John Folby and Lonna Malmsheimer, March 28, 2013, Harrisburg, PA, History Project.

13. Hill and Brennan, "History of Dignity."

14. Richard Hause, interview by Nancy Datres, September 20, 2013, Harrisburg, PA, History Project.

15. Group interview by William Burton, June 16, 2016, Harrisburg, PA, History Project.

16. Ibid.

17. Barns, interview.

18. *Harrisburg Patriot-News*, January 24, 1984.

19. John Folby, interview by Blake Barker, March 26, 2014, Harrisburg, PA, History Project.

20. Mary Nancarrow, interview by Lonna Malmsheimer, February 24, 2015, Carlisle, PA, History Project.

21. Daniel Miller, interview by Andrew C. Miller, March 15, 2014, Harrisburg, PA, History Project.

22. Metropolitan Community Churches website, accessed May 16, 1019, https://www.mccchurch.org.

23. "Our History," Metropolitan Community Church of the Spirit, accessed May 16, 2019, http://www.mccofthespirit.org/ourhistory1.

24. Ibid.

25. Material in the following paragraphs is derived from Mary Merriman, interview by Mark Stoner, August 28, 2013, Lancaster, PA, History Project.

26. The Pennsmen website, accessed February 6, 2018, http://www.pennsmen.com.

27. Richard Twaddle, interview by Barry Loveland, November 10, 2014, Harrisburg, PA, History Project.

28. Ibid.

29. The Reading Railmen website, accessed February 6, 2018, http://www.readingrailmen.net /home.html; see also the Bucks County Motorcycle Club website, accessed October 15, 2019, https://bucksmc.org.

30. Material here and in the following paragraphs is derived from Lorraine Kujawa, interview by William Burton, October 28, 2015, Provincetown, MA, History Project.

31. *Lavender Letter*, March 1984, History Project.

32. Kujawa, interview.

33. Ibid.

34. Material here and in the following paragraphs is derived from David Leas, interview by Barry Loveland, June 1, 2017, Harrisburg, PA, History Project.

35. *Gay Era*, LGBT-001, box 1, Joseph W. Burns Periodicals Collection, History Project.

36. Ibid.

37. Material here and in the following paragraphs is derived from Leas, interview.

38. Material in this section is derived from Joe Burns, interview by Lonna Malmsheimer, May 24, 2013, Boiling Springs, PA, History Project.

39. D'Emilio, *Sexual Politics, Sexual Communities*, 67.

Chapter 3

1. Warren J. Blumenfeld, "Urning/Urningin, Homosexual, Homophile, LGBT, Queer: A History of Youth Activism," *Academia*, accessed March 30, 2017, http://www.academia.edu/7623089/ Urning_Homosexual_Homophile_LGBT_Queer_A_ History_of_Activism_and_Identity_Catagorization.

2. Ibid.

3. "This Is Penn State," Penn State University, accessed October 15, 2019, http://www.psu.edu /thisispennstate.

4. *Alternative* 2, no. 1 (1971): 1, PSUA 450, Homophiles of Penn State Records, Special Collections Library, Penn State University Libraries, University Park, PA (hereafter cited as HPSR).

5. *Alternative* 1, no. 1 (June 1, 1971): 1, HPSR.

6. *Alternative* 2, no. 1 (September 3, 1971): 1, HPSR.

7. *Alternative* 1, no. 1 (June 1, 1971): 1, HPSR.

8. *Alternative* 2, no. 1 (September 3, 1971): 1, HPSR.

9. Jim Wiggins, "Homosexuals Shed Secrecy," *Daily Collegian*, May 19, 1971, 1, Pennsylvania Newspaper Archive, accessed October 15, 2019, https://panewsarchive.psu.edu/lccn/sn85054904.

10. Gary Mayk, "HOPS Denied Student Charter," *Daily Collegian*, September 19, 1971.

11. *Alternative* 2, no. 1 (September 3, 1971): 1, HPSR.

12. *Alternative* 2, no. 2 (January 21, 1972): 1, HPSR.

13. "HOPS Win Charter Right," *Daily Collegian*, January 25, 1973.

14. "Overview: The Case of Joe Acanfora," accessed May 1, 2019, www.joeacanfora.com /overview.html.

15. Quoted from the article by Craig Simpson, "MoCo Gay Teacher Fired 1972: Justice Denied for Forty Years," *Washington Area Spark* (as originally reported in the *Pennsylvania Mirror*), accessed May 1, 2019, https://washingtonspark .wordpress.com/2012/12/20/ mocogayteacherfired1972justicedeniedfor40years.

16. "Overview."

17. Simpson, "MoCo Gay Teacher Fired."

18. Ibid.

19. "Overview."

20. Simpson, "MoCo Gay Teacher Fired."

21. Ibid.

22. Ibid.

23. "Overview."

24. Ibid.

25. Simpson, "MoCo Gay Teacher Fired."

26. Ibid.

27. Ibid.

28. Ibid.

29. "Overview."

30. Simpson, "MoCo Gay Teacher Fired."

31. "Overview."

32. Simpson, "MoCo Gay Teacher Fired."

33. "Overview." *Certiorari* is a legal term. If the Supreme Court had granted certiorari, it would have meant that the court would have been willing to review the lower court's ruling and hear Joe's case.

34. Simpson, "MoCo Gay Teacher Fired."

35. *ZAP!* (monthly newsletter of Homophiles of Penn State), April 1972, 1, HPSR.

36. *ZAP!*, May 1972, 1, HPSR.

37. *ZAP!*, April 1972, 1, HPSR.

38. Gay Liberation Festival flyer, HPSR.

39. Anthony Silvestre, interview by Barry Loveland, September 21, 2016, Pittsburgh, PA, LGBT Center of Central PA History Project, Archives and Special Collections, Dickinson College, Carlisle, PA (hereafter cited as History Project).

40. Ibid.

41. Flyer for "Gay Awareness Festival," HPSR.

42. Material here and in the following paragraphs is derived from Mary Margaret Hart and Lynn Daniels, interview by Barry Loveland and William Burton, April 25, 2017, Bellefonte, PA, History Project.

43. Louise A. Blum, *You're Not from Around Here, Are You? A Lesbian in Small-Town America* (Madison: University of Wisconsin Press, 2001), 187.

44. Material in this section is derived from Daniel Maneval, interview by Barry Loveland, July 24, 2015, Harrisburg, PA, History Project.

45. Tina Fetner, *How the Religious Right Shaped Lesbian and Gay Activism* (Minneapolis: University of Minnesota Press, 2008), 24.

46. Amin Ghaziani, *The Dividends of Dissent: How Conflict and Culture Work in Lesbian and Gay Marches on Washington* (Chicago: University of Chicago Press, 2008), 34.

Chapter 4

1. Marc Stein, *Rethinking the Gay and Lesbian Movement* (New York: Routledge, 2012), 79.

2. Shapp biodata, ca. 1971–79, Manuscript Group 309, Milton J. Shapp Papers, Pennsylvania State Archives, Harrisburg.

3. Ibid.

4. Mark Segal, *And Then I Danced: Traveling the Road to LGBT Equality* (Brooklyn: Akashic Books, 2015), 65.

5. Ibid., 66–67.

6. Ibid., 82, 83, 88.

7. Mark Segal, interview by William Burton, July 20, 2016, Philadelphia, LGBT Center of Central PA History Project, Archives and Special Collections, Dickinson College, Carlisle, PA (hereafter cited as History Project).

8. Lillian Faderman, *The Gay Revolution: The Story of the Struggle* (New York: Simon and Schuster, 2015), 123, 124.

9. Segal, interview.

10. Ibid.

11. Segal, *And Then I Danced*, 108–9.

12. Segal, interview.

13. Samuel Deetz, interview by Lonna Malmsheimer, October 27, 2013, Carlisle, PA, History Project.

14. "Governor Milton Shapp (D) 1975-5," *LGBTQ Discrimination in Pennsylvania*, Suburban and Rural

Alliance of Pennsylvania, accessed May 10, 2017, https://sarapennsylvania.org/nondiscrimination/.

15. Craig A. Rimmerman, Kenneth D. Wald, and Clyde Wilcox, *The Politics of Gay Rights* (Chicago: University of Chicago Press, 2000), 272.

16. "Shapp Orders Homosexual Equal Rights," *Philadelphia Inquirer*, April 26, 1975, 1.

17. Mary Nancarrow, interview by Lonna Malmsheimer, February 24, 2015, Carlisle, PA, History Project.

18. Segal, *And Then I Danced*, 110.

19. LGBTCentralPA, "LGBT History Project: 40th Anniversary of PA Council for Sexual Minorities" (ceremony at the State Museum of Pennsylvania, commemorating the council's pioneering efforts in LGBT rights), video, 2:23:56, May 19, 2016, www.youtube.com/watch?v=l8Bpvwar9ZA.

20. Ibid.

21. Ibid.

22. "The Issue Is Equal Rights," *Philadelphia Inquirer*, October 18, 1975, 6.

23. Anthony Silvestre, interview by Barry Loveland, September 21, 2016, Pittsburgh, PA, History Project.

24. William Ecenbarger, "To Penna. Legislators, Gay Rights Are Wrong," *Philadelphia Inquirer*, June 20, 1976, 9.

25. Silvestre, interview.

26. See LGBTCentralPA, "LGBT History Project."

27. Silvestre, interview.

28. See LGBTCentralPA, "LGBT History Project."

29. Ibid.

30. Sam Deetz, notes, Pennsylvania Youth Action Conference, hosted by Pennsylvania Student Equality Coalition in 2015 at Juniata College, Huntingdon, Pennsylvania.

31. Ibid.

32. Minutes of Meetings and Correspondence, October 17–18, 1975, Manuscript Group 10.204, Records of the Pennsylvania Council for Sexual Minorities, Pennsylvania State Archives.

33. Senate Bills 83, 196, and 743, 1976, Pennsylvania State Legislature, Pennsylvania State Archives.

34. Nancarrow, interview.

35. Deetz, interview.

36. Ibid.

37. Silvestre, interview.

38. Deetz, interview.

39. Rural Gay Caucus, newsletter, June 1977, LGBT-001, folder 72, box 3, History Project.

40. Deetz, interview.

41. *Gay Era*, November 1977, History Project.

42. Faderman, *Gay Revolution*, 259.

43. *Gay Era*, November 1977, History Project.

44. Ibid.

45. *Gay Era*, December 1977, History Project.

46. Harry H. Long, "Impressions of Pride," *Gay Era*, May 1978, History Project.

47. Ibid. The Equal Rights Amendment to the US Constitution, passed by both houses of the US

Congress in 1972, sought to end legal distinctions between men and women in terms of divorce, property, employment, and other matters. The amendment failed to receive the necessary passage of thirty-eight states for ratification by the deadline of March 1979.

48. Rural Gay Caucus, newsletter, January 1977, LGBT-001, folder 67, box 3, History Project.

49. Rural Gay Caucus, newsletter, July 1978, LGBT-001, folder 41, box 3, History Project.

50. Harry H. Long, "Rural Caucus Dissolved," *Gay Era*, October 1978, History Project.

51. Material in this section is derived from Silvestre, interview.

52. "Anthony J. Silvestre, PhD," *Pitt Public Health*, University of Pittsburgh, accessed May 17, 2019, www.publichealth.pitt.edu/home/directory /anthony-j-silvestre.

53. Material in this section is derived from Nancarrow, interview.

Chapter 5

1. John-Manuel Andriote, *Victory Deferred: How AIDS Changed Gay Life in America* (Bangor: Booklocker, 2011), 58–59.

2. Amin Ghaziani, *The Dividends of Dissent: How Conflict and Culture Work in Lesbian and Gay Marches on Washington* (Chicago: University of Chicago Press, 2008), 75, 76.

3. "Thirty Years of HIV/AIDS: Snapshots of an Epidemic," Amfar, accessed May 9, 2017, www.AmFar.org/thirtyyearsofhiv/aidssnapshots ofanepidemic; "HIV Surveillance Reports," Centers for Disease Control and Prevention, accessed May 9, 2017, www.cdc.gov/hiv/library/reports/hiv surveillance.html. Philadelphia and Pittsburgh were the epicenters for the epidemic in Pennsylvania, accounting, respectively, for 75 percent and 12 percent of AIDS cases.

4. In 1985, polls showed "that 72 percent of Americans favored mandatory testing and 51 percent supported the quarantining of people with AIDS." See Ghaziani, *Dividends of Dissent*, 76.

5. Andriote, *Victory Deferred*, 81.

6. Ghaziani, *Dividends of Dissent*, 77.

7. Deborah B. Gould, *Moving Politics: Emotion and ACT UP's Fight Against AIDS* (Chicago: University of Chicago Press, 2009), 65.

8. Material here and in the following paragraphs is derived from HIV/AIDS Story Circle, January 22, 2015, Harrisburg, PA, LGBT Center of Central PA History Project, Archives and Special Collections, Dickinson College, Carlisle, PA (hereafter cited as History Project).

9. "Penn File," Department of State, Commonwealth of Pennsylvania, accessed May 9, 2017, www.corporations.pa.gov/Search/CorpSerch.

10. See "Thirty Years of HIV/AIDS"; "HIV Surveillance Reports."

11. Peg Dierkers, interview by Andrea Glass, March 21, 2014, Harrisburg, PA, History Project.

12. Group interview, by William Burton, June 16, 2016, Harrisburg, PA, History Project.

13. Deb Fulham-Winston, interview by Amanda Donoghue, March 19, 2017, Carlisle, PA, History Project.

14. Ibid.

15. Jay Tennier, "Betty Finney House Corp.," *Points of Light*, March 18, 1998, www.pointsoflight .org/programs/recognition/dpol/awards/1075.

16. Ibid.

17. Jerre Freiberg, interview by Mary Merriman, December 3, 2014, Lancaster, PA, History Project.

18. CDC National Prevention Information Network, "Pennsylvania: Betty Finney House Closes Doors; Agency Sends Its HIV/AIDS Clientele to the Gathering Place," The Body: The HIV/AIDS Resource, April 2, 2002, www.thebody.com/content /art22754.html.

19. Ibid.

20. Marty Tornblom, interview by Corine Lehigh, June 9, 2017, New Cumberland, PA, History Project.

21. Ibid.

22. Fulham-Winston, interview.

23. "Ryan White HIV/AIDS Program: Legislation," Health Resources and Services Administration, February 2019, https://hab.hrsa .gov/aboutryanwhitehivaidsprogram/ryanwhite hivaidsprogramlegislation.

24. Fulham-Winston, interview.

25. Eric Selvey, interview by Jennifer Ott, April 9, 2015, Harrisburg, PA, History Project.

26. HIV/AIDS Story Circle.

27. Ibid.

28. Paul Foltz, interview by Brian Pidgeon, March 20, 2015, Carlisle, PA, History Project.

29. Material here and in the following paragraphs is derived from Phil Wenger, interview by Michele Metcalf, March 23, 2015, York, PA, History Project.

30. David Leas, interview by Barry Loveland, June 1, 2017, Harrisburg, PA, History Project.

31. HIV/AIDS Story Circle.

32. Alder Health Services website, accessed June 24, 2017, https://alderhealth.org.

33. "A Timeline of HIV and AIDS," *HIV Basics*, accessed June 24, 2017, www.hiv.gov/hivbasics /overview/history/hivandaidstimeline.

34. Material in the following paragraphs is derived from John Folby, interview by Blake Barker, March 26, 2014, Harrisburg, PA, History Project.

35. Material in this section is derived from Joy Ufema, interview by Jennifer Ott, April 29, 2015, York, PA, History Project.

36. Rebecca Bricker, "Joy Ufema's Work with the Dying Has Inspired Controversy, a TV Film, and Immeasurable Gratitude," *People*, January 19, 1981, https://people.com/archive/joyufemasworkwiththe dyinghasinspiredcontroversyatvfilmandimmeasurable gratitudevol15no2.

37. Ufema, interview.

38. Bricker, "Joy Ufema's Work," 8; for this quotation and the following material, see Ufema, interview.

39. Material in this section is derived from Rick Schulze, interview by William Burton, March 12, 2017, Lock Haven, PA, History Project.

Chapter 6

1. Amin Ghaziani, *The Dividends of Dissent: How Conflict and Culture Work in Lesbian and Gay Marches on Washington* (Chicago: University of Chicago Press, 2008), 128–29.

2. Ibid., 135.

3. Eric Marcus, *Making History: The Struggle for Gay and Lesbian Equal Rights, 1945–1990* (New York: HarperCollins, 1992), 135.

4. Ghaziani, *Dividends of Dissent*, 138.

5. Ibid., 144–45.

6. Marcus, *Making History*, 258.

7. Randy Myers, "Council Approves Anti-Bias Rule," *Harrisburg Evening News*, March 9, 1983, B1.

8. Ibid.

9. Ibid.

10. Randy Myers, "Gays Cheer as Council OKs Anti-Bias Rule After Heated Debate," *Harrisburg Patriot-News*, March 9, 1983, C5.

11. Rick Schulze, interview by William Burton, March 12, 2017, Lock Haven, PA, LGBT Center of Central PA History Project, Archives and Special Collections, Dickinson College, Carlisle, PA (hereafter cited as History Project).

12. Ghaziani, *Dividends of Dissent*, 144.

13. Mary Merriman, interview by Mark Stoner, August 28, 2013, Lancaster, PA, History Project.

14. Mark Stoner, interview by Mary Merriman, August 29, 2013, Lancaster, PA, History Project.

15. Merriman, interview.

16. Lancaster City Council, meeting notes, May 14, 1991, City Clerk Office, City of Lancaster, PA.

17. Ibid.

18. Ibid.

19. Nathan Lee Gadsden, "Sexual Orientation Bias Banned in City," *Intelligencer Journal*, May 15, 1991.

20. William Tuthill, "County Finalizes Split on City Sex Bias Stand," *Intelligencer Journal*, August 15, 1991.

21. Ibid.

22. Jon Rutter, "Klan Marches to Jeers," *Lancaster Sunday News*, August 25, 1991, A1.

23. Ibid.

24. Ibid.

25. Ibid.

26. Cindy Lou Mitzel, interview by Debbie Gable, March 29, 2015, York, PA, History Project.

27. William Althaus and Rev. James Grove, "Gay Rights: Does York Need to Protect Its Sexual Minorities?," *York Sunday News*, January 10, 1993, A13.

28. Ibid.

29. Ibid.

30. Ibid.

31. Ibid.

32. American Psychological Association, "Official Reports and Proceedings," *Footnotes* 15, no. 2 (February 1987): 14.

33. Peg Welch, interview by Debbie Gable, March 22, 2015, York, PA, History Project.

34. The mayor claimed that York was the first capital of the United States because the "Articles of Confederation" by the First Continental Congress were written in York. "History of York," *York Daily Record*, September 14, 2008.

35. David Fleshler, "York Takes a Stand on Gay Rights," *York Daily Record*, February 17, 1993, A1.

36. Ibid.

37. David Fleshler, "'Symbolic' Ordinance Has Opened the Closet Door a Crack," *York Daily Record*, March 17, 1994, A1.

38. Ibid.

39. Ibid.

40. Ibid.

41. Mitzel, interview.

42. Barry Loveland, interview by Korie Lain, March 22, 2014, Harrisburg, PA, History Project.

43. Ibid.

44. Sharon Potter, interview by Barry Loveland, October 10, 2014, Harrisburg, PA, History Project.

45. Loveland, interview.

46. Material here and in the following paragraphs is derived from Potter, interview.

47. "'Jim in Bold' Looks at Life as a Gay Teen, Past and Present," *Augusta Chronicle*, October 20, 2003, accessed May 17, 2017, http://chronicle.augusta.com/stories/2003/10/20/mov_397810.shtml.

48. Ibid.

49. Material here and in the following paragraphs is derived from Bobbi Carmitchell, interview by Mary Merriman, June 26, 2013, Washington Borough, PA, History Project.

50. "Bobbi Carmitchell Music," accessed April 4, 2017, www.bobbicarmitchellmusic.com/disc.html (site discontinued).

51. Carmitchell, interview.

52. See "Bobbi Carmitchell Music."

53. Material here and in the following paragraphs is derived from Carmitchell, interview.

54. Material in this section is derived from Nancy Helm, interview by William Burton, January 16, 2016, Lancaster, PA, History Project.

55. Maria Coole, "New Bookstore Serves Gay Clientele," *Intelligencer Journal*, June 16, 1991, D1.

56. Ibid.

57. Helm, interview.

58. Ibid.

59. Nathan Gadsden, "Was Blast at Bookstore Incident of Gay Bashing?," *Intelligencer Journal*, June 25, 1991, A1.

60. Helm, interview.

61. Ibid.

62. Tim Buckwalter, "2nd Explosion Damages Windows at Gay Bookstore," *Lancaster New Era*, August 15, 1991, A1.

63. Helm, interview.

64. Ibid.

65. Ibid.

66. Roger Clinton, "Bookstore Bombers Arrested," *Intelligencer Journal*, June 5, 1992, A1.

67. Helm, interview.

68. Clinton, "Bookstore Bombers Arrested," A1.

69. Helm, interview.

70. Ibid.

71. Material in this section is derived from Daniel Miller, interview by Andrew C. Miller, March 15, 2014, Harrisburg, PA, History Project.

72. James B. Stewart, "Gentlemen's Agreement," *New Yorker*, June 13, 1994, 75.

73. Material in the next several paragraphs is derived from D. Miller, interview.

74. Stewart, "Gentlemen's Agreement," 78.

75. Ibid.

76. Ibid.

77. D. Miller, interview.

78. Ibid.

79. Stewart, "Gentlemen's Agreement," 80.

80. Ibid., 81.

81. Ibid.

82. D. Miller, interview.

83. Ibid.

Chapter 7

1. John D'Emilio, *Sexual Politics, Sexual Communities: The Making of a Homosexual Minority in the United States, 1940–1970* (Chicago: University of Chicago Press, 1983), 232.

2. Lillian Faderman, *The Gay Revolution: The Story of the Struggle* (New York: Simon and Schuster, 2015), 116.

3. Marc Stein, *Rethinking the Gay and Lesbian Movement* (New York: Routledge, 2012), 111.

4. Faderman, *Gay Revolution*, 117–18.

5. Ibid., 119–20.

6. Ibid., 120–22.

7. Stein, *Rethinking the Gay and Lesbian Movement*, 81.

8. LGBT-001, LGBT Center of Central PA History Project, Archives and Special Collections, Dickinson College, Carlisle, PA (hereafter cited as History Project), 2-12.

9. Scrapbook, LGBT-011, History Project, 22.

10. LGBT-001, History Project, 1-94.

11. Scrapbook, LGBT-011, History Project, 19.

12. Nikki Knerr, interview with Barry Loveland, October 9, 2016, Harrisburg, PA, History Project.

13. Ibid.

14. Ibid.

15. Peg Dierkers, email correspondence to Barry Loveland, April 26, 2016.

16. "Why Should the Public Pay?," *Lancaster New Era*, October 4, 1991, Commentary, A9.

17. Jeanette Krebs, "Gay, Lesbian Pride Festival Set," *Harrisburg Patriot-News*, July 19, 1992, Central PA, B4.

18. The Harrisburg Men's Chorus was reluctant to call themselves the Harrisburg Gay Men's Chorus because of socially conservative nature of the central Pennsylvania region.

19. *Harrisburg Patriot-News*, July 23, 1993, Weekend, C9.

20. Rebecca Logan, "Candace Gingrich Comes Home to Gay Pride Event," *Harrisburg Patriot-News*, July 31, 1995, State/Local, B1.

21. LGBT-012, 4.1, History Project.

22. Sandy Cullen, "2 Area Women to Be Honored for Their Positive Contributions to Midstate During Pride Week," *Harrisburg Patriot-News*, July 21, 1996, Living, J10.

23. Jeff McGaw, "Gathering with Pride," *Harrisburg Patriot-News*, July 27, 1997, Central PA, B1.

24. Founded by Cleve Jones, the Names Project developed the AIDS memorial quilt, composed of thousands of individual three-by-six-foot fabric panels, each inscribed with the name of someone who had died of AIDS. Amin Ghaziani, *The Dividends of Dissent: How Conflict and Culture Work in Lesbian and Gay Marches on Washington* (Chicago: University of Chicago Press, 2008), 119.

25. McGaw, "Gathering with Pride."

26. Jamal Jones, "Event Promotes Pride, Unity of Gay, Lesbian Community," *Harrisburg Patriot-News*, July 26, 1998, Central PA, B9.

27. Ibid.

28. Jeff McGaw, "Pride Fest Goes Out in the Open of '99," *Harrisburg Patriot-News*, August 1, 1999, Central PA, B5.

29. Jane Garisto, "Gay Pride Festival Was Shameful," *Harrisburg Patriot-News*, August 11, 1999, Editorials, A12.

30. Edward T. Hoffman, "Cafeteria Christianity," *Harrisburg Patriot-News*, August 8, 1999, Editorials, B14.

31. Shevin Spruill, "Festival Offers Opportunity for Gay Pride, Activism," *Harrisburg Patriot-News*, July 29, 2001, Local/State, B1.

32. Diana Fishlock, "Pride Festival Attendance, Goals Grow," *Harrisburg Patriot-News*, July 26, 2002, Insideout, I41.

33. Diana Fishlock, "PrideFest to Celebrate a Landmark Year," *Harrisburg Patriot-News*, July 25, 2003, Insideout, I40.

34. Prasana William, "PrideFest Pushes for Unity," *Harrisburg Patriot-News*, July 26, 2007, Go!, G32.

35. Laura Vecsey, "Pride Celebrations Have Affirming Role," *Harrisburg Patriot-News*, July 24, 2010, A1.

36. Julianne Mattera, "We Want to Be Equal," *Harrisburg Patriot-News*, July 28, 2013, A3.

37. Lori Van Ingen, "Group Plans Summer Gay Festival Here," *Intelligencer Journal*, February 7, 2007, A1.

38. Ibid.

39. Lori Van Ingen, "Gay Pride Festival Moves to Millersville," *Intelligencer Journal*, June 8, 2007, B1.

40. Lori Van Ingen, "Gay Pride Festival Canceled," *Intelligencer Journal*, June 14, 2007, B1.

41. Suzanne Cassidy, "One Amazing Day," *Intelligencer Journal*, June 22, 2008, sec. B1.

42. Ibid.

43. York LGBTQIA Resource Center, accessed September 27, 2017, http://equalityfestyork.com.

44. See Brandie Kessler, "Equality Fest York Scheduled for Aug. 7," FlipSidePA, July 26, 2016, www.flipsidepa.com/story/entertainment/2016/07/26/equalityfestyorkscheduledaug7/87404724.

Chapter 8

1. Sheryl Gay Stolberg, "Obama Signs Away Don't Ask, Don't Tell," *New York Times*, December 22, 2010.

2. Greg Botelho, "Federal Judge Rules Same-Sex Marriage in Pennsylvania Is Unconstitutional," CNN, May 21, 2014, https://edition.cnn.com/2014/05/20/us/Pennsylvaniasamesexmarriage.

3. "State Overview: Pennsylvania," *Out for America*, Victory Institute, accessed June 24, 2019, https://outforamerica.org/state/pennsylvania.

4. "LGBTQ Non-discrimination Laws in Pennsylvania," Pennsylvania Youth Congress, accessed June 24, 2019, https://payouthcongress.org/paequalitycenter/nondiscrimination.

5. Kristine E. Newhall and Erin E. Buzuvis, "(e)Racing Jennifer Harris: Sexuality and Race, Law and Discourse in *Harris v. Portland*," *Digital Commons*, Western New England University School of Law, accessed February 8, 2018, https://digitalcommons.law.wne.edu/facschol/40.

6. "University Concludes Investigation Claims Against Women's Basketball Coach," *Penn State News*, Penn State University, April 18, 2006, http://news.psu.edu/story/203885/2006/04/18/universityconcludesinvestigationclaimsagainstwomensbasketballcoach.

7. Chuck Finder and Cindi Lash, "Penn State's 'Mommy Coach' a Bigot?" *Pittsburgh Post-Gazette*, April 29, 2006, www.postgazette.com/sports/psu/2006/04/30/PennStatesmommycoachabigot/stories/200604300213.

8. Ibid.

9. "Harris Claim Settled," *Penn State News*, Penn State University, February 5, 2007, https://news.psu.edu/story/198428/2007/02/05/harrisclaimsettled.

10. Newhall and Buzuvis, "(e)Racing Jennifer Harris."

11. Jill Lieber, "Harris Stands Tall in Painful Battle with Penn State Coach," *USA Today*, May 11,

2006, https://usatoday30.usatoday.com/sports/college/womensbasketball/20060511jenniferharris_x.htm.

12. Newhall and Buzuvis, "(e)Racing Jennifer Harris."

13. Ibid.

14. Ibid.

15. Tim Ford and Justin Kenkel, "Portland Accused of Anti-Gay Remarks," *Daily Collegian*, October 12, 2005.

16. Jon Blau and Andre Straub, "PSU Finds Portland in Violation of Policy," *Daily Collegian*, April 19, 2006.

17. Ibid.

18. Ibid.

19. Mark Viera and Joseph Dolan, "Portland Resigns," *Daily Collegian*, March 23, 2007.

20. Ibid.

21. Lieber, "Harris Stands Tall."

22. Campus Pride, accessed November 24, 2017, www.campuspride.org/campusprides2017bestofthebesttop25lgbtqfriendlycollegesuniversities (now offline).

23. Amin Ghaziani, *The Dividends of Dissent: How Conflict and Culture Work in Lesbian and Gay Marches on Washington* (Chicago: University of Chicago Press, 2008), 226.

24. Mara Keisling, interview by William Burton, September 15, 2017, Philadelphia, PA, LGBT Center of Central PA History Project, Archives and Special Collections, Dickinson College, Carlisle, PA (hereafter cited as History Project).

25. Renaissance Transgender Association website, accessed February 8, 2018, www.ren.org.

26. "Pennsylvania: LGBTQ Non-discrimination in the States," Freedom for All Americans, accessed June 24, 2019, www.freedomforallamericans.org/category/states/pa.

27. "One Year After Military Ban Announcement, Transgender Veterans Explain the Importance of Protecting All Americans from Discrimination," Freedom for All Americans, accessed June 24, 2019, https://freedomforallamericans.org/onveteransdaytransgenderveteransexplaintheimportanceofprotectingallamericansfromdiscrimination.

28. "Pennsylvania."

29. Material here and in the following paragraphs is derived from Jeanine Ruhsam, interview by Liam Fuller, August 23, 2017, Carlisle, PA, History Project.

30. Gretchen Little, interview by Sarah Goldberg, November 19, 2015, Harrisburg, PA, History Project.

31. Joanne Carroll, interview by Barry Loveland, November 18, 2016, Lancaster, PA, History Project.

32. Ruhsam, interview.

33. Ibid.

34. Ibid.

35. Carroll, interview.

36. Little, interview.

37. Ibid.

38. Ibid.

39. Ruhsam, interview.

40. Carroll, interview.

41. Rachel Levine, interview by Barry Loveland, February 6, 2017, Harrisburg, PA, History Project.

42. National Center for Transgender Equality website, accessed June 25, 2019, http://transequality.org.

43. Material here and in the following paragraphs is derived from a group interview by William Burton, June 16, 2016, Harrisburg, PA, History Project.

44. Ruhsam, interview.

45. Material in this section is derived from MJ Dougherty, interview by Marjorie Forster, November 22, 2014, Honey Brook, PA, History Project.

46. Material in this section is derived from Keisling, interview.

Conclusion

1. Beth Skwarecki, "This Map Shows Which States Protect LGBT People from Discrimination," Lifehacker, March 15, 2017, https://lifehacker.com /thismapshowswhichstatesprotectlgbtpeople fromdi1793305575.

2. Marc Stein, *Rethinking the Gay and Lesbian Movement* (New York: Routledge, 2012), 194.

3. Equality Pennsylvania, accessed February 6, 2018, www.equalitypa.org/municipalitieswith nondiscriminationordinances (now offline).

4. Ibid.

5. Pennsylvania Youth Congress website, accessed February 6, 2018, http://payouthcongress. org.

6. Alex Reber, interview by Barry Loveland, October 4, 2017, Harrisburg, PA, LGBT Center of Central PA History Project, Archives and Special Collections, Dickinson College, Carlisle, PA.

7. The gay candidates elected to local offices in Harrisburg are Dan Miller, city council member, controller, and treasurer (2017); John Campbell, treasurer (2011); and Ben Allatt, city council member (2014).

selected bibliography

Andriote, John-Manuel. *Victory Deferred: How AIDS Changed Gay Life in America*. Bangor: Booklocker, 2011.

Blum, Louise A. *You're Not from Around Here, Are You? A Lesbian in Small-Town America*. Madison: University of Wisconsin Press, 2001.

Boyd, Nan Alamilla, and Horacio N. Roque Ramírez. *Bodies of Evidence: The Practice of Queer Oral History*. New York: Oxford University Press, 2012.

Bronski, Michael. *A Queer History of the United States*. Boston: Beacon Press, 2011.

D'Emilio, John. *Sexual Politics, Sexual Communities: The Making of a Homosexual Minority in the United States, 1940–1970*. Chicago: University of Chicago Press, 1983.

———. *The World Turned: Essays on Gay History, Politics, and Culture*. Durham: Duke University Press, 2002.

Faderman, Lillian. *The Gay Revolution: The Story of the Struggle*. New York: Simon and Schuster, 2015.

Fetner, Tina. *How the Religious Right Shaped Lesbian and Gay Activism*. Minneapolis: University of Minnesota Press, 2008.

Ghaziani, Amin. *The Dividends of Dissent: How Conflict and Culture Work in Lesbian and Gay Marches on Washington*. Chicago: University of Chicago Press, 2008.

Gould, Deborah B. *Moving Politics: Emotion and ACT UP's Fight Against AIDS*. Chicago: University of Chicago Press, 2009.

Herring, Scott. *Another Country: Queer Anti-urbanism*. New York: New York University Press, 2010.

Marcus, Eric. *Making History: The Struggle for Gay and Lesbian Equal Rights, 1945–1990*. New York: HarperCollins, 1992.

Meyerowitz, Joanne. *How Sex Changed: A History of Transsexuality in the United States*. Cambridge, MA.: Harvard University Press, 2002.

Rimmerman, Craig A., Kenneth D. Wald, and Clyde Wilcox, eds. *The Politics of Gay Rights*. Chicago: University of Chicago Press, 2000.

Segal, Mark. *And Then I Danced: Traveling the Road to LGBT Equality*. Brooklyn: Akashic Books, 2015.

Stein, Marc. *Rethinking the Gay and Lesbian Movement*. New York: Routledge, 2012.

index